The Basques

The Peoples of Europe

======

General Editors
James Campbell and Barry Cunliffe

The Basques

Roger Collins

Basil Blackwell

First published 1986
First published in the USA 1987

Basil Blackwell Ltd
108 Cowley Road, Oxford OX4 1JF, UK

Basil Blackwell Inc.
432 Park Avenue South, Suite 1503,
New York, NY 10016, USA

British Library Cataloguing in Publication Data

Collins, Roger
    The Basques.———(The Peoples of Europe)
    1. Basque Provinces———History
    I. Title   II. Series
    946'6   DP302.B47
    ISBN 0-631-13478-6

Library of Congress Cataloging in Publication Data

Collins, Roger.
    The Basques.

    (The Peoples of Europe)
    Includes index.
    1. País Vasco (Spain)———History.   2. Pays Basque
    (France———History.   3. Basques———History.
    I. Title.   II. Series.
    DP302.B49C65   1986   946'6   86-8285
    ISBN 0-631-13478-6

Typeset by Freeman Graphic, Tonbridge
Printed in Great Britain by
Butler & Tanner Ltd, Frome and London

For John and Madge Collins
with gratitude and affection

Contents

Maps and Genealogies

Maps

Genealogies

Preface

This book is as much about region as about a people, but uniquely in Europe this is a case in which the two cannot be separated one from another. The Basques as a people are known in no other geographical context than that of the western Pyrenees, where also they have no clearly discernible predecessors as the human occupants of the region. Thus the study of the land and of its habitation is at the same time the study of the continuity of a culture. To some degree this makes it hard to divide up the history of the area into discrete chronological sections or justify anything less than a comprehensive coverage from dimmest antiquity right up to the present day. However, such an all-embracing approach would require an omnicompetence and a size of volume to which neither the author nor this series of books would wish to aspire. In practice, what is offered here is a study in detail of the history of the Basques and of the western Pyrenees in the period between the Roman conquest, when they first emerge clearly into historical record, and the late twelfth century, by which time the basic political divisions and many of the salient features of their society have been established. Moreover, as far as the evidence allows, an even-handed treatment of the areas to both the north and the south of the Pyrenees is at least attempted — something that the national historiographical traditions of both Spain and France are often reluctant to consider. Such chronological selectivity may seem eccentric; general historical treatments of Basque history or of the individual Basque provinces prefer to relegate the whole medieval period to the compass of usually little more than a single chapter. It is hard not to find some sympathy with such an approach. The scant, fragmentary and frequently contradictory evidence for the earliest recorded periods of Basque history is almost too frail to bear any substantial construction and can reduce the aspiring chronicler to the rank of novelist.

However, for all that, what has been attempted here needs doing. The period treated is a crucial one in which, solely amongst all of the former pre-Indo-European peoples of Europe, the Basques were able to survive, to resist cultural assimilation and to retain a language divorced in its origins and its linguistic character from all other living speeches of the continent. At the same time these centuries saw the failure of the Basques to develop political unity or even to feel the impulse to do so. Their cultural tenacity was thus totally separate from any form of political cohesion based upon independent self-government or the growth of nationhood. Nor, unlike that of most of the other peoples of Europe, has Basque ethnogenesis anything to do with the formation of a sense of identity based upon that of a social elite. The latter was the process taking place amongst the Basques' immediate neighbours and elsewhere in Europe during the centuries considered here. What the Basques were up to at this time thus takes on a peculiar significance. In general, the history of these early centuries has a surprising degree of relevance to some of the most insistent political arguments of the present in the Basque lands both south and north of the Pyrenees. This in itself implies the danger of a degree of political implication being put upon otherwise seemingly abstruse historical discussion. At the same time myth and misapprehension can become almost inextricably entangled with scholarly interpretation, all the more so when the latter has to be as cautious and tentative as the nature of the evidence for early Basque history requires. Any excessive argumentativeness in this book should be put down to the need to keep both of these tendencies in check; though to readers unfamiliar with the specialized bibliography concerned with the Basques in the early Middle Ages, some of it may seem rather like tilting at windmills.

Even the most quixotic of authors benefits from the guidance of teachers and friends and from the generous material assistance of learned societies. I am grateful to the British Academy for a substantial research grant in 1983 that took me to many parts of the western Pyrenees, and I am delighted to be able to acknowledge the assistance so professionally provided by the Archivo Historico Nacional in Madrid, the Archivo General del Reino de Navarra in Pamplona and the Musée Basque in Bayonne. I should like to thank D. Jose Goñi Gaztambide, Archivist of Pamplona Cathedral, for valuable discussion of some problems relating to early Navarrese history and particularly the charter evidence. I benefitted greatly from the advice of Professor John Morby on matters of regnal dating and from that of Dr Margaret Collins and Peter Essam on those of archaeology and geology respectively. I should like to give particular thanks to Dr Chris Wickham for allowing me to read his important and stimulating article on pastoralism in early medieval Europe well in advance of its publication as part of the proceedings of the 1983 Spoleto conference; this article enormously clarified my thinking. To John Davey of Basil Blackwell I am most grateful for the spur to translate this book from concept to reality by his offer to include it in this series, and to its editors James Campbell and Barry Cunliffe for the numerous improvements that they have wrought upon it. It is a source of particular sorrow that my tutor, supervisor and friend Professor Michael Wallace-Hadrill did not live to be able to read this book, let alone detect its errors. As always my wife, Dr Judith McClure, has throughout kept an improving oversight on both the book and its author. Finally, the dedication marks but a small acknowledgement of a great debt.

Acknowledgements

The author and publishers are grateful to the following for permission to reproduce illustrations in this book. J. Allan Cash (p. 203); Archivo História Nacional, Madrid, Sección de Clero, Carpeta 1404, doc. 4 (p. 162), doc. 5 (p. 205), doc. 14 (p. 171), doc. 19 (p. 225); Bibliothèque Nationale, Paris, Ms. Latin 2855, fol. 73 (p. 213), Ms. Latin 8878, fol. 52v (p. 178); Bodleian Library, Oxford, Antiq C.B. 1571.1 (p. 257); Crown copyright reserved, University of Cambridge, Committee for Aerial Photography (p. 44); Diputacion Foral de Alava (pp. 246, 247); Escudo de Oro (pp. 136, 146, 232); Fotografia cedida y autorizada por el Patrimonio Nacional, Madrid, Codice Virgiliano: d.I.2, fol. 428 (p. 167); Germanisches National Museum, Nuremberg (p. 253); Hirmer Fotoarchiv (pp. 188, 190); Les Editiones d'Art Yvon (p. 237); Museo Arqueologico Nacional, Madrid (p. 42); Museo Provincial Arqueologia de Alava (pp. 23, 25, 27, 29, 39, 41, 49, 50, 60, 77, 147, 153); Roger-Viollet (pp. 118, 175, 219); Stadsarchief, Bruges (p. 242); Wines from Spain (p. 62). Map 2 on p. 6 and map 15 on p. 105 are from J. Bernard and J. Ruffie, 'Hématologie et culture', *Annales — Économies, Societes, Civilisations*, 31, 1976. All other illustrations have been supplied by the author.

1

An Ancient People

For few other peoples of the world, and surely no other in Europe, can the scholarly study of their origins and earliest history be a matter of such direct and contemporary importance, linked at not many removes to political debate and even terrorism, as is the case with the Basques. Admittedly, for various minorities and in some instances whole populations of independent states, appeals to history and to their particular past have been used to justify resistance to oppressors, real or imaginary, and to help provide a focus for national identity. But in few such cases do the arguments get taken as far back as by the Basques, or does the antiquity of a people have so direct a relationship with its present. More recent phases of their history are, of course, also held to be of crucial significance, but what is tantamount to a politicization of normally abstruse and recherché anthropological arguments about the Stone Age is a distinctive feature of the ideological underpinning of modern Basque nationalism, in which the longevity of the people and the continuity of their occupation of their western Pyrenean home-lands are arguments of central importance.

At the simplest level the Basque claim to have inhabited uninterruptedly more or less the same areas of the Iberian peninsula in which they are still to be found since the neolithic

Note on references: For a substantial general bibliography relating to all aspects of Basque history, society and literature recourse should be made to the ten volumes of *Eusko-Bibliographía*, eds C. Cuerpo and J. Bilbao (San Sebastián, 1960—75). For more recent publications, see the annual bulletins provided in *Anuario de Bibliografía Vasca*, ed. J. Bilbao (Vitoria-Gasteiz); vol. I (1983) contains publications of 1981, and so on. Only references of immediate relevance are given in the footnotes to this book.

Map 1   The Basque provinces and their capitals

(*c.* 4000 BC) or even the palaeolithic (ends *c.* 9000 BC) periods
marks them off from the rest of the inhabitants of Spain,
relative newcomers on the scene and of different racial and
cultural origin (see map 1). Similarly, what might appear to be
purely linguistic arguments relating to the theory of Vasco-
Iberism, which will be discussed below, can rapidly take on a
political complexion when it is appreciated that this hypothesis
that Basque is the last surviving vestige of a language once
spoken throughout the whole of the Iberian peninsula can be
used to imply a closer historical relationship between Basques
and other Spaniards than some of the former are currently
prepared to accept. Such drawing out of implications and
undertones from scholarly debates otherwise far removed from
the concerns of daily life may seem far-fetched, even rather

paranoid, but the present state of Basque nationalist arguments and the counter-thrusts of its centralizing opponents are such that few statements relating to the people, their history and their language can be treated as being politically neutral. How such a state of affairs came into existence may in part be explained by some of the processes studied in this book, though it is important to stress that the current extreme form of some of the manifestations of nationalism, both in intellectual argument and in the recourse to violence and terror, are very recent developments. For the present it is sufficient to appreciate the need to be wary of the covert significance of arguments that might otherwise seem to be scholarly, rarefied, or even just boring. Thus current discussions of the origins and antiquity of the Basques must be approached with considerable caution, and it is probably sensible to try to reformulate the questions in as neutral a way as is possible.

Anthropology

The first problem is therefore one of definition: what criteria should be employed in the delineation of the Basque national identity? Some of the most successful peoples of the world (in terms of longevity at least), such as the Chinese or relatively more recently the Arabs, have maintained their existence and sense of racial unity, despite largeness of numbers and breadth of geographical extension, by their ability to absorb new elements of population of initially different cultural and racial origin. Acceptance of a common language and a common material culture, and also in some though not all cases of a common religion, has enabled other racial elements to be absorbed despite or possibly assisted by protestations of exclusivity on the part of the absorbing culture. Thus the Chinese have been able to engulf several waves of invading, and indeed conquering nomadic peoples in the course of an existence of over 4000 years. The Arabs, conquerors themselves, have achieved a similar result in the opposite direction by absorbing large numbers of very varied subject populations, largely on the basis of the acceptance of a language and a religion. Even more remarkable is the case of the Jews who, despite nearly two millennia of the Diaspora and an apparently total racial and religious exclusivity, have been able to absorb elements of population as various as the Russian Ashkenazim, some of whom are perhaps of central Asian origin, and the Ethiopian Falashas, whilst the very existence of such a process is vociferously denied. In contrast, though, the Basques, few in number and geographically highly localized, would seem to represent the opposite polarity: a people who have successfully resisted absorption by a succession of conquering or neighbouring cultures, and one who, despite the loss of their political independence, have preserved not only a unique language and material culture but also a distinctive physical identity that marks them off from the rest of mankind.

Such a claim to physiognomic distinctiveness is not unique to the Basques, though it is usually expressed in very generalized terms and breaks down on close inspection. It often consists of no more than a fairly loose notion of a racial stereotype, which allows for a substantial amount of variation within the bounds of certain rather broad limitations. Thus within the Chinese self-delineation as 'the black-haired people', a ginger-headed China-man is inconceivable. Similarly, from the other end of the world, the red-haired Umayyad caliph of Spain Abd ar-Raḥmān III found it expedient to have recourse to black hair dye, doubtless so as not to strain credibility within the very loose, but clearly finite, perceptions of Arab physical self-imagery. The Basques, however, have in recent times advanced a series of very specific and supposedly scientific claims about the nature of their physical make-up. It should be stressed that no evidence suggests that they defined themselves in such terms in any previous stage in their history. These claims are relatively straightforward in so far as they relate to what is supposed to represent a specifically Basque physiognomic type, with distinctive cranial formation and hair and eye colouring. However, the quest has been as much pursued inside the body as without: the Basques have claimed, *vis-à-vis* other European peoples, to have a distinctive blood.[1]

Tests have been used to show that a disproportionately high percentage of Basques have blood of group O: 55 per cent as

[1] J. Altuna, 'La race basque', in *Être Basque*, ed. J. Haritschelar (Toulouse, 1983), pp. 89—105.

opposed to 40 per cent of Spaniards and 43 per cent of Frenchmen. Similarly, it appears that the blood groups B and AB are proportionately even rarer amongst Basques than amongst their fellow western Europeans:

Blood group	Basques	Spaniards	Frenchmen
B	3%	9%	10.5%
AB	1.5%	4.5%	4.5%

Equally significant are held to be the results of tests conducted via the rhesus system, and the overall conclusions of this research have recently been summed up as follows:

Cette composition sanguine indique aussi que la population basque est la moins hybride de l'Europe. Les autres races européennes, à l'origine plus proches de celle des Basques, seraient parvenues à leur état actuel par la réception des gènes provenant des invasions asiatiques. Le peuple basque serait celui qui s'est maintenu le plus pur, s'affirmant plus impénétrable aux courants d'immigration.[2]

The invoking of such notions as that of 'purity' of blood and the implication that most of the rest of the population of western Europe constitute genetic mongrels of basically asiatic origin will hardly endear such arguments to the reader, well enough aware of the appalling consequences of such thinking for the history of the continent in the earlier part of this century. However well grounded the research — and the sample was a relatively small and almost exclusively urban one — some of the interpretations put upon it are dangerously fanciful and have been harnessed to ends that are neither objective nor scientific. However, more extensive testing of larger samples and over longer periods was carried out by French scientists in the area of the northern slopes of the Pyrenees in the 1940s and 1950s with almost identical results. But they have related their work not to broader theories of the movement of racial groups but rather to other anthropological and place-name research concerned with the same regions.[3] Their studies provide further support for the notion that the proportions of the different genetic and blood types found in the areas of occupation of Basque speakers are

[2] Ibid., p. 102.
[3] J. Bernard and J. Ruffié, 'Hématologie et culture: le peuplement de l'Europe de l'ouest', *Annales — Économies, Sociétés, Civilisations*, 31 (1976), pp. 661—76.

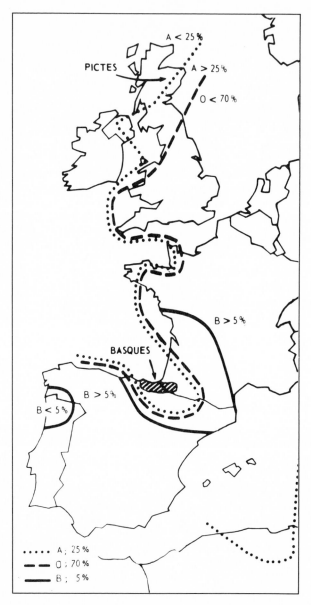

Map 2   Blood group variations: a European perspective

notably different from those encountered in many though not all (see map 2) of the other parts of western Europe. However, their most direct value has been in respect of the corroboration they can give to hypotheses under consideration in other disciplines, such as that of an earlier and wider diffusion of a Basque population throughout southern Aquitaine than purely literary sources of evidence can indicate.

Particularly important, too, is the appreciation that this predominance in statistical terms of particular blood groups in no way corresponds to any expectation of the existence of a uniform skull type. Thus there is a marked difference between the dominant skull shape to be found on the northern slopes of the western Pyrenees and that to be encountered on the southern, the former being generally brachycephalic or 'short-headed' and the latter dolichocephalic or 'long-headed' (these being determined by the relative proportions of breadth to length in any given skull). It is indeed now accepted that cranial structures are only imperfectly controlled by hereditary factors, and that little reliance can therefore be placed upon arguments for long-term continuity of a human group on the basis of skull formation.

In the Basque case this has again been taken to extremes in recent arguments of an otherwise rarefied anthropological kind. The discovery of a few fragments of a single skull of a late Cro-Magnon man (*c.* 9000 BC) in the Basque region has been held to establish that the cranial formation of the inhabitants of the western Pyrenees in the palaeolithic period is identical to that of their modern counterparts. From this is deduced a direct continuity of occupation of the region by the Basques and their prehistoric forebears from the very earliest period.[4] That a conclusion of such magnitude could be based upon so little evidence, too small even to constitute a representative sample, is quite breath-taking, and must inevitably arouse the suspicion that it is being dictated by the predetermined requirements of nationalist ideology rather than by processes of rational deduction. Once again it is necessary to recognize that flawed methodology is being employed to arrive at conclusions that are, if not totally impossible, at least in the highest degree

---

[4] Altuna, 'La race basque', pp. 90—5; but see Bernard and Ruffié, 'Hématologie', p. 665 and the bibliography cited there for the dangers of such an approach to the evidence of skull type.

improbable, and which will only convince those already committed to them for other reasons.

Ultimately, it looks as if an exclusively anthropological approach to the questions of Basque origins and self-definition fails to carry conviction, as a result of a lack of sufficient evidence. Basque identity thus has to be defined in cultural rather than physical terms. Even here, though, problems abound. It is almost impossible to talk about Basque material culture, not only in terms of prehistoric periods, but also for those of classical antiquity and the Middle Ages. This is a difficulty, therefore, that will accompany every stage of this investigation. Its causes are various, and change from period to period. There has been some excellent archaeological work done on the various prehistoric stages of human occupation of the western Pyrenees, but there is nothing intrinsic to the material remains of the megalithic and cave cultures thus investigated which proves these to be the products of societies lineally related to that people later known as the Basques.[5] In so far as that can and has been suggested it is purely by inference and on other grounds. Hence, for example, the far-reaching claims made for the Cro-Magnon skull. On the other hand, and not immediately relevant here, is the fact that for later periods, when historical and documentary evidence makes it certain that the Basques were firmly settled in the Pyrenean and Biscayan regions, there has been virtually no archaeological investigation conducted into the material remains of their society. Roman urban and villa sites have been excavated and work has been done on some later medieval towns, but for a variety of reasons Basque rural society is at the moment archaeologically non-existent.

Language

This then leaves language as the sole satisfactory tool with which it is possible to approach the questions of Basque identity and origins. This obviously has authority in its own right but, as

[5] For the French Pyrenees in particular see P. G. Bahn, *Pyrenean Prehistory* (Warminster, 1984), and for the Spanish Basque provinces the extensive archaeological bibliographies in *Eusko-Bibliographia* eds C. Cuerpo and J. Bilbao (San Sebastián, 1960—75), especially for the work of J. M. de Barandiarán, the doyen of Basque archaeologists.

has been suggested, for the period before the first appearance of documentary records relating to the Basques (which is to say roughly the beginning of the Christian era) it has to stand alone as the means of analysing these complex and currently highly controversial problems. It must be admitted that it proves far from satisfactory as the sole means of support for a weighty edifice. Ancient records of the Basque language are non-existent, and the earliest surviving texts written in it date only from the late Middle Ages; to which can probably be added a section from an eleventh-century charter that appears to be in Basque or represents an attempt to write it.[6] Thus, although 'those who speak the Basque language' is probably the safest or indeed the only workable definition of the Basque people, historical references to the existence of the Basques by outsiders predate by at least a millennium the first extant examples of the language in its written form.

Moreover, the peculiarity of the language is such that it has so far defied acceptable classification. Theories as to its relationship to other language groups certainly abound, but none of them has yet achieved sufficient consensus of scholarly opinion in its favour to be regarded as orthodoxy, however temporary. Indeed the linguistic analysis of Basque remains a peculiarly controversial field of endeavour. Leaving aside views already discredited, some of which were highly ingenious, only two lines of enquiry are being currently pursued. On the one hand there is the Vasco-Iberist theory, that sees Basque as the last remnant of a language spoken in most, if not all, parts of the Iberian peninsula before the Roman conquest. Basically this would imply that the Basques are the descendants of the Iberians, a significant if shadowy people, perhaps of north African origin, who occupied most of south and central Spain in the opening half of the first millennium BC, and who exercised substantial cultural and linguistic influence on the other main body of immigrant population, the Celts. The evidence on which such an argument is based is necessarily limited, in that other traces of the Iberian language are remarkably few, and consist effectively of some inscriptions on coins and some place-names. A number of effective counters to the Vasco-Iberist

---

[6] See below, p. 194.

thesis have been launched on historical and linguistic grounds, and, although not yet defunct, it must be said of it that its credibility has been seriously undermined.[7]

The other direction which the enquiry has taken has been towards certain, rather limited, points of similarity between Basque and some of the Caucasian languages of the Kartvelian class — that is to say, those such as Georgian and other smaller related languages of non-Indo-European origin.[8] Although suggestive, the similarities have been too few to afford conclusive evidence of affinity, and by some the whole relationship is firmly denied.[9] Another and parallel line of approach has been through languages which no longer exist as spoken tongues, but which can be reconstructed on the basis of modern languages in which certain elements of them are believed to be encapsulated. Such a line of enquiry depends upon the acceptability of this theory of substrate languages, in which it is held that features of extinct tongues are lurking beneath some modern ones and are capable of identification and isolation by linguistic analysis.[10] This has led to attempts to relate Basque to substrate elements in languages otherwise as far removed as old Irish and Berber.[11] However, it must be confessed that substrate theory has by no means won universal acceptance, and its application to the Basque problem has proved to be far from satisfactory. Basque itself has had to be used in the isolating of substrate features in other languages, and thus to turn them back upon themselves to help in the classification of Basque can give a certain circularity to the line of argument! Also the supposed relationships between peoples thus detected by substrate theory can on occasion

---

[7] J. Caro Baroja, 'Sobre la hipótesis del Vascoiberismo', *Emerita*, 10 (1942), pp. 236—86; 11 (1943), pp. 1—59; reprinted in his *Sobre la lengua vasca* (San Sebastián, 1979), pp. 11—120.

[8] C. C. Uhlenbeck, 'De la possibilité d'un parenté entre le basque et les langues caucasiques', *Revista internacional de estudios vascos*, 15 (1924), pp. 565—88; R. Lafon, 'Basque et les langues Kartvèles', ibid. 24 (1933), pp. 150—75; R. Lafon, *Études basques et caucasiques* (Salamanca, 1952).

[9] M. Díez, F. Morales and A. Sabin, *Las lenguas de España* (Madrid, 1977), pp. 301—25.

[10] J. Hubschmid, *Pyrenäenwörter, vorromanischen Ursprungs und das vorromanische Substrat der Alpen* (Salamanca, 1954); J. Hubschmid, *Mediterrane Substrate, mit besonderer Berücksichtigung des Baskischen und der west-östlichen Sprachbeziehungen* (Bern, 1960).

[11] H. Wagner, 'Common problems concerning the early languages of the British Isles and the Iberian peninsula', in *Actas del I Colloquio sobre lenguas y culturas prerromanas de la península ibérica* (Salamanca, 1976), pp. 387—407.

stretch credibility to breaking point, or be justified only by recourse to some very odd history.[12]

On one thing at least there is no disagreement, which is that Basque is a non-Indo-European language, and as such the only one extant in western Europe. There are a small number of others in the continent as a whole, including Hungarian, Finnish and Estonian, but all of these are to be found on its easternmost fringes, and the establishment of their speakers in their current homelands occurred within the historical period and can be more or less fully documented from existing records, as for example with the establishment of the Magyars in the first half of the tenth century on the plains of Hungary. Although all of these languages have certain points of superficial similarity to Basque, as for instance the immediately obvious fact that they are all aglutinating (that is to say, they make more specific or augment the meaning of words by suffixing additional elements to the original word rather than by putting them in apposition to them) the relationship is basically insignificant. Even in historical terms it is clear that the Basques were established in the Pyrenean homelands at least a millennium before the arrival of the Magyars in eastern Europe.

Thus Basque is the sole surviving, anciently established, non-Indo-European language of Europe. Even in other areas as physically isolated and apparently resistant to change, such as Albania and Sardinia, the spoken languages, not only at the present but also as far back as they can be recorded, belong to the Indo-European linguistic family, and are therefore directly related to the majority languages of the continent. Only substrate theorists have been able to isolate certain limited elements in them that are, perhaps, indicative of an earlier pre-Indo-European linguistic level. The only partial exception to the linguistic isolation of Basque — and this relates to the speech of a people who lost their separate identity about 1000 years ago — might be made in respect of Pictish. Here is an area in which caution is immediately necessary. Over-enthusiastic scholars at the end of the last century sought to reconstruct the Pictish language on the basis of assumed parallels with Basque, but so effectively did they discredit themselves that even today to

---

[12] For example, the use Wagner (ibid.) has to make of the theories on migrations of T. F. O'Rahilly, *Early Irish History and Mythology* (Dublin, 1946).

include the words 'Basque' and 'Pictish' in the same sentence is sufficient to arouse suspicions of eccentricity.[13] For Pictish is only represented by a small number of ambivalent inscriptions, certain elements of which seem to be clearly identifiable as Celtic. Indeed, although persuasive arguments exist for regarding the historical Picts, who flourished from *c.* AD 200 to *c.* AD 900, as having combined sections of both pre-Indo-European and Celtic population, at least one recent study has denied the existence of the former at all, and has sought to regard the Picts as a purely Celtic and therefore Indo-European people.[14] The present state of Pictish studies and the extremely limited nature of its evidence relevant to this enquiry makes it too frail to support a major role in the investigation of Basque origins.

This in practice leaves Basque linguistically isolated, which in itself is a feature likely to be indicative of considerable antiquity on the part of the language. For languages do not develop in isolation, and the lack of obvious cousinage suggests a longevity that has seen the demise of previous near-relatives. In itself this is important, as it is true of only a limited number of languages. Furthermore, on the basis of comparison between the earliest available Basque texts, admittedly only of late medieval date, and current usage it has become clear to linguists that this is a language that is highly resistant to significant grammatical change, and is thus likely, even in its present state, to be much closer to its original form than is, for example, modern to ancient Greek or modern to biblical Hebrew.[15] It should be said that this conservatism does not extend to vocabulary, in which the limitations of Basque social and political structures have led to the need for extensive verbal borrowing, and neologisms have been coined in large numbers from the Middle Ages onwards, above all in the nineteenth century.[16]

---

[13] K. H. Jackson, 'The Pictish language', in *The Problem of the Picts*, ed. F. T. Wainwright, 2nd edn (Perth, 1980), pp. 129—66, especially pp. 130—1, 152.

[14] A. P. Smyth, *Warlords and Holy Men: Scotland AD 80—100* (London, 1984), pp. 45—50.

[15] A. Tovar, *The Ancient Languages of Spain and Portugal* (New York, 1961), pp. 127—37.

[16] R. M. de Azkue, *Diccionario Vasco-Español-Francés* (2 vols, Bilbao, 1969), pp. xv—xxi.

Survivors or migrants?

Where, though, does this all lead in historical terms? One obvious explanation for this linguistic isolation and the antiquity of the language is that the Basques constitute the sole survivors of the pre-Indo-European population of Europe. Thus they somehow succeeded in surviving the period of Indo-European migrations in the Bronze Age (*c.* 2500—1000 BC) that otherwise swamped the material and linguistic culture of their late Stone Age relatives, leaving them a peculiar island of antiquity in a sea of newer peoples. Their survival in an apparently remote, mountainous and probably densely forested part of Europe might support such a view. However, it is important to note from the start that the Basque-inhabited regions of the Pyrenees and northern Spain are not as isolated as they may appear superficially to be. As is clear from more recent periods, the lines of communication across the western Pyrenees were not difficult of use, and it is certain that terrain much more resistant to penetration did not enable other pockets of pre-Indo-European population to survive elsewhere in Europe. Nor, when the Romans encountered them, were the Basques substantially different in material culture and social organization from the other peoples of northern Spain, whose lifestyles were recorded in the writings of the classical geographers. In other words, if they really had dwelt in the Pyrenees since the Stone Age, this had not been at the cost of remaining uninfluenced by their neighbours.

The archaeological record of the Basque regions from the neolithic to the Roman occupation indicates considerable regional variety within the area and, at least in respect of burial customs, fluctuation and change. As has been mentioned, in itself archaeology can give no answer to the question of whether the populations practising various forms of mound and tumulus building were Basque or not. That is part of the interpretative framework to be drawn from other sources, in relation to which the archaeological evidence may be considered. It does, however, indicate that these regions were not culturally isolated, and that those developments within them that have been studied are

more or less congruous with ones occurring at the same periods
in other parts of southern France and northern Spain. Unfortunately, the evidence does become exceedingly sparse for the
crucial Bronze Age stage, when the greatest differentiation
between Indo-European migrants with a new technology and
older elements of indigenous population, as the Basques are
held to be, might be expected or sought for. In fact the
association of the Indo-Europeans with the new metallurgy and
its dissemination is by no means assured, and periodization of
this kind on the basis of a supposedly dominant technology may
prove to be something of an intellectual strait-jacket. At any
rate the question of possible Basque continuity across a notional
neolithic/Bronze Age divide cannot be answered in archaeological
terms.

If it be thought that Basque survival in these regions from
virtually the earliest periods of antiquity is inexplicable or
unacceptable as an hypothesis, what then can the alternative
be? The only other explanation for their presence must be that
they represented an alien element of population somehow
carried along in the phase of the Indo-European migrations,
who, for whatever reasons, finally came to rest in the western
Pyrenees — probably therefore at some point in the second
millennium BC or possibly even more recently.[17] It might be
objected that the existence of such a non-Indo-European component in an otherwise linguistically and culturally homogenous
movement of migration is inherently improbable, and at the
very least it should have been subsumed into the majority
culture. However, a parallel case may be that of the Alans, an
almost certainly non-Indo-European people, who accompanied
the Germanic Vandals and Sueves in their migrations in the
early fifth century AD.[18]

Thus there are problems and objections to be faced on both
lines of argument, and there is insufficient evidence to provide a
satisfactory resolution. This may all seem unduly pessimistic,
but there is little point in pretending to a certainty that is
unjustified. Perhaps the balance of probability might favour the
idea of long-term continuity of the Basque occupation of the

[17] Wagner, 'Common problems', pp. 390—1.
[18] B. Bachrach, *A History of the Alans in the West* (Minneapolis, 1973), especially
pp. 26—73.

western Pyrenees from at least the neolithic, though almost certainly not the palaeolithic, for which period there is only very slight evidence of any human habitation of the region.[19] The conservatism and relative purity of the language might tend to favour such a view, as language can prove fragile in periods of upheaval and population mobility, as, for example, the fate of Gothic might indicate. However, it is all too clear that no answer can hope to be considered as being definitive, and recourse might usefully be made instead to an expedient adopted in the study of an equally enigmatic though ultimately less successful people — the Picts. This is to make a sharp divide between the period in which their society can be studied on the basis of historical records, however scanty and albeit not of their own making, and that for which there is no such basis for investigation.[20] The Pictish problem is, in this respect at least, identical to the Basque one: the genesis of the Picts in the prehistoric period is impossible to trace, and the surviving evidence is of the kind that it makes the question not only unanswerable but also irrelevant. This also must be the verdict for the Basques, despite much ingenuity and wishful thinking.

The evidence just does not exist, be it anthropological, archaeological or linguistic, on which it would be possible to state where the Basques came from, and when and how they established themselves in the western Pyrenees. Not until the period for which we have our first written accounts of them, which is to say around the beginning of the Christian era, do the Basques take on a clear historical dimension. In this respect the Basques seem to prove Bishop Berkeley's line of argument: they only exist when we can see them! Thus, although they may well have occupied their lands for 2000 or more years by the time they first make their mark in the historical record, those earlier phases of their existence have to be assumed rather than proved. In the case of the Picts this earlier prehistorical phase has been conveniently labelled 'proto-Pictish', and has been left open-ended. It is perhaps wise or indeed necessary to do likewise with the Basques and to refer to that period of their existence before

[19] J. M. de Barandiarán, *La prehistoria en el pirineo vasco: estado actual de su estudio* (Zaragoza, 1952), p. 9 and map 1.

[20] F. T. Wainwright, 'The Picts and the problem', in *Wainwright, The Picts*, pp. 1—53.

they are clearly vouched for in the historical record as 'proto-Basque'. This would be a regrettable but sensible expedient.

Although this particular cutting of the Gordian knot resolves the difficulty of having to ask questions which the available information is unsuited to answer, and at the same time effectively divides Basque history and prehistory into two separate and more manageable units, it does not entitle us to dismiss the 'proto-Basque' period as being now irrelevant to our purposes. For one thing the ethnographic composition of the western Pyrenees was exceedingly complex by the time it first came under the scrutiny of Greek and Roman travellers and geographical writers. As will be seen their reports are far from unambiguous as to the distribution and differentiation between peoples in these regions. As a result there is distinct uncertainty as to which of the numerous tribes they refer to were Basque and which were not. Even taking the minimal definition of 'Basqueness' as being the common use of the Basque language, and allowing that there was much similarity in material culture between Basque and non-Basque peoples in the general region of the western Pyrenees at the beginning of the Roman period, some resolution of the problem is necessary if the subsequent history of the Basques is to be followed.

Proto-Basque: the archaeological evidence

As has been seen, it is impossible to pick out the Basques on *a priori* grounds. Instead it is necessary to cast an eye over the general development of the area in the 'proto-Basque' period to see if from the archaeological evidence a picture emerges that makes sense when it is assumed that amongst the various cultures of the region, and in a span of time extending from either the neolithic or at the latest the Bronze Age, there existed a distinctive and continuing body of population who represent the ancestors of the Basques. Such an enquiry can be geograph-ically restricted: we are not expecting to find our 'proto-Basques' in Scandinavia, for example. Whatever theoretical model may be taken to explain how they got there, their presence is only going to be detectable in areas contiguous with the western Pyrenees. Here the Basques have been found ever since the beginning of the first millennium AD, and it is here that any hunt for the fossil impression of their ancestors must begin. It is indeed a fossil that is being sought because, for the reasons previously given, the living presence of the Basques in their prehistorical phase cannot be found, and we are reduced to looking for the impression they left in the overall pattern of the human societies that existed in these regions during antiquity. In practice this is only likely to be found in an area covering Aquitaine south of the river Garonne, if not the Loire, the whole of the middle and upper Ebro valley, all of the central and western Pyrenees, and the whole of the eastern half of the north coastal region of the Iberian peninsula. This represents the greatest extent of the territories in which Basque-speaking populations have been found or have been claimed to have been found in the course of the last three millennia. Even if the Vasco-Iberist argument be accepted — and there are fairly strong grounds for not doing so — a wider Basque presence within Spain cannot be postulated within this timespan, and a larger extension of Basque occupation in France has never been claimed.

The area under consideration is easily subdivided. The chain of the Pyrenees runs almost directly across its centre, and exercises a decisive influence on climate, communications and forms of human society in the region. Within the mountains themselves the history of man has largely been the history of valleys, micro-worlds whose geographical configuration often makes them easier of access from related valleys across the watershed than from those parallel to them on their own side of the mountains (see map 3). The line of the mountains runs roughly east to west along the 43rd parallel from the Mediterranean to the Bay of Biscay; however, just before it reaches the latter, the watershed is deflected towards the south and runs to meet the mountains of Cantabria, which extend along most of the northern coast of Spain. This has created three separate but related additional regions and areas of human settlement: the almost flat and low-lying alluvial plains of southern Aquitaine, cut by the Adour and the Garonne and their tributaries; the broad but relatively arid valley of the upper Ebro, to the south of the Pyrenees and east of the point at which the watershed turns towards Cantabria; and finally the narrow coastal strip at

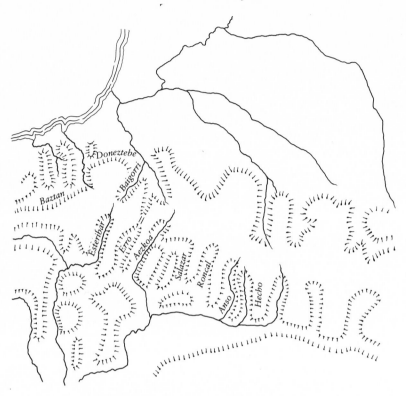

Map 3   Principal valleys of the western Pyrenees

the western end of the mountains and north of the watershed. Both the first and the third of these regions receive a high rainfall from the Atlantic, effected by the mountains, whilst the Ebro is poorly watered. The latter region is most open to human penetration from the east, along the open line of the valley extending down to the Mediterranean, but there are also limited but usable lines of communication between the valley and southern Aquitaine and also the coastal area via a number of passes across the mountains.[21] (The principal river systems of Navarre are shown in map 4.)

[21] For a study of the interrelationship of the valleys to the north and to the south of the Pyrenees in recent centuries, see H. Cavaillès, 'Une fédération pyrénéenne sous l'Ancien Régime: les traités de liès et de passeries', *Revue Historique*, 105 (1910), pp. 1—34, 241—76. The best geographical study of the region is that of D. A. Gómez-Ibañez, *The Western Pyrenees* (Oxford, 1975).

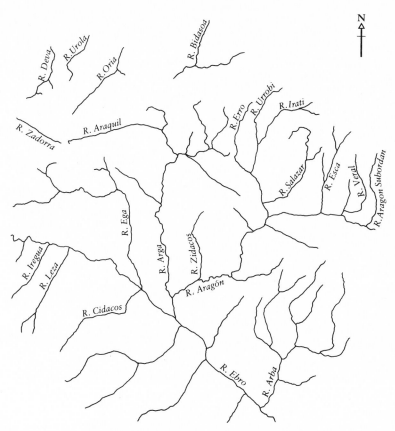

Map 4   Principal river systems of Navarre

Although the present heavily wooded appearance of the coastal and north Pyrenean regions of the Basque lands is the product of extensive reafforestation in the last century, climatic conditions are such that this heavy vegetation has probably always been a natural feature of these areas; it seems likely that birch was once the dominant form of tree, but it has now been largely replaced by beech.[22] This will have served as a further check on communications, already restricted by the mountainous terrain. Although the average height of the mountains declines progressively from the central Pyrenees to the Biscayan coast,

[22] Gómez-Ibañez, *The Western Pyrenees*, p. 17.

ending in a series of relatively small and isolated massifs, it is likely that in the absence of sea-borne communications the coastal strip was the remotest and least easily penetrated of all these regions, not even forming part of the normal land route across the Pyrenean chain. On the northern and southern fringes of the area as a whole the swampy sand dunes (now forested) of the Landes, and the high southern wall of the Ebro valley, served to delimit it from its neighbours.

The evidence for the earliest period of human occupation of these areas, which occurred in the last glacial period (*c.* 40,000— 10,000 BC), is extremely sparse, and is represented by little more than a couple of find sites in Alava, four in Navarre and an important cave painting in Aragón.[23] Only if we are prepared to accept the anthropological argument for continuity, to whose difficulties we have previously referred, would it be possible to consider these Cro-Magnon men to be the lineal ancestors of the later Basque inhabitants of the region. Even if that were admissible, the social and economic discontinuities are so great that such a supposed relationship would be meaningless, except conceivably for the arguments of modern nationalism. Additionally, it is thought highly probable that the last Ice Age marked a lacuna in human habitation in these parts.[24] Finds from the post-glacial final stage of the palaeolithic and from the succeeding mesolithic, if slightly more numerous than for the previous period, are still relatively rare and are highly localized (see map 5).

The ensuing neolithic, which lasted roughly from 4000 to 2000 BC, is far better represented in the archaeological record, and may have seen an effective repopulating of most of the area. There are, however, notable regional variations. In the more fertile Alava, around the upper Ebro, the culture of the neolithic may be said to be fully developed by the mid fourth millennium BC, whilst in much of Navarre it looks to have been a much slower process. One of the most distinctive features of the material culture of the neolithic is the first emergence of pottery.

[23] I. Barandiarán Maestu, 'Las primeras formas de organización del hábitat y del territorio en el País Vasco', in *El Hábitat en la Historia de Euskadi* (Bilbao, 1981), pp. 11—30; A. Baldeón Iñigo et al., *Museo de Arqueología de Alava* (Vitoria-Gasteiz, 1983), pp. 20—1; A. F. Samanes and A. M. Duque (eds), *Atlas de Navarra*, 2nd edn (Barcelona, 1981), p. 39.

[24] Baldeón Iñigo et al., *Museo de Arqueología de Alava*, p. 16.

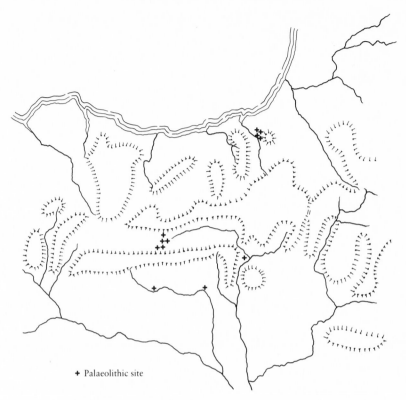

+ Palaeolithic site

Map 5   Major palaeolithic find sites in the western Pyrenees

While a large number of simple pots have been recovered in Alava, principally from cave habitation sites, only one such source of ceramics is recorded as having been found in Navarre.[25] Even more striking are the conclusions drawn by recent work on the French western Pyrenees in respect of another distinctive feature of this period in western Europe — the development of cultivation. This transformation of the basis of human society away from total dependence upon hunting and towards a mixed economy of farming, hunting and stock rearing has been labelled 'the neolithic revolution', and it obviously had crucial effects, not least in the development of fixed settlement sites and the growth of more complex forms of social organization.

[25] This is the cave site of Zatoya; see Samanes and Duque, *Atlas de Navarra*, p. 69 and map on p. 39.

However, it seems that, unlike much of the rest of the continent, such innovations do not manifest themselves in the northern regions of the Pyrenees before the succeeding period of the Bronze Age (*c.* 2000—900 BC), and that the older style of a purely pastoral economy survived undisturbed.[26] It would seem likely that similar conclusions might be drawn from the Navarrese evidence, whilst the indications of a more settled agrarian economy have been detected in certain parts of Alava.[27]

There are other cultural distinctions, the precise significance of which are not always clear, to be drawn between different parts of the region at this period. Firstly there exist basically two different forms of habitation site, one in caves and the other in the open air.[28] This may well not mark a distinction between two different cultures, but may rather represent the difference between winter and summer settlements within a transhumant economy. Climatically conditions in the western Pyrenees may have been more extreme than at present, with longer, harder and colder winters. Cave sites obviously presented the best seasonal protection, whilst the pastoral mode of subsistence will have necessitated the creation of temporary (though perhaps recurrent) dwelling sites away from the roots of the mountains. On the other hand, some of the 'open air' sites, particularly in Alava, may represent places of permanent habitation linked to crop raising.

Another marked regional distinction is the clear division of the whole area into two sections according to whether or not dolmens are present (see map 6).[29] In general this coincides with a separation of the mountains proper from the lower lands

[26] P. G. Bahn, 'The neolithic of the French Pyrenees', in *Ancient France, 6000—2000 BC*, ed. C. Scarre (Edinburgh, 1984), pp. 184—223.

[27] Even in Alava there is no evidence of the domestication of fowl before *c.* 500 BC: J. Altuna, 'Los restos mas antiguos de gallo doméstico en el País Vasco', *Estudios de Arqueología Alavesa*, 11 (1983), pp. 381—6.

[28] E. Vallespi, 'Talleres de silex al aire libre en el País Vasco', *Estudios de Arqueología Alavesa*, 3 (1968), pp. 7—27; A. Baldeón Iñigo, 'Contribución al estudio de yacimientos al aire libre. Landa y Saldaroa', ibid., 9 (1978), pp. 17—45; J. M. Apellániz, 'Organización del territorio, arquitectura y concepto de espacio en la población prehistórica de cavernas del País Vasco', in *El Hábitat en la Historia de Euskadi* (Bilbao, 1981), pp. 31—48.

[29] For the distribution of dolmens see J. M. de Barandiarán, *La Prehistoria en el Pirineo Vasco* (Zaragoza, 1952), map 2; for those in Alava see the bibliography in Baldeón Iñigo et al., *Museo de Arqueología de Alava*, pp. 214—15; for Vizcaya see J. Gorrochategui and M. J. Yarritu, *Carta Arqueológica de Vizcaya II: Materiales de Superficie* (Bilbao, 1984), pp. 7—113.

The dolmen at Sorginetxe

surrounding them to north and south. The dolmens, or megalithic burial mounds, are found only in the mountainous areas, that is to say northern Navarre, Aragón, northern Alava, the coastal region north of the watershed, and also the southern parts of the French Pyrenees. The areas in which dolmens are found do not coincide exactly with the limits of cave settlement sites, but most of the 'open air' sites are found outside of the dolmen region. This may all indicate a division of the region as a whole

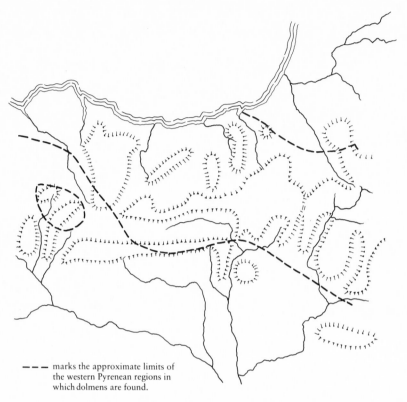

--- marks the approximate limits of
the western Pyrenean regions in
which dolmens are found.

Map 6   Dolmens: general pattern of distribution

between two basic culture groups: one cave-dwelling, dolmen-
building pastoralists, with little or no use for pottery and
farming, and the other following a mixed economy, employing
pottery and living in the 'open air' occupation sites. This is
conceivable, but an alternative explanation would be to unite
all of these elements within a single ecosystem, not fundamentally
different to that which functioned in the Basque areas in historic
times, and in which the cultural differences would be explained
by the requirements of transhumance linked to some limited
agricultural production. The mountains would be inhabited on
a seasonal basis for summer pasture, and with the flocks
accompanied by herders, whilst other members of the kin
groups remained in the valleys engaged in agriculture. Such a

The cave of Los Husos, Alava

model would explain the uneven pattern of the distribution of pottery, as well as the variation in occupation sites. The dolmens might seem, as a distinctive and localized form of burial practice, to present an insuperable obstacle for such a hypothesis. However, it has recently been suggested that they are not funerary monuments but, from their positioning on the crest line paths in the mountains, may instead have been erected to provide seasonal shelters for the pastoral herders, who would employ them on a regular annual basis.[30] Obviously such views result from an extrapolation from the economy of the region in more recent periods, but in so far as the fundamental geography and climate of the region have powerful determining effects upon the nature of the societies and the forms of the economies they can practise, such parallels should be taken seriously.[31] As for size of population, although such figures are not easy to substantiate, it has been estimated that the inhabitants of the

[30] Bahn, 'The neolithic of the French Pyrenees'.
[31] Gómez-Ibañez, *The Western Pyrenees*, pp. 24—8.

Basque regions to the south of the Pyrenees numbered roughly 9000 at any given point in the neolithic.[32]

In general, occupation and burial sites of the neolithic are to be found widely diffused over virtually all parts of what were later to be the Basque regions, and in several instances there is evidence of continuity of habitation across the notional divide between it and the ensuing Bronze Age.[33] As has been mentioned, the distinguishing of these chronological spans in technological terms is to some degree artificial. Flint instruments continued in use into the period of the Bronze Age (*c*. 2000—900 BC), and, as previously referred to, one of the major social transformations of the neolithic in other parts of Europe may only have established itself in the Pyrenean regions in the succeeding age. It is often suggested that the European Bronze Age resulted from migrations of peoples from further east, who introduced the metal technology into their new areas of occupation. This may not have been the case in the western Pyrenees, where there is more evidence of continuity and less of innovation. Furthermore, settlement and occupation sites increase in number and are to be found in more marginal areas that lack evidence of a previous neolithic phase of habitation.[34] This suggests the existence of an expanding population, whose developing skills enabled them to exploit parts of the region either not needed by or beyond the possible use of their ancestors. Thus the beginnings of metal technology in the Basque regions probably result from cultural diffusion from without rather than from the migration of new population into the area.

This may in part be confirmed by a comparison with the establishment of the two succeeding waves of Iron Age culture (*c*. 900—600 BC and *c*. 500—200 BC), which are represented only in sites situated well away from the mountains and principally found in the Ebro valley, in those of its tributaries and to the north of the Adour (see map 7). Virtually no Iron Age traces have been uncovered in the former 'dolmen region' of the

[32] A. C. F. Galilea, 'Aproximación a la demografía en Euskalerria sur durante el III—II milenio AC', *Estudios de Arqueología Alavesa*, 11 (1983), pp. 357—80.

[33] For example the cave site of Los Husos in Alava, on which see the annual reports by J. M. Apellániz in *Estudios de Arqueología Alavesa*, 2—7 (1967—74).

[34] For a comparative distribution of sites see the maps in Samanes and Duque, *Atlas de Navarra*, p. 39.

A carving of an Iron Age Celtic warrior, from Iruña

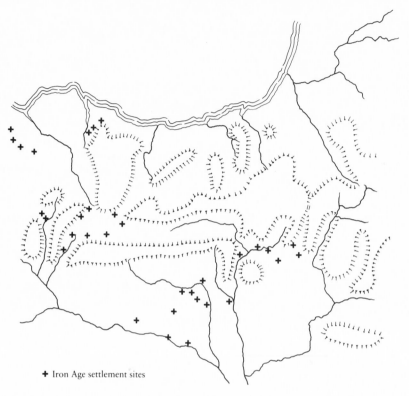

+ Iron Age settlement sites

Map 7   Iron Age settlements

mountainous spine of the Pyrenees. Iron Age sites are considerably fewer in number than for the previous Bronze Age, and
generally take the form of fortified settlements.[35] That these
represent the intrusion of a new and alien population, perhaps
established as a conquering aristocracy ruling over a subject
body of the earlier inhabitants, is a theory that is at least
plausible. The geographically limited traces of this otherwise
dominant culture, which survived until the imposition of Roman
rule, and which is generally congruous with that of other
neighbouring peoples in western Europe, notably the Celts,
would suggest that it is not that of our 'proto-Basques'.

[35] For a substantial account of a castro-culture site, see A. Llanos, J. M. Apellániz, J.
A. Agorreta and J. Fariña, 'El castro del castillo de Henayo. Alegria (Alava). Memoria
de excavaciones. Campañas de 1969—70', *Estudios de Arqueología Alavesa*, 8 (1975),
pp. 87—212.

The Castro de las Peñas de Oro, an Iron Age fortified settlement site

Moreover Alava, which contains numerous traces of these Iron Age cultures, looks from recent linguistic analysis to have undergone a period of profound Indo-Europeanization in the course of the first millennium BC.[36]

Thus parts of the areas for which in subsequent periods and in extant historical records it is possible to show that there was a substantial Basque presence, and which are marked by the existence of place-names of Basque origin, were directly affected by the two phases of Iron Age culture, of which the second was that of the Celt-Iberians.[37] These areas of occupation also more or less correspond to those in which crop raising appears first to have been practised. These are lands best able to support a more developed economy, and are also those most immediately open to penetration from outside the western Pyrenean region, being basically the river valleys draining away to the north and to the south of the mountains. The lack of penetration by the Iron Age

[36] M. L. Albertos, 'Alava prerromana y romana: estudio lingüístico', *Estudios de Arqueología Alavesa*, 4 (1970), pp. 107—223.
[37] J. J.-B. Merino Urrutia, *La lengua Vasca en la Rioja y Burgos*, 3rd edn (Logroño, 1978), pp. 9—76.

cultures of the mountain regions proper surely indicates that it
is not amongst them that we should be looking for the ancestors of
the Basques. It should be noted that this is not to imply that iron
objects, and possibly even the technology itself, did not establish
themselves in those areas of the Pyrenees not dominated by the
society of the conquering 'Iron Age' town dwellers. That the
Basques have descended from the indigenous neolithic/Bronze
Age inhabitants of the mountainous zones thus looks a reasonable hypothesis as far as the archaeological evidence is concerned.
There seems to have been a continuity of population in those
areas from the period of stone into the period of bronze, and by
and large the impact of the establishment of new peoples in the
Iron Age looks to have been localized geographically. This then
is conceivably the niche into which to place the society of the
'proto-Basques'; this is their fossil imprint. There remains the
question of those areas that were later clearly in Basque
occupation, such as the upper Ebro valley and other parts of
Alava, but which in the first millennium BC came under the
domination of cultures socially, economically and linguistically
alien to that of the Basques. Did these cultures achieve only a
temporary dominance and fail to assimilate an essentially
'proto-Basque' subject population, or is the clear Basque imprint
in such regions the product of a later phase of expansion? The
evidence of subsequent periods, for which for the first time
written records exist, may help to solve such problems. With the
ending of the pre-Roman Iron Age the Basques make their first
unambiguous mark upon the historical scene.

2

The Basques and Rome

Tribal origins

In about AD 7, roughly a quarter of a century after the completion of the protracted Roman conquest of the Iberian peninsula, a Greek historian and geographical writer called Strabo (*c.* 64 BC to *c.* AD 24) composed his *Geography* in 17 books, of which the third was devoted to Spain. Although he himself had travelled widely, his personal experience was probably limited to the eastern Mediterranean and Italy and for his accounts of western lands he turned to earlier sources, notably the otherwise now lost writings of the philosopher Poseidonius (*c.* 135—50 BC), together with those of the Greek geographer Artemidorus of Ephesus (*c.* 100 BC). Both of these contributed to his description of Spain, though he does not always specify his source for any particular section of his work. The main focus of attention is the south of the peninsula, and only relatively brief treatment is afforded to the north and to the area of the western Pyrenees in particular. However, it is in this work of Strabo that we encounter the first literary reference to the Basques.[1]

Such a statement depends upon a not unreasonable willingness to concede that the people he refers to as the Ουασκωνους, usually translated as 'Vasconians', are to be identified with those later to be referred to by Latin authors as the Vascones.[2]

---

[1] G. Aujac (ed.), *La Géographie de Strabon*, vol. I (Paris, 1969), introduction, pp. vii—xlvii.

[2] Strabo, III.iii.7, F. Lasserre (ed.), *La Géographie de Strabon*, vol. II (Paris, 1966), p. 59.

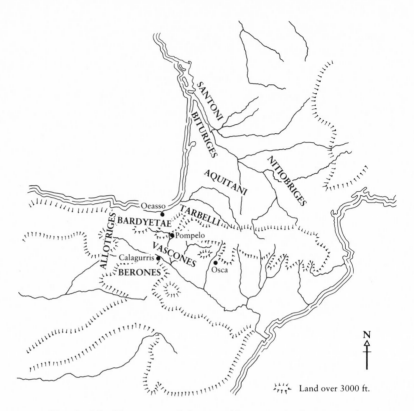

Map 8   The Vascones and their neighbours, according to Strabo

Both names can plausibly be derived from the Basques' own
word for themselves, the Euskaldunak. Strabo locates his Vasconians more or less in the area of later known Basque
settlement along the slopes of the western Pyrenees (see map 8).
In his account their zone of occupation extends westwards as
far as 'the Ocean', here indicating the Bay of Biscay.[3] However,
other (slightly later) classical authors designate the coastal
region, north of the Pyrenean watershed, as being the homeland
of peoples whom they distinguish from the Vasconians or
Vascones, and as will be seen this can cause some confusion. It
must be admitted that Strabo did not care to be too specific in
such matters, and he is more than a little arch in his ethnographic

[3] Strabo, III.iv.10, ibid., vol. II, p. 70.

treatment of the mountainous zones of northern Spain, hinting at the existence of numerous tribal divisions that he does not care to go into in detail, though this may be a cover for confusion or inadequacy in his sources: 'I shrink from giving too many of the names, shunning the unpleasantness of writing them down — unless anyone can derive pleasure from hearing Pleutarous and Barduetas and Allotrigas and other worse and obscurer names.'[4]

What at least he does condescend to is the provision of some useful pieces of information about the settlements of the region, and also a rather generalized description of certain features of the society and lifestyles of the inhabitants of the mountainous regions of northern Spain. The latter, however, is extended to embrace all of the peoples living in an area that extends from Galicia to the central Pyrenees, thus making it difficult to assess how much of his account is an accurate reflection of Basque society in particular. He does specify that Calahorra, Pamplona and Oiasona (probably Oyarzun, near Irun in Guipúzcoa) were the cities (πόλεις) of the Vasconians. This might seem to run counter to the image just elaborated of the Basques as being fundamentally different to the late Iron Age town-centred populations of the Ebro valley. However, Pamplona, as its name in its earliest form as Pompeiopolis indicates, was a Roman foundation, established by Pompey *c.* 77 BC, and Calahorra (Calagurris) was a Celt-Iberian settlement captured by the Romans, again under Pompey *c.* 75 BC. The early history of Oyarzun, if it is to be identified with Oiasona or the later Oeasso, remains obscure, but it is likely to follow a pattern similar to that of the other two of being effectively a Roman settlement, either created or transformed as part of the process of the Romanization of the indigenous population.

The notices given by the classical historians and geographers to the Basque regions, brief as they seem to be, are by no means free from ambiguity. As has been mentioned, although Strabo, the earliest source, only refers specifically to the Vasconians, and locates them in an area extending from Calahorra and the central Pyrenees to the Bay of Biscay, other writers introduce different peoples into the same region. The Spanish Roman

---

[4] Strabo, III.iii.7, H. L. Jones (tr.), *The Geography of Strabo*, vol. II (Loeb Library, 1923), p. 77.

geographer Pomponius Mela, writing *c.* AD 45, refers in his *De Chorographia* to a people called the Varduli, whom he situates between the lands of the Cantabrians and the Pyrenees.[5] The same people feature in the listings in the *Geographia* of Claudius Ptolemy, written in upper Egypt in the second century AD, and a number of names of their settlements are recorded in his account, in which they receive separate treatment from the Ouascones, doubtless Strabo's Vasconians.[6] Indeed it is clear from a passing reference in Strabo's work that these Varduli are the same people as his Bardyetans, whom he could not believe his readers would have wished to hear more about.[7] Oiasona, which he places near to 'the Ocean', is therefore one of their settlements.

Another people whom Strabo does not care to elaborate on are the Allotriges. Once again later accounts help to locate them, and it seems likely that they are to be identified with the Autrigones, referred to by Pliny the Elder in his *Natural History*.[8] They appear to have been established in an area extending from the headwaters of the Ebro to the Bay of Biscay in the region around the later sites of the modern cities of Bilbao and Santander. Their lands may also have extended into the Castilian plains as far as the vicinity of Burgos. Thus the geographers subsequent to Strabo seem to present a slightly more complex and, in terms of the evidence of location, more detailed picture of these regions than does he. They allot the coastal lands north of the Pyrenean watershed and the beginnings of the Cantabrian mountains to two peoples, the Varduli and the Autrigones or Allotriges, whom they distinguish from the Vascones, placed to the south of the watershed, and with a frontier between the two somewhere between the sites of the modern cities of San Sebastián and Bilbao. This suggests that their territories were very roughly equivalent to the later provinces of Guipúzcoa and Vizcaya, though neither of these were to be heard of for another thousand years. This dichotomy between Strabo and the subsequent writers does not imply that

[5] Pomponius Mela, III.i.15, G. Ranstrand (ed.), *De Chorographia* (Göteborg, 1971), p. 49.

[6] Ptolemy, II.vi.67, C. F. A. Nobbe (ed.), *Geographia* (Hildesheim, 1966), p. 96.

[7] Strabo, III.iv.12, Lasserre (ed.), p. 72.

[8] Pliny, III.27, H. Rackham (ed.), *Naturalis Historia*, vol. III (Loeb Library, 1942), p. 22.

dramatic events had occurred in the meanwhile. For one thing both Strabo and certainly Pomponius Mela used the same century-old information taken from Poseidonius. It is just that some of his successors lacked Strabo's squeamishness in presenting his readers with barbaric tribal names.

However, there does exist a real problem for the historian of the Basques: how are the Varduli and Allotriges to be related to the later unequivocally Basque population of the areas these tribes once inhabited, and how, if at all, were they connected to the Vascones? It is easy enough to see that the distribution of these three peoples corresponds reasonably closely to the later provincial divisions of Guipúzcoa, Vizcaya and Navarre (including the Rioja and Aragón). It is normal to regard the Varduli and the Allotriges as the ancestors of the modern Basque inhabitants of the former two provinces, and thus to see these fundamental territorial divisions within the overall Basque regions as reflecting distinctions that existed at the earliest period of their recorded history.[9] This may be wishful thinking, but there is no evidence to advance against such a view. Even Strabo seems to make a distinction between two sets of his Vasconians, referring to those of the region of Pamplona (and Calahorra) and distinguishing them from those 'further' Vasconians who lived on the edge of 'the Ocean'.[10] It is a reasonable hypothesis to accept either that the Varduli and Allotriges constituted tribal subdivisions of the Vascones, or that all three were peoples formally quite separate but linked by at least a common language, which at the same time divided them off from all other neighbouring groups.

Imprecise as is Strabo's information about tribal locations, and however capable of amplification by his successors, his work stands alone in respect of its provision of ethnographic detail. Generalized and in some features demonstrably anachronistic as is his description of the society of the mountain peoples of northern Spain, it is effectively all that we have, and there are certain aspects of it that are particularly worthy of

[9] L. Valverde, *Historia de Guipúzcoa* (San Sebastián, 1984), pp. 25—9; F. García de Cortázar and M. Montero, *Historia de Vizcaya* (2 vols, San Sebastián, 1980), vol. I, pp. 13—15. For the opposing view, see C. Sánchez-Albornoz, 'Divisiones tribales y administrativas del solar del País Vasco y sus vecindades en la época romana', *Boletín de la Real Academia de la Historia*, 95 (1929), pp. 315—95.
[10] Strabo, III.iv.10, Jones (tr.), vol. II, p. 99.

note. The recording of their diet as consisting for the most part of goats' meat and a kind of nut bread may well be accurate, but to talk of them sacrificing rams to Ares is not for our purposes a very helpful delineation of their religion. Here Strabo has just assimilated a local divinity to its nearest equivalent in the classical pantheon, in typical Graeco-Roman fashion. It may at least suggest the existence of worship of a male deity and one whose functions, like those of Ares/Mars, were particularly related to war. However, this is probably also an example of the limited utility of such descriptions in the work of classical geographers, in that it is hard to envisage the existence of a uniform worship of one particular divinity with common forms of religious practice, in an area extending from the Atlantic to the central Pyrenees.[11] In general, the items chosen for notice by Strabo, which range from forms of dance to the treatment meted out to parricides, may seem occasionally eccentric and certainly ill assorted, and the intrusions of comparisons with contemporary Greek and Egyptian practices distinctly unhelpful, though all of this would have had a significance for his readership at the time. Neither Strabo nor, perhaps more strikingly, Pomponius Mela, who actually lived in Spain, felt it necessary to have first-hand knowledge of the peoples they were describing, and they were quite content to use the accounts of Poseidonius, which were well over a century old.

Even so, and tiresome as a lot of Greek and Roman ethnography may be, there is generally some element of reality hiding under accounts that seem ambiguous, derivative and stylized. Thus Tacitus's *Germania* has served as a valuable source for some aspects of the tribal distribution, if not necessarily of the social organization, of the early Germans. One important area into which Strabo may lead us is that of the special role of women in (some of) the societies he describes so generally in northern Spain: 'It is the custom among the Cantabrians for the husbands to give dowries to their wives, for the daughters to be left as heirs, and the brothers to be married off by sisters. The custom involves, in fact, a sort of woman-rule — but this is not

---

[11] It would also run counter to the impression of the cults of northern Spain to be gained from J. M. Blázquez Martínez, *Religiones Primitivas de Hispania*, vol. I (Rome, 1962), pp. 27—40.

at all a mark of civilisation.'[12] Now, although this is specifically related of the Cantabrians, in other words the western neighbours of the Basques, this is usually held to apply to the latter as well, and to provide the earliest evidence of their matrilineal social organization. If so, it is obviously something of a burlesque of standard matrilinear inheritance customs, and it is clear that Strabo is introducing the topic to highlight the supposed barbarism of these peoples. However, he hints at features still detectable in Basque society a millennium later.

There is a danger that, because of an interpretative model that presents the Indo-European peoples as being distinguished by worship of 'sky father' divinities, by social organization centred on a warrior aristocracy, by the practice of patrilineal inheritance customs and so forth, the non-Indo-European societies with which they came into contact are expected to display fundamentally opposite characteristics.[13] Just because their language is non-Indo-European we should not therefore require the Basques to follow matrilineal customs, worship 'earth mothers', and generally constitute themselves as a matriarchal society.[14] The same kind of expectations have been held of the Picts. In the case of the latter some aspects of the thesis have recently been subjected to useful scrutiny and found, if not wanting, certainly in need of cautious reappraisal. So too with the Basques; it would be unwise on the basis of Strabo's words, which, as has been mentioned, are related specifically to the Cantabrians, to try to erect an image of their society solely on the strength of theories of how non-Indo-European societies *ought* to behave. It is better, therefore, to postpone consideration of the supposedly matriarchal nature of early Basque society until a point is reached when it can be subjected to scrutiny on the basis of internal evidence. Because of the nature of our sources, this means the tenth century AD at the earliest. For now it would be more fruitful to consider the relationship of the Basques with the first outside power that can be shown to have exercised its authority over most of their region.

[12] Strabo, III.iv.18, Jones (tr.), vol. II, p. 115.
[13] J. Haudry, *Les Indo-Européens* (Paris, 1981).
[14] J. Caro Baroja, *Los pueblos del norte de la península ibérica*, 2nd edn (San Sebastián, 1973), especially pp. 25ff.

Roman military rule

Roman military contact with the various Basque tribes seems to have dated back to at least the first quarter of the first century BC. Gaius Marius, the political opponent of the patricians, is reported by Plutarch to have owned a band of Vardulian slaves, doubtless prisoners of war.[15] In the same period his supporter, the rebel general Sertorius, gained control of the Ebro valley and drew support from some of the native population in his resistance to the Roman oligarchy; it was in the aftermath of the suppression of his revolt, and doubtless in consequence of it, that Pompey founded the Roman settlement at Pamplona *c.* 77 BC. At what stage the Romans first put roads into the region is uncertain, but after Caesar's conquest of Gaul the lines of communication between the Ebro valley and southern Aquitaine became increasingly important. What is known of the Roman road system in the Basque region indicates that the maintenance of trans-Pyrenean communications was its principal function, and the provision of access to local settlements only of secondary importance. Indeed, apart from Pamplona, and Calahorra in the Ebro valley, few towns of any significance existed. Whatever Oeasso may have been in the time of Strabo, it seems to have dwindled or disappeared by the period of the late empire. Conversely, by then a handful of other sites look to have developed, notably Lapurdum, probably on the site of the later Bayonne, which first came into existence as military bases and forts, especially for the defence and overseeing of the roads across the mountains.

None of the Roman settlements in the Basque region appears to have been of any considerable size (see map 9). It was once thought that Pamplona might have been equivalent in its dimensions to Zaragoza (Caesaraugusta), the principal city of the Ebro valley, but recent investigation suggests that it was considerably smaller.[16] Unfortunately urban continuity, par-

---

[15] Plutarch, *Life of Marius*, R. Flaceliere and E. Chambry, *Plutarque, Vies*, vol. VI (Paris, 1971), pp. 150, 152.

[16] M. A. Mezquíriz de Catalán, *Pamplona Romana* (Pamplona, 1973); M. A. Mezquíriz, 'Notas sobre la antigua Pompaelo', *Principe de Viana*, 15 (1954), pp. 231—47.

The Roman bridge at Iruña

ticularly in Pamplona, has limited the opportunities for detailed archaeological work, and only one town site in the Basque region has ever been subjected to extensive excavation. This is Iruña, the Roman Veleia, in Alava, a small settlement classified as an *oppidum*, situated on a strategic site at the confluence of two rivers and the intersection of two roads, one of which was the principal highway across the region from Astorga to Bordeaux.[17] In the case of both Iruña and Pamplona the most impressive monumental remains date from the second century AD, but both have also revealed small finds of pre-Roman date, indicative of earlier occupation of their sites. In the case of Pamplona the evidence consists of small amounts of imported pottery dating from roughly the mid second century BC.

The Iruña excavations, conducted in the 1950s, give the impression or have achieved the effect of having been undertaken

[17] G. Nieto Gallo, *El Oppidum de Iruña* (Vitoria, 1958); A. Baldeón Iñigo et al., *Museo de Arqueología de Alava* (Vitoria-Gasteiz, 1983), pp. 139—60.

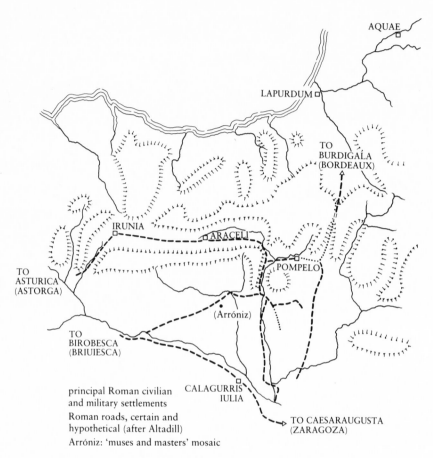

AQUAE

LAPURDUM

TO
BURDIGALA
(BORDEAUX)

IRUNIA

ARACELI

TO
ASTURICA
(ASTORGA)

POMPELO

(Arróniz)

TO
BIROBESCA
(BRIUIESCA)

principal Roman civilian
and military settlements

Roman roads, certain and
hypothetical (after Altadill)

Arróniz: 'muses and masters' mosaic

CALAGURRIS
IULIA

TO CAESARAUGUSTA
(ZARAGOZA)

Map 9   Roman roads and settlements

more for the sake of 'finds' than for the presentation of a
coherent picture of urban development on the site. Admittedly
archaeological emphases have changed, and the site itself is an
extensive one, but in practice the result is that all too little can
now be known about the dynamics of town life in Iruña-Veleia
in the Roman period. Moreover, greater emphasis seems to
have been placed on the excavation of prehistoric rather than
Roman sites in general in the Basque regions, and in Alava only
two other Roman settlements have been subjected to systematic
study: part of a small town at Arcaya and a villa site

The site of the Roman town at Iruña

at Cabriana.[18] The amount of similar investigation undertaken in Navarre and the other two Basque provinces is roughly comparable.

Little of real opulence, in terms of either buildings or, on a smaller scale, items of personal property and adornment, has been uncovered. There is relatively little fine pottery, which would have had to have been imported from Gaul, and the quality of bronze working and marble sculpture, of which few examples are known, never rises above the purely 'provincial'. There is little evidence of import from metropolitan workshops. Likewise, unlike those of some of the villa sites further down the Ebro or on the Castilian plains, few of the generally fragmentary mosaics uncovered in these parts display any great distinction. One exception to the latter stricture is the exceedingly fine fourth-century AD 'muses and masters' polygonal mosaic from

[18] Baldeón Iñigo et al., *Museo de Arqueología de Alava*, pp. 170—82; M. Torres, 'Los mosaicos descubiertos en el siglo xviii en la villa de Cabriana (Alava)', *Estudios de Arqueología Alavesa*, 10 (1981), pp. 311—40. For an overall listing of the Roman sites in the Basque regions, see the appendix to P. Narbaitz, *Le Matin Basque* (Paris, 1975), pp. 423—65.

The 'Muses and Masters' mosaic from Arróniz, Navarre

Arróniz in Navarre, now in the Museo Arqueológico in Madrid. This really represents the final northwards extension of the society of the great villas of the middle Ebro. In general there is little evidence for much importing of luxury goods or the employment of skilled craftsmen from outside the region, and, although it is only fair to recall how limited has been the work undertaken so far, such a conclusion is not a surprising one. With the exception of parts of southern Alava, none of these areas provided particularly rich land and, as has been mentioned, they did not support any substantial settlements. Even the military presence of the Romans was a limited one, and no equivalents to the major legionary fortresses of Braga, Astorga and León existed in the region. Thus there was little conspicuous consumption and insufficient locally created wealth to sustain an indigenous or an import trade in luxury goods. Even in comparison with some of the other less urbanized parts of the Roman Empire, such as northern Gaul, the western Pyrenean area looks 'provincial' and under-developed.

This is not, however, the same as to say that it was un-Romanized. Few as the excavations may have been, the existence of numerous Roman sites, mainly small townships and villas, has been recognized. Incidental finds over a wide area indicate the impact of Roman material culture. A major imperial highway passed directly through the region, and the general road network may have been more extensive than we think.[19] Those settlements that have been studied show that all the basic features of Roman town life were present, and that baths and temples, however small scale, were to be found in them. Low level as much of the evidence may be in artistic terms, the wide distribution and varied range of the traces of the Roman cultural impact is what is most striking. It must be remembered also that the Roman presence was first felt in the area by the beginning of the first century BC at the latest, and by the end of direct imperial rule in AD 411 it had lasted for over half a millennium. It is thus probably wrong to concentrate too much on a supposed Basque resistance to Rome or to stress continuity of conflict as the principal feature of the area. Much more significant is the evidence for close interrelationship, especially in particular aspects of social and economic organization.

Perhaps the most obvious feature of this is the use of auxiliary troops recruited from identifiably Basque tribes by the Roman army. Even before that process was initiated, probably at the time of the reorganization of the army by the Emperor Augustus, the military potential of the Basques seems to have been appreciated by some Roman commanders at least. Gaius Marius, who had campaigned in Spain, had a bodyguard of several thousand slaves, drawn from the Bardyetans, now recognizable as the Varduli, from the region of the modern province of Guipúzcoa. These he brought with him from Africa to terrorize his political opponents in Rome on his return from exile in

[19] J. Altadill, 'De re geografía-historica: vias y vestigios romanos en Navarra', in *Homenaje a D. Carmelo de Echegaray* (San Sebastián, 1928), pp. 480—8.

Bremenium, a Roman fort at High Rochester, Northumberland, England

87 BC. So outrageous did their behaviour become that eventually Sertorius had them massacred.

The Varduli also came to contribute forces to Rome in a more institutionalized way through the recruiting of at least one cohort of auxiliary mounted infantry from amongst them. Interestingly, this unit spent the only periods for which we have any records of it in northern England, based principally at the auxiliary fort at High Rochester, 23 miles NNW of Corbridge in Northumberland. A number of inscriptions from the early third century AD found in this fort refer to I Fida Vardullorum Equitata. In particular these take the form of dedicatory inscriptions to emperors of the Severan dynasty, notably Caracalla (211—17), Elagabalus (218—22) and Severus Alexander (222—35). The first of these seems to have rewarded the unit by granting it the use of the epithet 'Antoniniana', taken from his own name of Marcus Aurelius Antoninus, which first appears on an inscription dated to AD 216.[20] Two of the inscriptions record the building of artillery platforms on the walls of the fort.[21] The clustered datings of these inscriptions in a period of *c.* 213—25 may well indicate that the Vardullian cohort was installed at High Rochester by the Emperor Septimius Severus as part of his campaign in Britain and the restoration of the defences in the north in AD 210—11. The earlier history of this unit is less clear, though an inscription from Belgium of the reign of Trajan (98—117) records incidentally that even then I Fida Vardullorum Civium Romanorum was stationed in Britain, and another inscription shows that at least a detachment of the unit served on Hadrian's Wall, probably in milecastle 19, in the course of the second century.[22] The 'Civium Romanorum' element in the Trajanic inscription indicates that the members of the cohort had been granted the privileges of Roman citizenship (on discharge), doubtless in reward for distinguished service. When citizenship was granted to all inhabitants of the empire by Caracalla, this distinction ceased to be significant, and the title was then dropped, soon to be replaced by the imperial 'Antoniniana'. The other epithet of 'Fida' or 'faithful' is more tantalizing, in that it must have been the reward for some act of conspicuous loyalty by the cohort before the time of Trajan, but what that was remains a mystery.

The final record of Cohors I Vardullorum is in the form of another inscription from High Rochester set up between AD 238 and 241, dedicated to the emperor (Gordian III) and to the standards of I Vardullorum and the Numerus of the Bremenium Scouts.[23] The latter was a detachment of Sarmatian cavalry, originally from across the Danube. With this image of Basques and trans-Danubian nomads sharing (doubtless extremely cold) quarters in the north of Britain, both in the service of Rome, we lose sight of Cohors I Vardullorum. Whether there was ever a Cohors II is unknown. The commanders of the unit, in so far as they are known, all bear Latin names, and would appear to be

---

[20] R. G. Collingwood and R. P. Wright (eds), *The Roman Inscriptions of Britain* (London, 1965) (henceforth *RIB*), no. 1279.

[21] *RIB*, nos 1280—1.

[22] *Corpus Inscriptionum Latinorum* (henceforth *CIL*), vol. XIII.

[23] *RIB*, no. 1262.

Roman career soldiers. Little hint of the exotic character of the troops may be found in the inscriptions, though the numerous altars dedicated to Minerva that have been uncovered in the fort would suggest the existence of worship of a female divinity assimilated into the person of the Roman goddess. The second-century inscription from milecastle 19 on Hadrian's Wall seems to suggest that the unit as a whole had placed itself under the spiritual protection of a group of female deities: 'To the Mother Goddesses, the detachment of the First Cohort of the Varduli erected this temple together with this altar, and willingly and deservedly fulfilled its vow.'[24] This is the only inscription to record a dedication by the troops as a body, rather than by one of their officers.

The cohort of the Varduli was not the only unit of Basque origin then serving in Britain. Two inscriptions, one of which is now lost, prove the existence of a body called Cohors II Vasconum Civium Romanorum. The first of these is in the form of a copper tablet, discovered in 1806 on Sydenham Common in Kent, and is a fragment of a long list of auxiliary units, dated to AD 105.[25] The second inscription, now lost, records the career of a certain Quintus Fulvius Euchir, who rose to command the Second Legion. He was probably a Spaniard, as the inscription was uncovered in 1767 near Seville, and in its list of his previous offices is recorded his service as prefect of Cohors II Vasconum Equitata.[26] From the epithet 'Equitata', it is clear that this unit, like that of the Varduli, was one of mixed mounted and ordinary infantry.[27] There is no evidence to link this cohort with any specific location or fort, and of a notional Cohors I Vasconum, that the existence of Cohors II would suggest, no trace remains.

The Basques were far from unique amongst the various tribal groups of the Iberian peninsula in contributing units to the Roman army. The Sydenham Common inscription of AD 105, incomplete as it is, also records the existence of Cohortes I Celtiberorum, I Hispanorum and (?) Asturum as being stationed in Britain, and similar units can be traced in other epigraphic

[24] *RIB*, no. 1421.
[25] *CIL*, vol. VII, no. 1194.
[26] *CIL*, vol. II, no. 1086.
[27] R. W. Davies, 'Cohortes equitatae', *Historia*, 20 (1971), pp. 751—63.

sources. What is important to note is that the Basques were no different to the rest in this respect. Furthermore, after their term of service, nominally of 25 years, although many may have remained in the lands in which they had been stationed, not least Britain, others will have returned to the western Pyrenees. It has been questioned as to how far such units were, after their initial formation, recruited exclusively from the areas which gave them their names, and there is no evidence to determine this one way or another.[28] Linguistic and cultural problems would doubtless have made it difficult to introduce new elements into some of the more exotic units, amongst which those of the Basques might well be counted; however, even if the racial exclusiveness of such units did decline, it is hard to imagine that Rome did not continue to draw upon the useful reserves of military manpower that northern Spain provided. It is likely that such recruiting remained a continuous process throughout the second and third centuries.

Little as we know of the details of the process, the very existence of these units of Basque origin makes it impossible to view Basque relations with Rome purely in terms of conflict or isolationism. That one of the contributory tribes should be the Varduli from Guipúzcoa would additionally suggest that this is not just a question of a Roman impact upon the easily accessible valley bottoms of Alava and the Rioja, but is rather a trans-cultural contact that could have made itself felt throughout all of the Basque areas. Similarly, the very limited military presence of other Roman forces in those Basque regions, in comparison not only with such frontier zones as northern Britain but also with other parts of Spain, notably those confronting the mountains of Galicia and the Asturias, must certainly suggest that Rome felt very little threat to its order from the possibility of depredations by the Basque mountain tribes. Such a view is confirmed by historical records, limited and sporadic as they may be for the early Roman Empire. There is no evidence of military conflict in the Basque region in the whole of a period extending from the ending of the Cantabrian Wars (*c.* 20 BC) up to the final collapse of centralized Roman government in the area in the early fifth century AD. This is in stark contrast to the

---

[28] G. Webster, *The Roman Imperial Army*, 2nd edn (London, 1979), pp. 145—6.

events of the succeeding 300 years. In comparison with the
recorded difficulties of the Visigoths in their dealings with the
Basques in the sixth to eighth centuries, this previous period
seems to have constituted nearly half a millennium of genuine
pax Romana.

When there was disturbance in the region it came from
outside. The third century AD was marked by periods in which
the frontiers of the empire proved vulnerable to pressure,
particularly on the part of Germanic tribes across the Rhine and
the Danube. The resulting military crises led on occasion to
political instability and the periodic breakdown of the authority
of the central government. One such crisis occurred in 259,
when the Rhine frontier was breached by migrating Franks,
who entered Gaul. In the ensuing disorder Postumus, one of the
commanders of the army on the Rhine, was proclaimed emperor
by the troops, and rapidly made himself master of Gaul and,
thereby, of Britain. His authority clearly extended to Spain,
though certainly not all of the parts of the peninsula. That the
western Pyrenees belonged to the short-lived 'Gallic Empire' of
Postumus seems clear from a milestone erected in his name,
discovered in Alava and now preserved in Vitoria.[29] His
successor Victorinus (268—70) lost control of all parts of Spain,
and the breakaway empire was suppressed in 273.

In its way this provincial regime may have proved more
effective than the central government in protecting the settlements of the west in this short-lived period of migration and
upheaval. For it is only for the succeeding decades (*c.* 280) that
evidence of destruction has been found in a number of sites in
both Navarre and Alava. Obviously the limited nature of the
excavations so far undertaken may mean that such indications
from both Pamplona and Iruña, as well as the villa site of
Cabriana, are the products of coincidence rather than evidence
of a wave of widespread destruction, but the possibility exists
that this represents the work of a body of invaders passing
through the region. Alternatively, of course, it could be argued
that, if this is evidence of more than a series of accidents, it is to
be attributed to raiding of the valley communities by the under-
Romanized Basque mountain dwellers. Certainty is not possible,

[29] Illustrated in Baldeón Iñigo et al., *Museo de Arqueología de Alava*, p. 165.

A Roman milestone in the name of the Gallic usurper Postumus (r. 259–68), whose rule extended over parts of Northern Spain

Fragments of earlier buildings re-used in the walls of Iruña, Alava (third century AD)

and there is a real danger of judgement being made on the basis of preconceived models of the nature of Basque—Roman relations, but if the latter explanation were the correct one it seems surprising how limited were the subsequent defensive undertakings by the central government to protect a region thus revealed as being under permanent threat. Nor does there appear to be either earlier or subsequent evidence of such large-scale devastation during the period of Roman rule. This appears to represent a unique occurrence in the history of the region during these centuries.

There are indications that a circuit of walls may have been erected at Pamplona in the very late third or early fourth centuries.[30] Certainly remains of an impressive town wall of this period may be seen at Iruña.[31] This was not out of step with what was happening elsewhere in the Iberian peninsula at this time, as instanced by the walls of Mérida as well as those of Lugo and other more vulnerable sites. Indeed these decades saw extensive programmes of town wall building throughout most

[30] Mezquíriz, *Pamplona Romana*, p. 30.
[31] J. C. Elorza y Guinea, 'A propósito de la muralla romana de Iruña', *Estudios de Arqueología Alavesa*, 5 (1972), pp. 183—94.

of the empire in the west, starting with Rome itself. More significant in the Basque region is the lack of additional garrisoning or stationing of additional forces in the area. Whilst the principal army units in the peninsula remained in the north-west, even after the reforms and redistribution of forces carried out under the Emperors Diocletian (284—305) and Constantine (307—37) the Pyrenees look to have been lightly garrisoned.

Records are far from satisfactory for most of the fourth century, but the existence of the *Notitia Dignitatum*, which recounts the disposition and structuring of the Roman army *c*. 410, presents a picture probably little changed from preceding decades. Whilst Galicia required the stationing of a legion and four additional cohorts, only one unit is to be found in the upper Ebro, the Cohors Prima Gallica, stationed at Veleia, in all probability Iruña in Alava, although the site has produced no evidence of the cohort's presence. There is one other unit recorded that is relevant to this picture — the Cohors Novem-populana, stationed at Lapurdum, a fort on or near the site of the later city of Bayonne.[32] Incidentally, neither Cohors I Vardullorum nor Cohors II Vasconum feature in the *Notitia*, disappearing, perhaps, in the collapse of the defences of Britain in 367.

The stationing of two cohorts, the second by its name locally raised, at either end of the routes across the western Pyrenees is certainly indicative of concern, and can only be related to the line of communications across the mountains. However, even allowing that they were both maintained at roughly full strength, this involves a force of no more than about 1000 men with divided command and stationed in two separate provinces. In other words these cohorts can have been expected to face no more than a small-scale threat, hardly likely to require co-ordination of their activities. Banditry along the line of the roads would seem to be the most likely challenge, and the lack of other military establishments further down the Ebro to protect the numerous towns and large villas of the valley would suggest the absence of the kind of danger of large-scale raiding that this area was to face in the seventh century (see map 10).

Thus, whilst it is important not to minimize the difficulties of

[32] O. Seeck (ed.), *Notitia Dignitatum*, oc. XLII 19 and 32 (reimpression of 1876 edn, Frankfurt, 1962), p. 216.

Foz (a ravine or defile) de Lumbier, Navarre: a ruined Roman bridge that once carried the old road between Pamplona and Aragón across the Río Irati

Map 10 Roman provinces

anchoring the Basque mountain tribes within the Roman world or to ignore the possibility of such people taking advantage of momentary weakness on the part of the central government to prey upon their settled neighbours, particularly travellers and perhaps the inhabitants of small settlements, there seems little evidence of their presenting a serious threat to the norms of urban life and the economy of the region. Indeed, as has been mentioned, the diffusion of Roman or Romanized material culture all around the fringes of the mountains does not leave the impression that this was a defensive frontier society, or that Romanization was superficial, at least in material terms. Roman military recruiting can only have developed ties of economic dependence between the mountains and their settled hinterland,

reinforcing links that already existed and which were created by
the basic economy of the mountain dwellers.

Basque life under the Romans

Archaeological evidence from the neolithic, particularly in the
better studied northern fringes of the Pyrenees, has indicated the
unusually extended survival of a pastoral economy, and the
relatively late and limited development of farming. Although
crop raising is long established and a central feature of the
agrarian economy of the western Pyrenees, pastoralism not only
still exists but retains the dominant hold in many parts,
particularly the areas more mountainous and less affected by
the growth of industry on the Spanish side of the modern
frontier.[33] There are good reasons for believing in the continuity
of this pastoral economy from the earliest times. It can also be
documented in a substantial body of medieval records and,
although such texts are not available for the Roman period,
there are no grounds for believing that the economy of the
mountains was any different then either. In practice this has
meant the existence of small family-centred settlements, as this
mode of production can hardly support larger units of population. Their flocks are pastured higher up the mountainside
during the summer months, the only time when conditions
render such areas usable; those animals not killed for preserving
and winter eating are taken down to the lower slopes or off the
mountainside during the months of the long hard winters. The
dependence upon animal produce has been supplemented,
doubtless since the Bronze Age, by limited arable farming,
though this is strictly conditioned by the poverty of the mountain
soils and the severity of the climate.

In itself such a pastoral economy is generally not self-
supporting, and even amongst genuinely nomadic peoples exchange is normally a necessary and regular feature of their
annual round.[34] Flocks produce only limited value in a closed
economy, in that they reproduce themselves in larger quantities

---

[33] D. A. Gómez-Ibañez, *The Western Pyrenees* (Oxford, 1975), pp. 24—8.
[34] C. Wickham, 'Pastoralism and underdevelopment in the early Middle Ages',
Settimane di Studio sull' Alto Medioevo, 31 (Spoleto, 1985), pp.401—51.

than is necessary for the subsistence of their owners in terms of meat eating and the consumption of such by-products as milk and cheese. With a surplus of livestock and also the problem of keeping the animals alive in large numbers through the difficult conditions of winter, it is clearly preferable for some of the flocks to be disposed of by means of exchange for other items that the pastoralists cannot provide for themselves. This might include alternative forms of food, and also weapons and other metal products. The transhumant pastoralism of the Basques is far removed from the full nomadism of various peoples of parts of central Asia and Africa. In the Roman period the culture of their settled, urbanized neighbours was close and accessible, and thus the markets for their surplus livestock, of immediate value to the towns for food and clothing, were readily available. The paucity of the evidence makes precision impossible, but the testing of such a model of economic interrelationship in better documented societies gives reasonable grounds for optimism that it may be applied to the Basques too.

The major towns such as Pamplona and the smaller civilian settlements are unlikely to have been the only potential markets for the surplus products of pastoralism. From parallels elsewhere in the Roman world it would seem likely that the army was also a potential purchaser, thus making the military bases at Veleia and Lapurdum important to the Basques not only because of the soldiers' policing activities but also for their active role in the functioning of the local economy.[35] Whilst the army may have been principally a consumer of grain, supplies of meat, hides and furs necessary for the maintenance of the troops and their equipment would in the western Pyrenees have been obtainable from the mountain-dwelling tribes. Thus, although substantial differences of lifestyle, economic activity and material culture doubtless did exist between the urban and rural population of the valleys on the one hand and the mountain-inhabiting pastoralists on the other, it would be wrong to envisage their interrelationship as being inevitably one of mutual antagonism and conflict. Rather they should be seen as the two complementary components of the overall economic and social organization of the western Pyrenees. Obviously the mountaineers

[35] R. MacMullen, *Soldier and Civilian in the Later Roman Empire* (Cambridge, Mass., 1967), pp. 2—4.

The foundations of a Roman villa at Foz de Lumbier, Navarre

could be dangerous, particularly in times when the central
government was not strong enough to curb localized and small-
scale banditry, or when adverse seasonal conditions produced a
temporary disruption in the normal pattern of their lives. It is
possible, too, that demographic pressures could lead to additional
encroachments on the agrarian lands of their lowland neighbours.

Clearly there were limits to the effective Roman penetration
of the mountains. The military presence was geographically
restricted, but civilian settlements, principally villa sites, have
been found in the mountain zones, indicating not only a relative
sense of security on the part of their owners, but also the
extension of features of Roman culture into such areas.[36] It is
possible that other such sites will be discovered, and that it may
be found that the network of Roman communications was even
more extensive than it now seems. The Roman material impact
is thus relatively easy to trace, but its effects in less tangible
cultural areas, such as language and ideas, principally religious,
are harder to delineate. Much scholarly attention has been

[36] A. F. Samanes and A. M. Duque (eds), *Atlas de Navarra*, 2nd edn (Barcelona,
1981), p. 40.

devoted recently to problems of the continuity of pre-Roman languages in various parts of the western empire. Basque, like British (Welsh) but unlike Punic, Gallic Celtic and others, is one of the few languages spoken by the indigenous inhabitants of an area of the Roman Empire that not only survived the imperial centuries but continued to flourish thereafter. The problem is not the straightforward one of whether or not Basque continued in use, as it is obvious that it did, despite the existence of Latin not only as the language of the conquerors but also and increasingly as the polite and learned language of the conquered. What is difficult to know is whether or not Basque speech survived in those parts of the western Pyrenees and upper Ebro valley that were in material terms thoroughly Romanized. Linguistic evidence suggests that it was eclipsed in Alava, but the question of the possible continuing use of Basque in Pamplona and other lowland regions is an important one in that it could shed light on the degrees of assimilation of or resistance to Roman culture by people who in material terms look well absorbed into the civilization of their conquerors.

Attempts to prove the survival of pre-Roman indigenous culture in lowland Britain, Gaul or coastal north Africa amongst other places look frankly not very convincing, although currently fashionable.[37] They depend upon a great deal of weight being placed upon limited and ambiguous evidence relating to the fifth century, since the proponents of such views have to admit that these hypothetical continuities are terminated by the Germanic migrations. It is thus perplexing to find societies and languages supposedly able to resist half a millennium of Roman rule and yet unable to hold out against the influence of the ruling people of successor states that are themselves half-Romanized and without a higher culture of their own to impose. There are obvious exceptions, notably in highland Britain, where Rome either never extended its sway or was content with no more than a military presence to protect more valuable settled regions in the lowlands. On the basis of such analogies, it would seem likely that the Basque language suffered an appreciable diminution in its sphere of influence in the settled regions of the western Pyrenees, and notably in the upper

[37] A. P. Smyth, *Warlords and Holy Men: Scotland AD 80—1000* (London, 1984), pp. 1—6.

Ebro valley. This is certainly borne out by the findings from Alava.[38] Such a contraction may have encompassed areas, like the valley of the river Aragón, to which the language was not to return. Others, such as Alava itself, were to be linguistically 're-Basqueized' in the course of subsequent centuries. The localized nature of Roman rule, and the limits of Roman interest in the region as a whole, clearly meant that the dominance of Basque in the mountains was never challenged.

Christianity

This may have had a direct bearing upon the spread of Christianity in the Basque areas. Of earlier religions once to be found there, all too little is known. Undoubtedly there existed temples in the principal towns devoted to some of the deities of the Roman pantheon, but no evidence survives to speak of particular dedications. There are also slight indications that some of the oriental cults, long established in Rome and which had devotees elsewhere in the peninsula, also attracted followers here.[39] There are a small number of altars set up to the *genii* of various settlements, but for the cult of indigenous deities of Basque origin evidence exists only for two of them: Ilurberrixus and Lacubegus. The latter may not even be a name of Basque origin, but it is attested to by an altar discovered at Ujue and now preserved in the Museo de Navarra in Pamplona. The inscription reads: 'COELI TESPHOROS ET FESTA ET TELE-SINUS. LACUBEGI EX VOTO.'[40] It was set up in fulfilment of a vow, and is undated. If the name be anything to go by the deity was probably an aquatic one, but the element on which this is based, the derivation of the first part of the name from Basque *lako* (canal), also suggests that the divinity was not genuinely Basque, as this looks like a loan word from Latin *(lacus)*. This just leaves Ilurberrixus Anderexus as the only historically attested Basque god. Evidence for this cult comes from both sides of the Pyrenees, taking the form of a badly

[38] M. L. Albertos, 'Alava romana y prerromana', *Estudios de Arqueología Alavesa*, 4 (1970), pp. 107—223.

[39] A. García y Bellido, *Les religions orientales dans l'Espagne romaine* (Leiden, 1967), p. 119.

[40] Blázquez Martínez, *Religiones*, pp. 176—7.

mutilated altar found near Saint Bertrand de Cominges and a better preserved if more laconic one from Escugnau in the Valle de Aran. The latter reads: 'ILURBERRIXO ANDEREXO'. It is thought that the name Ilurberrixus means 'the new hawthorn' (from *ilurri-berri*), and that Anderexus is an epithet signifying 'flowering'.[41] This may seem like some form of confirmation of the view that the later importance of special trees, such as the Oak of Guernica, has its origin in earlier Basque tree worship.[42] Such arguments are superficially attractive, but should be approached with a fair measure of caution. Despite much ingenuity, no other evidence or convincing argument has been produced to show that the Basques did venerate sacred trees or worship tree gods in their pre-Christian phase. There also exists a distressing tendency to use modern Basque folklore, by means of a kind of substrate theory, as a source of evidence for the earlier paganism, and a whole pantheon of supposed Basque gods has been brought into existence this way despite the insecure nature of the methodology involved.[43]

The question of the Christianizing of the Basque regions has recently become a more contentious issue amongst scholars than hitherto. From the sixteenth to the nineteenth centuries, in a time of considerable self-consciousness and antiquarian interest amongst the Basques, confident and often absurd arguments were advanced to show that Basque was the language that had been spoken in the Garden of Eden, and that certain linguistic keys could be used to show that the Christian revelation had been accepted by them almost before any other people.[44] Better, if more mundane, scholarship has dispelled such delightful illusions, and instead emphasis has come to be placed upon the relative lateness of the final conversion of the Basque regions to Christianity, and the completion of this process has been put as late as the eleventh or twelfth centuries.[45] Folklorists and others

[41] Ibid., pp. 68—9.

[42] J. Caro Baroja, 'Culto a los árboles y mitos y divinidades arboreas', in his *Sobre historia y etnografía vasca* (San Sebastián, 1982), pp. 135—52.

[43] For Basque folklore see J. M. de Barandiarán, *Mitología vasca*, 2nd edn (San Sebastián, 1979), and J. M. Satrústegui, *Mitos y Creencias*, 2nd end (San Sebastián, 1982).

[44] For the earlier and more picaresque beliefs about the Basque language see A. Tovar, *Mitología e ideología sobre la lengua vasca* (Madrid, 1980).

[45] J. M. Lacarra, 'La Cristianización del País Vasco', in his *Vasconia Medieval — Historia y Filología* (San Sebastián, 1957), pp. 51—70.

*An early medieval funerary inscription, carved on a fragment of a Roman altar
dedicated to Jove and Sol*

would like to put it even later, if only to justify their extravagant
expectations of legend and folk-memory as sources for Basque
indigenous religion. However, recently attempts have been
made to suggest that this is an unduly pessimistic view, and that
the conversion of the Basques *en masse* occurred more or less at
the same time as did that of most of the rest of the inhabitants of
the peninsula, that is to say in the fourth and fifth centuries.[46]

It hardly needs to be said that in all of this the availability of
evidence has been slight and that the role of assertion has been
high. It is worth reviewing the information upon which an
interpretation must be built. In general the fourth century saw
the establishment of bishoprics in most of the principal towns of
the peninsula, and it was to be a Spanish emperor, Theodosius I
(378—95), who in 392 decreed an absolute prohibition on all
forms of pagan worship within the Roman Empire. However,
there are indications that the institutional development of

[46] A. E. de Mañaricua, 'Introdución del Cristianismo en el País Vasco', in *I Semana de
Estudios de Historia Eclesiástica del País Vasco* (Vitoria, 1981), pp. 27—42.

Christianity was slower in the north of Spain, particularly in Galicia, and the completion of the diocesan structure was only achieved in the fifth century or possibly later.[47] In terms of numbers and percentages it is hard to say how many Christians there were in the peninsula at this time.

It is clear that some parts of the Basque regions were rapidly Christianized, at least in institutional terms. A diocese existed at Calahorra by the end of the fourth century, but the earliest record of a bishop of Pamplona comes in the attestation by one 'Liliolus Pampilonensis Ecclesiae Episcopus' of the acts of the Third Council of Toledo in 589.[48] This, though, was the first such general council of the Church in Spain to which bishops from most of the peripheral regions of the peninsula came, and, as signatures to conciliar *acta* constitute our principal source for episcopal continuity, the lack of earlier indications of this sort does not necessarily imply that the diocese of Pamplona was then but newly founded. Indeed some would insist that it was not and that its origins must be sought in the third century at the latest. Such a view is based upon acceptance of the fundamental historicity of the legend of St Firminus, 'San Fermín', the patron saint of Pamplona.[49] In brief this story states that a local senator by the name of Firmus was persuaded of the truth of Christianity by a priest called Honestus, but determined only to accept baptism at the hands of Bishop Saturninus of Toulouse. The latter was prevailed upon to come to Pamplona, and there his preaching led to his baptizing of 40,000 people in the city in the course of a mere three days. Firmus's son Firminus was taught by Honestus, and at the age of 31 was sent by him to be consecrated by Honoratus, the successor of Saturninus as bishop of Toulouse. Firminus went on to preach in northern Gaul, and was particularly associated with Amiens, before suffering persecution and martyrdom. In this tale there exists not an iota of truth, and attempts to determine whether it was the Decian or the Diocletianic persecution that proved fatal to Firminus are just so much wasted effort. At the very earliest the legend cannot date from before the ninth century, and it should

---

[47] M. C. Díaz y Díaz, 'Los orígenes Cristianos de Lugo', in *Actas del Colloquio Internacional sobre el Bimillenario de Lugo* (Lugo, 1977), pp. 237—50.

[48] J. Vives (ed.), *Concilios Visigóticos e Hispano-Romanos* (Barcelona—Madrid, 1963), p. 138.

[49] V. Ordóñez, *San Fermín y sus fiestas* (Pamplona, 1967).

The cathedral at Calahorra

be seen as a very successful part of the attempt by the archdiocese of Toulouse to link or create cults in related regions that would be subsidiary to that of its own patron saints, principally Saturninus. Such hagiographic manipulation to suit the requirements of ecclesiastical politics can be paralleled elsewhere in the eleventh and twelfth centuries, as for example in the creation in northern France of a legend of a St Eugenius I of Toledo, a mythical disciple of St Denis of Paris. As with Eugenius, it is extraordinary to see the alien cult coming to be accepted in the notional and distant homeland of the non-existent saint. Thus in 1186 Bishop Pedro de Artajona of Pamplona, previously a student in Paris, obtained a relic of Firminus from the church of Amiens, and it is probably from this that the cult of San Fermin in Pamplona stems.[50] Although interesting in itself, and the excuse for a major fiesta, this legend has nothing to do with the true origins of Christianity in Navarre.

Calahorra, on the other hand, does possess a genuine cult of early martyrs, vouched for in the work of one of the most distinguished literary figures the region ever produced, the Christian poet Prudentius (*fl. c.* 400). Of his life his works are the sole record.[51] The relative frequency of his references to saints associated with Zaragoza has led some scholars to regard him as a native of that city, but more recently and reasonably it has been argued that he came from Calahorra. Indeed medieval tradition has it that he was born at Armentia, a site now represented only by a fine Romanesque church, on the outskirts of Vitoria in Alava. This particular belief may have arisen when the see of Calahorra was possibly transferred to Armentia in the aftermath of the Arab conquest of Spain in 711. Prudentius's body is also recorded in the tenth century as having been preserved in the Riojan monastery of San Prudencio de Laturce.[52]

It is thought that he composed his *Peristephanon*, his Latin verse celebration of the martyrdoms of Spanish and other saints in 12 parts, for the consecration of Calahorra cathedral *c.* AD 400. His work is the earliest literary evidence for the cult of those

[50] There is an excellent discussion of the legend in J. Goñi Gaztambide, *Historia de los obispos de Pamplona* (2 vols, Pamplona, 1979), vol. I, pp. 31—5; and for Bishop Pedro see ibid., pp. 33—78.

[51] Prudentius, *Works*, ed. and tr. H. J. Thomson (2 vols, Loeb Library, 1949—53).

[52] *Cartulario de Albelda*, ed. A. Ubieto Arteta (Zaragoza, 1981), doc. 19 (of AD 950), pp. 28—30.

Iberian saints, such as Eulalia of Mérida, whom he includes. Amongst others are SS Emeterius and Celidonius, the patrons of Calahorra, and indeed it is with them, appropriately enough, that the poem begins. According to Prudentius's account these two brothers were soldiers who refused to sacrifice to the pagan gods, and as a result suffered torture and martyrdom.[53] The poet himself has to admit that the record of their deeds and sufferings was sparse, and he puts it down to deliberate suppression of their memory by the authorities. The outline of the story would seem to fit the standard pattern of martyrdom accounts of the Decian (*c.* 250) or Diocletianic (*c.* 303—6) persecutions. Interestingly, the cult looks to have had a relatively slow dissemination in Spain, in that the two saints do not figure in the León antifonal or the Tarragona *Liber Orationum*, suggesting that their feast was unknown to or unrecognized by the churches of Toledo and Tarragona in the Visigothic period, although the former was the metropolitan see under which Calahorra was somewhat distantly placed. Only from the ninth century did it come to be generally included in the Spanish liturgy.[54] On the other hand the two saints were known to Gregory of Tours (d. 594—5) in Gaul, explicitly on the authority of Prudentius.[55]

In the concluding lines of the poem devoted to them, Prudentius makes clear both his own association with Calahorra, and also the fact that, as in Strabo's day, it was still regarded as a city of the Vascones:[56]

> Believe ye now, ye Vascones, once dull pagans,
> how holy was the blood which cruel superstition sacrificed.
>
> ★ ★ ★
>
> This blessing the Saviour himself bestowed for our advantage
> when He consecrated the martyrs' bodies in our town,
> where they now protect the folk who dwell by Ebro's waters.

The implication is also clear that the Vascones he addresses are now Christians.

---

[53] Prudentius, *Peristephanon*, vol. I, ed. and tr. H. J. Thomson, pp. 98—109.

[54] C. García Rodríguez, *El culto de los santos en la España romana y visigoda* (Madrid, 1966), pp. 321—4.

[55] Gregory of Tours, *Liber de Gloria Martyrum*, 93, *Patrologia Latina*, LXXI, cc. 786—7.

[56] Prudentius, *Peristephanon*, vol. I, Thomson, p. 107.

Prudentius himself is the best testimony as to how sophisticated a Romanized provincial from one of the towns of the Basque region could become in the late fourth century. It is likely that he was born in 348, and the lack of any reference to a conversion has led it to be believed that he was the son of Christian parents. His education, which he alludes to, was of the standard late Roman kind and led finally to legal training and practice. He probably also served in the imperial administration, and may have obtained the honorific title of *comes* (count) from the Emperor Honorius. He was thus a layman of some social standing, at least in provincial terms, and was not afraid to confront the possibly still predominantly pagan senate of Rome in his verse *Contra Symmachum*, a reply to the arguments in favour of toleration of paganism advanced to the Emperor Valentinian II by the urban prefect Quintus Aurelius Symmachus in 384. Prudentius was admittedly writing *c.* 400, a few years after Symmachus's death, but the latter's memory was still venerated and he had left influential heirs.

On another level Prudentius is marked out for the quality of his verse, and the wide range of subjects and forms in which he employed it. Previous specifically Christian poetry, of which not a lot existed, had been largely confined to the composition of metrical versions of scriptural books, notably represented by the works of the Spanish priest Juvencus (*c.* 340).[57] The writing of metrical hymns was also developing, particularly under the influence of Ambrose of Milan (d. 397), and Prudentius composed some of these too. More original were his extended theological writings in verse, as evidenced in his *Apotheosis*, that attacks contemporary heresies, and the polemical *Contra Symmachum*. Unique and highly personal as Prudentius's talent was, it is important to note that his grounding in Christian doctrine and in the poetic forms he so ably combined in his work seems to have been available to him in Calahorra, 'city of the Vascones'.

Prudentius and Calahorra may indeed have been at the forefront of provincial Christianity, at least in the western half of the empire, in the late fourth century, but this does not imply that such enlightenment had extended itself to the whole of the Basque region. It is impossible to be confident about the

[57] J. McClure, 'The Biblical epic and its audience in late antiquity', *Papers of the Liverpool Latin Seminar*, 3 (1981), pp. 305—21.

bishopric of Pamplona before 589, and although other dioceses came into existence on the northern fringes of the Pyrenees, this was only the periphery of the Basque area. It is impossible to speak with confidence of a bishopric at Bayonne before the tenth century.[58] From the lands between Pamplona and the river Adour, and between Pamplona and the Bay of Biscay, there exists no evidence for the person of a single Christian in this period. The indications of the very late development of monastic institutions in comparison with the rest of Spain and France, and the delayed appearance of virtually all of the other dioceses of the Basque areas, must put the onus of the argument on to those who would like to claim that the existence of Christianity in fourth-century Calahorra establishes proof of its contemporaneous flourishing in Guipúzcoa, Vizcaya and the French Basque provinces. As has been seen in other respects, the Basque regions can be divided into two interrelated but distinct highland and lowland zones. Calahorra, on the southernmost fringe of the Basque lowland area, was open to currents of influence from further down the Ebro and from the Mediterranean. Such currents cannot but have become attenuated or have extinguished themselves in the mountains. Thus the question of the full and final Christianization of the Basques has to await its resolution in a later period.

[58] See below, pp. 101, 176.

3

The Parting of the Ways

At some point, probably in the second decade of the fifth century, a letter was sent in the name of the western emperor Honorius (395—423) via a certain Sabinianus, who held the honorific title of patrician, to the militia of Pamplona. The letter itself is somewhat obscure in its content and may have become garbled in its later transmission, but seems to be a general introduction to the imperial forces in Spain of their new commander or *magister utriusque militiae*, in the person of Sabinianus.[1] The body of the text is thus the imperial letter proper, and the introductory formulae that of the particular copy sent to the troops in Pamplona. Other units will doubtless have received similar versions personally addressed to them, but none of these has survived. Indeed, it is little short of miraculous that the Pamplona letter has been preserved, as it is the sole such ephemeral administrative document to have survived from the western empire in this period. For reasons that cannot be known it was preserved in Navarre, probably in Pamplona itself, long enough to have been copied into a manuscript of genealogical and historical texts written in the tenth century, probably at the royal court, then centred at Nájera.[2]

Unfortunately, the introductory phrases fail to specify the

[1] E. Demougeot, 'Une lettre de l'empereur Honorius sur l'*hospitium* des soldats', *Nouvelle revue historique de droit français et étranger*, 4th series, 34 (1956), pp. 26—49; A. H. M. Jones, 'A letter of Honorius to the army of Spain', in *Xe Congrès international des études byzantines* (Istanbul, 1957), p. 223.

[2] Text in J. M. Lacarra, 'Textos navarros del Códice de Roda', *Estudios de Edad Media de la Corona de Aragón*, vol. I (1945), pp. 268—70.

nature and composition of the forces then constituting the militia of Pamplona, and the generalized text of the letter proper, full of obscure references and corruptions introduced by later scribal error, sheds no additional light on purely Pyrenean conditions; though the initial reference to 'an infestation of barbarians' would seem to refer to the period following the first overrunning of the peninsula by Germanic tribes in 409. Related to the letter in the manuscript is a separate short piece constituting a description of the city of Pamplona. The tenth-century scribe obviously regarded the two texts as forming a unity, or received them thus in the manuscript transmission, and he entitled the composite work *De Laude Pampilone Epistola*, or 'Letter in praise of Pamplona'. This second part of the work, the description of the city, was almost certainly written in the seventh century, some 200 years after its companion piece was sent from Rome. It was thus composed when the Visigoths, the heirs and conquerors of those earlier Germanic invaders of the beginning of the fifth century, were masters of the Iberian peninsula. Under their rule many features of late Roman urban life were preserved, and the literary and intellectual heritage of antiquity continued to exert a direct influence, at least upon some sectors of society. Thus the anonymous author of the description of Pamplona unconsciously offers a symbol of such urban continuity in his account of the city's 84ft high walls with their 67 towers, survivals of the Roman defensive *enceinte*.

Defence is indeed the dominant theme of this brief *Laudatio*, and to such material protection as the walls and towers are added the spiritual ones of the bones of the martyrs reposing within the city. Just as the defences are twofold, so likewise are the enemies of Pamplona, in the persons of heretics and Vascones.[3] It should not be inferred that the author made a distinction and saw the relics of the martyrs (unfortunately unspecified) as the city's protection against heresy and its fortifications as its shield against the Basques. Both were inextricably linked, and the role of a city's patron saints as its defenders against both material and spiritual harm can be paralleled not only elsewhere in Spain but more widely through-out the Mediterranean world, and not least in the city of

---

[3] Ibid. pp. 269—70.

Constantinople, at this period.[4] The heretics in this instance may have been Arians, though it is impossible to say whether or not this is a reference to some specific threat or episode or a more generalized fear of the effects of heresy. More tangible is the mention of the danger posed by the Vaccaei, a name either synonymous with or representative of a distinct portion of the Vascones. Against them the protection of the many-towered walls and of the sacred relics had to be invoked. Again this could refer to a general threat or a particular incident.

From Roman to German

It is striking to juxtapose this text with the reference to the Vascones in Prudentius's *Peristephanon*. In the latter the Vascones were, as in the work of Strabo, identified with the city dwellers of Calahorra, and as Christians under the special protection of the patron saints Emeterius and Celidonius. In the Pamplona text, on the other hand, they are the outsiders, the rural threat, the enemies of the citizens and allies of heresy. How had such a transformation of image come about? This contrast highlights a process that can also be documented from other sources. In the Roman period, as has been seen, there is no evidence that the Basque region presented special problems of order or government to the imperial administration and its delegates in the peninsula. On the other hand, in the sixth and seventh centuries whenever the Basques feature in the extant historical sources it is always in the context of military activity being directed against them by the Visigothic and Frankish rulers of Spain and Gaul, and this, it is clear, is in response to raids made by them on settled areas as far down the Ebro valley as Zaragoza or deep into the plains of southern Aquitaine. Although the limited nature of the evidence for the Roman period may conceal some elements of a greater continuity in the security problem, there are good grounds for suspecting that the sixth- and seventh-century conditions are new ones, and it is

[4] For a Spanish parallel see R. Collins, 'Mérida and Toledo, 550—585', in E. James (ed.), *Visigothic Spain: New Approaches* (Oxford, 1980), pp. 194—8. For Constantinople see A. Cameron, 'The *theotokos* in sixth-century Constantinople: a city finds its symbol', *Journal of Theological Studies*, new series, 29 (1978), pp. 79—108.

therefore necessary to seek an explanation of why such a fundamental change came about.

In the last days of the year 406 pressure that had been mounting on the Rhine frontier of Rome over the preceding half century finally overwhelmed the empire's defences when the river froze, allowing a confederacy of peoples, the Vandals, Sueves and Alans, to cross into Gaul.[5] Within the next three years they had made their way across the Gallic provinces, and in the autumn of 409 were admitted into Spain through passes across the Pyrenees, almost certainly at the western end. What destruction their passage wrought in the Basque regions is not known, and it is important to regard them as more than mere looters and scavengers. Nor was it just their irruption that affected the military and governmental structures of the western Pyrenees. In the aftermath of the breaking of the Rhine frontier, a rebel emperor in Britain, Constantine III, was able to cross into Gaul, and make himself master of it in 407. He had extended his power to the Spanish provinces as well before the Vandals, Sueves and Alans crossed the Pyrenees, but having been faced with opposition by members of the family of the legitimate emperors, who were of Spanish origin, he had replaced the garrison troops holding the passes over the mountains with contingents of barbarian mercenaries, on whose loyalty he more closely counted. It was these forces who, by deliberate design or incompetence, allowed the Vandals and others into Spain in September or October of 409.

Despite problems closer to home, notably the Visigothic invasion of Italy in 408 and sack of Rome in 410, the imperial government proved sufficiently resilient to be able to launch a counter-offensive; in 411 the regime of Constantine III, centred at Arles, was overthrown, and that of Maximus, set up in Barcelona in rebellion against the rebel Constantine, collapsed. In the aftermath the units of the Roman army in Spain, which had been led into Gaul as part of the civil war between the rival usurpers, were not returned to the Iberian peninsula. In practice these events marked the end of direct rule by Rome over most of Spain. Although the Vandals, Sueves and Alans, who under

[5] For a fuller account of this period, particularly in respect of Spain, see R. Collins, *Early Medieval Spain: Unity in Diversity, 400—1000* (London and Basingstoke, 1983), pp. 14—21.

their kings had made themselves masters of most of the peninsula, were curbed by the Visigoths, who in 416 invaded Spain as the allies of Rome, this proved only partially effective. The Visigoths, who showed ambitions of transferring themselves to the rich province of Africa, source of much of the western empire's grain, had to be withdrawn, and in 418 were established in southern Aquitaine as the result of a treaty with Rome. As a result the Hasding branch of the Vandal confederacy emerged as the dominant power in Spain, but even after they successfully migrated into Africa in 429, control of the south and the west of the peninsula passed into the hands of the Sueves. The latter made themselves masters of the provinces of Galicia, Lusitania and Baetica, with direct Roman rule limited to no more than Tarraconensis and the coastal parts of Carthaginiensis. The upper Ebro valley and the Basque regions south of the Pyrenees, forming part of the province of Tarraconensis, thus remained under nominal imperial rule, and Zaragoza was even to receive an imperial visitor in the person of the Emperor Majorian in 458.[6] But to the north of the mountains lay the newly formed Visigothic kingdom in Aquitaine, with its capital at Toulouse.[7] Thus if Calahorra and Pamplona still paid taxes to Rome, it was from the very fringe of a much diminished empire, with the valley of the Ebro as the only direct line of communication between governors and governed.

The Aquitanian settlement: city and mountain

One crucial development in this period, already alluded to, which was to be of the greatest significance for the future history of the whole of the Iberian peninsula, was the settlement of the Visigoths in southern Aquitaine in 418, and this may have been brought about in response to events in the Basque region. The reasons behind this particular piece of imperial policy have aroused considerable discussion amongst historians. It looks clear enough that in this instance Rome's hand had not

[6] J. Orlandis, 'Zaragoza visigótica', in his *Hispania y Zaragoza en la antigüedad tardía* (Zaragoza, 1984), pp. 16—17.
[7] On the Visigothic kingdom in Aquitaine see A. M. Jiménez Garnica, *Orígenes y desarrollo del Reino Visigodo de Tolosa* (Valladolid, 1983).

been forced. The Visigoths were deliberately extracted from Spain in order to move them to Aquitaine.[8] That this was a way of neutralizing the threat of their moving southwards to Africa may have been one factor, but the choice of Aquitaine as the area in which to establish them on a permanent basis after nearly a quarter of a century of instability and movement on their part was clearly calculated. One explanation, long and forcefully advanced, is that the underlying purpose was to use their military strength to protect the estates of the Aquitanian landowners from the depredations of the Bagaudae.[9] Here problems begin. The question of who the Bagaudae were has not yet, and may never be, fully answered. Our sources are all too brief and elusive on the subject. The name itself is not self-explanatory.[10] It may be of Celtic origin, but there is no certainty that the people to whom it was applied by various Latin authors would have used it of themselves. The geographical locations of the recorded Bagaudae are less problematic. They are found in the northern Alps in the late third century; in Armorica, the later Brittany, in the first half of the fifth century; and in the Spanish province of Tarraconensis in the 440s and 450s.[11] With such a distribution in time and place it is clear that this is not a homogeneous group, and the employment of the name Bagaudae in a diversity of sources probably indicates that this was a label, perhaps deriving from the perpetrators of the first outbreak, in Savoy *c.* 286, that continued to be applied by Roman authors to similar and subsequent but unrelated phenomena.

The points of similarity between the various instances of Bagaudic activity would suggest that they represent acts of banditry on a large scale. In 286 the Emperor Maximian had his baggage train looted in the Alpine passes. In 417 and in the 430s and 440s estates in Armorica were being looted, and in

---

[8] For a recent discussion of the processes involved see W. Goffart, *Barbarians and Romans, 418—584: the Techniques of Accommodation* (Princeton, N.J., 1980), pp. 103—26.

[9] E. A. Thompson, 'The settlement of the barbarians in southern Gaul', *Journal of Roman Studies*, 46 (1956), pp. 65—75; see also the arguments to the contrary in J. M. Wallace-Hadrill, *The Long-Haired Kings* (London, 1961), pp. 26—9, and the riposte in the appendix to E. A. Thompson, *Romans and Barbarians* (Madison, 1982), pp. 251—5.

[10] C. E. Minor, 'Bagaudae or Bacaudae', *Traditio*, 31 (1975), pp. 318—22.

[11] A. H. M. Jones, *The Later Roman Empire* (3 vols, Oxford, 1964), pp. 35, 38, 99, 187—90, 199, 406, 811—12.

Spain in 449 Bagaudae killed the bishop of Tarazona. For most of these episodes particular leaders of the Bagaudae are recorded: Amandus in Gaul in 286, Tibatto in Armorica in the 430s and Basilius in Tarazona in 449. In all cases relatively large-scale military action by imperial or federate troops was required to suppress and massacre the Bagaudae. It has been argued, more on the grounds of prior ideological conviction than on those of the evidence, that these Bagaudae were oppressed peasants, driven by the harshness of the Roman fiscal and social systems into revolt against the upper classes and into attempts to create new forms of society divorced from Roman rule.[12] However, Bagaudic activity was localized and restricted to certain marginal areas in which it was difficult to maintain the normal working of law and order in times of weakness on the part of the central government. In such areas local and short-term conditions could lead to a growth of banditry that immediately available resources were insufficient to repress. Such conditions cannot be assumed to be endemic in the whole of western Roman society in the late imperial period.

The question of the Bagaudae needs to be aired here, problematic and controversial as it might be, for two reasons. Firstly, it has been suggested recently that the Visigoths were established in southern Aquitaine not to contain the threat of the Armorican Bagaudae but to counter that presented by the Basques. Secondly, it has also been argued that the Bagaudae recorded as being active in Tarraconensis were none other than the Basques under another name.[13] Certainly the explanation of the Aquitanian settlement in terms of the Bagaudae in Armorica does not convince. To put defenders in Toulouse against a threat anticipated as coming from north of the Loire must seem eccentric, and however odd Roman notions of geography may now seem, they did have a realistic awareness of distances. Further, if a problem existed that required a military solution, why were the apparently quite tractable Visigoths not sent to Armorica itself? The only counter-argument must be that the

[12] E. A. Thompson, 'Peasant revolts in late Roman Gaul and Spain', *Past and Present*, 2 (1952), pp. 11—23.

[13] R. Collins, 'The Basques in Aquitaine and Navarre', in *War and Government in the Middle Ages*, eds J. Gillingham and J. C. Holt (Ipswich, 1984), pp. 3—17, many of whose conclusions are here modified; J. Orlandis, 'Bagaudia hispánica', *Revista de Historia del Derecho*, 2 (1977).

Visigoths were settled where they were to deter Aquitanian peasantry and *coloni* from breaking out into Bagaudic risings of their own against the landowning classes of the province, affected as it were by contagion from Armorica. For such a view no evidence exists, and it can only be supported by *a priori* assumptions about the nature of the Bagaudic phenomenon and the social conditions held to have caused it.

It is probably necessary to be equally wary of believing that the Spanish Bagaudae were Basques. Only three references to the former exist, all of which come from the *Chronicle* of the Galician bishop Hydatius (d. *post* 469).[14] The first records the despatch in 441 of Asturius as *dux utriusque militiae* (commander of cavalry and infantry) to Spain and his subsequent slaughter of a multitude of Bagaudae in the province of Tarraconensis. Secondly, in 449 a certain Basilius, having re-formed the Bagaudae, massacred a body of federate troops in the church at Tarazona, in the course of which its bishop, Leo, was killed. This episode may conceivably have been an act of vengeance for the massacre of 441. Finally, in 454 the Tarraconese Bagaudae were slaughtered in the name of Rome by the Visigothic commander Frederic, brother of King Theoderic II. Laconic as are Hydatius's entries, it is reasonable to suspect that a continuity underlies his three references to the Bagaudae of Tarraconensis, and that it was the band reconstituted by Basilius that was eliminated by Frederic in 454. There is only one point of geographical localization in the three entries, and that is the reference to Tarazona, on the southern wall of the Ebro valley, about 35 miles south of Calahorra, and roughly equidistant between Pamplona and Zaragoza (see map 11). This would seem to place the sphere of Bagaudic activity and the campaigns against them within this central Ebro region, and thus on the very outskirts of the Basque areas. But with Tarazona as the only point of reference, it is also conceivable that the Bagaudae operated further south still, in the Sierra de Moncayo and Llanos de Plasencia, or further west towards Soria and the Peña Turquillo, all good guerrilla country, and all beyond the zones of Basque occupation. Equally significant is the fact that Hydatius did *not* call them Vascones, although he was well enough aware

---

[14] A. Tranoy (ed.), *Hydace, Chronique*, 125, 141, 158 (2 vols, Paris, 1974), vol. I, pp. 138, 142, 148.

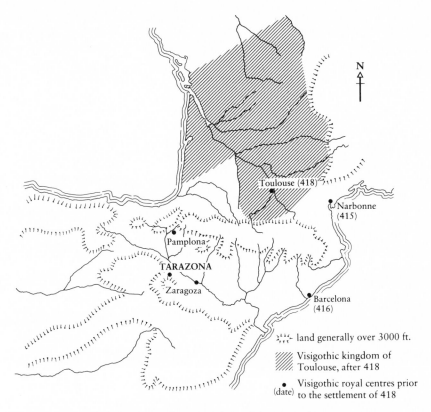

Map 11   The Visigoths and the Bagaudae

of the existence of the Vasconias, the lands of the Basques. Thus in general there is not enough reason to believe that the Spanish Bagaudae were the Vascones, although there may have been individual Basques amongst them.

If that be the case, there is no evidence to show that even by the middle of the fifth century the mountain-dwelling Basque tribes had become the threat to the settled communities of the Ebro valley and southern Aquitaine that they certainly were to be by the end of the sixth. Indeed in the records of this period they only feature as being attacked by others. In February 449 the Suevic king Rechiarius is recorded by Hydatius as having both married the daughter of the Visigothic monarch Theoderic

I (419—51) and ravaged the territories of the Vascones.[15] Geographically, this may seem a rather strange combination of actions on his part, as at this time the Sueves only controlled the south and west of the peninsula, with the capital of their kingdom being Mérida.[16] It is conceivable, therefore, that Rechiarius had made his way to the Visigothic court at Toulouse for the nuptials, and then looted his way through the Basque regions with his followers on his way home. The very early season of the year, as reported by Hydatius, might confirm such a view, as it was not normal campaigning time. The effective independence, even hostility, of both Suevic and Visigothic monarchies towards Rome at this point would explain why notional imperial subjects could be treated in this way. On the other hand, if the Basques were posing a threat to southern Aquitaine, now firmly under Visigothic sway, this ravaging could have been part of a campaign to contain them. However, there are no other such indications, and such looting by passing Germanic armies was a not uncommon feature of this period. It was certainly not in response to any aggression that a fleet of Heruls carried out raids on the coasts of Cantabria and the land of the Varduli in 455.[17] It is therefore only on the basis of extrapolating from conditions that existed a century or two later that a case can be made out for seeing the Basques as being either expansionary or a threat to local order in the middle of the fifth century. There are thus no contemporary intimations of the problems to come.

The notional threat of the Vascones must join that of the Bagaudae as an unsatisfactory explanation for the Aquitanian settlement of the Visigoths.[18] Overall it is likely that conditions in the western Pyrenees altered in the course of the first half of the fifth century. There were periods of disruption and destruction, as in the passage of the Vandals, Sueves and Alans in 409, and the ravaging by Rechiarius in 449. Damage to settlements clearly occurred, and future excavation may reveal more of this. Pamplona survived, as did Calahorra, but Iruña seems to have been abandoned at a point no later than these decades, and the same is true of a number of villa sites. It is conceivable too that

[15] Tranoy, *Hydace*, 140, vol. I, p. 142.
[16] Collins, *Early Medieval Spain*, pp. 19—24.
[17] Tranoy, *Hydace*, 171, vol. I, p. 152.
[18] In opposition see Collins, 'The Basques in Aquitaine and Navarre', p. 6.

A Roman or early medieval discoidal funerary monument found near Iruña (Alava). Such grave markers have continued in use among the Basques to the present day

the amount of land under cultivation contracted, not least with the removal of the garrisons in 411. Urban disruption and the disappearance of the army also involved a decline in the market for the surplus products of the Basque pastoral economy. Although none of this can be quantified, and its very existence only inferred, the events of this period cannot have failed to have had a significant impact upon a long established pattern of town—country relationships. In the case of a pastoral economy the decline or disappearance of normal markets would have a profound effect in that there was no alternative system of production to turn to instead. The geography of the mountain region made more intensive use of agriculture or greater diversification impossible. Thus, if thwarted of the possibility of obtaining what they needed or were used to by the exchange of their surplus products, pastoralists have tended to resort to alternative means, notably taking what they want by force, not least because the conditions in the lands in which they live, and which require them to subsist in the manner in which they do, also render them less vulnerable to retaliatory action on the part of the settled neighbours on whom they are driven to prey. In the case of the Basques the densely vegetated mountains of the western Pyrenees provided such opportunities. In addition, the attacks to which they themselves were subjected on a number of occasions by passing armies or sea-borne raiders such as the Heruls cannot but have developed their own aggressive reactions, little needed in the previous period of Roman order. Thus in general it is possible to suggest that the peculiar conditions that characterized the Basque regions in the sixth and seventh centuries and the attitudes that accompanied them should be seen as resulting from the events of the immediate post-imperial period rather than as manifestations of an unchanging pattern of conflict between the Basques and all and any of their neighbours.

It is possible to envisage how the conditions of the first half of the fifth century brought about a crucial transformation in the economic relations and mutual regard of the Basque mountain dwellers and their lowland neighbours. This is what lies behind the crisis of identity that seems to have overtaken the city dwellers of the upper Ebro at this time. As has been mentioned, Calahorra was for Strabo a 'city of the Vasconians', and four centuries later Prudentius could still identify the Vascones with the city, but this was to be the last time any such association could be made. All references to the Vascones in the Visigothic period are to a dangerous rural population emerging from the mountains to threaten the settled inhabitants of the valleys.[19]

[19] Ibid., pp. 11—13.

The only context in which they are found linked to towns is that of the threat they pose to the citizens. The author of the *De Laude Pampelone* was not alone in his attitude towards the Vaccaei. Gone is any sense of common identity as fellow Vascones.

It might be thought that language has a part to play in this, and that such feelings reflect a loss of community of speech. This is possible. There is no easy way of telling how the Basque language had fared during the Roman period. That Latin had become the polite speech of the educated urban elites is a reasonable supposition, but how far they had retained a bilingualism cannot be judged. Their late medieval equivalents seem to have been able to do this, but such an analogy cannot prove the case. It is hard to believe, though, that Latin made as much impact on the rural population of the valleys, let alone those of the mountains. Even if there was a linguistic divide, and whether they spoke Basque primarily or at all, Prudentius's Calahorran fellow citizens were clearly content to think of themselves and be addressed as Vascones; within a century, or two at the most, such an epithet would be insulting.

This period also sees the disappearance of the references to the various tribal subgroupings. The Varduli can appear in Hydatius's *Chronicle*, but are not heard of again, any more than are the Autrigones.[20] This may be just a quirk of the survival of evidence, but the same phenomenon is to be detected elsewhere in the Roman world and even in areas such as Scotland outside the formal structures of the empire but within its cultural orbit. Thus north of Hadrian's Wall the extensive list of tribes known in the Roman period is reduced to only two in the aftermath of the imperial collapse. Likewise in the Pyrenees the generic name of Vascones comes to be applied where once a more varied range of tribal labels had existed. This is certainly not to imply some act of conquest by which one dominant tribe swallows up the rest.[21] It is conceivable that a brief recrudescence of indigenous cultures, which like the Basque language had survived the centuries of Roman uniformity, occurred in certain parts of

---

[20] Tranoy, *Hydace*, 171, vol. I, p. 152.
[21] For an opposed view see C. Sánchez-Albornoz, 'Los vascones vasconizan la depresión vasca', in his *Orígenes de la nación española* (3 vols, Oviedo, 1972—5), vol. I, pp. 101—6.

the former western empire in the wake of its dissolution, only to give way in turn before the reassertion of a common Christian *Romanitas* when confronted with the challenge presented by the new Germanic overlords. Certainly it was not a survival of Celtic culture in Gaul or Spain that moulded the Franks and the Visigoths into modest imitators of Roman examples. Such processes are hard to fathom, the more so for occurring in a period so signally lacking in records, but it is against a background of this sort that the developments in the Basque regions must be put.

Previously, two loosely interrelated forms of society and economic organization had been able to coexist in the western Pyrenees and upper Ebro valley, with mutual benefit, and under the cover of a single racial name and conceivably united by a common language. In the course of the fifth and sixth centuries such community broke down. The town dwellers, and no doubt those who lived in the associated rural hinterlands, were prepared to abandon their identity as Vascones, and to co-operate with the newly established central authority in the peninsula, the Visigothic kingdom, as a way of defending certain values and ways of life, to which the mountain dwellers, now the sole bearers of the name of Vascones, were not only alien but also a threat. Defence against the Vascones was probably the greatest cement of political loyalty in the towns of the western Pyrenees, which, unlike those at the eastern end of the range, rarely flirted with rebellion or the alternative attraction of Frankish rule. Thus the growing apart of the two societies in the western Pyrenees was a response to change on the part of both of them. The town dwellers of the lowlands no longer lived in the centre of a large empire, with security as well as communications stretching away from them both to north and south: they had instead become frontiersmen. The mountaineers were perched between two hostile but vulnerable lowland societies, that in the sixth century were themselves to become mutually antagonistic.

Presented thus, it is easier to see both how the once wider geographical extension of Vasconia contracts at this time to exclude the urbanized and settled areas once contained within it, and how the Basque identity continued to survive. Unusual in terms of their racial longevity and non-Indo-European origin as

the Basques are, they were but one of the various peoples of
Spain under Roman rule; yet, together with the similarly placed
Cantabri, further to the west, they alone retained that identity
across the whole span of the imperial period. It is not their
inaccessibility or continuity of hostility to Rome that explains
this. It is clear enough that the western Pyrenees were quite
penetrable, and the Roman presence in the area is marked.
Resistance to Rome, and indeed a position beyond its frontiers,
did not preserve the only other non-Indo-European people of
western Europe, the Picts. Nor is the intractability of the
language an explanation: for exceptional as Basque is in linguistic
terms, it was in practice no odder to a Latin speaker than the
equally 'barbarous' Gallic Celtic or Gothic. The survival of the
Basques at this crucial time, when so many of the other tribal
and linguistic identities of early Europe were being lost, cannot
be understood in terms of physical or cultural isolation. Any
acceptable explanation must be a positive one, dependant upon
the way in which significant changes offered a variety of
possible alternative reactions. In the case of the Basques, it is
arguable that altered circumstances led to an internal confron-
tation between two contrasting forms of social and economic
organization within their area of habitation. As a result, one
group abandoned all elements, cultural and probably therefore
linguistic also, of the former common identity, whilst the other
embraced it all the more closely, subordinating to it previous
tribal subdivisions that may once have played an important role
in expressing separation in geographical rather than socio-
economic terms.

All of this is rather theoretical, but throughout its great
chronological span the history of the Basques presents many
problems and very few answers. Resort has to be made to
models of interpretation that can embrace all of the available
information and yet not put too much strain upon common
sense. What is clear is that the Basques did not become masters
of the art of survival by acting as if the rest of the world was
empty — not that some of the more aggressive elements of that
outside world were slow to make their presence felt in the
passes of the western Pyrenees. In 456 the Visigothic king
Theoderic II (453—66) invaded the Iberian peninsula, probably
at the behest of the vestigial imperial government in Rome, and

destroyed the Suevic kingdom of his brother-in-law Rechiarius, who in the previous year had eliminated one of the last Roman footholds in Spain by overrunning the province of Carthaginiensis.[22] As the fighting involved took place in the north-west, in the vicinity of Astorga, it is likely that the Visigothic forces, coming from Aquitaine, crossed the Pyrenees by the western passes. They did so again in the reign of Theoderic's brother Euric (466—84), when a Visigothic army descended the Ebro valley to unite with another force that had come around the eastern end of the mountains, and thus finally extinguish Roman rule in the peninsula.[23] Henceforth the Basques were, in theory at least, the subjects of the Visigothic kings.

From the termination of Hydatius's chronicle in 469 up to the resumption of historical writing in the peninsula *c.* 590, and the composition of Gregory of Tours' *Ten Books of History* (583—94), there is a lack of contemporary reference to events in the Basque regions on both sides of the Pyrenees. When the Vascones re-emerge into the light of history it is in a new role. The lacuna in our evidence makes it hard to know precisely when to start this new phase in their history; it could be as much as a century earlier than the point at which we first have notice of it. What is clear though, is that in this time they have become — to reverse a dictum used, not very sensibly, of the Vikings — 'raiders not traders'. To put this in context, it is necessary to look at some of the wider developments in western Europe that were to exercise an influence upon events in the Pyrenees.

Frank and Visigoth: the Basque frontier

The complete subjection by the armies of Euric of the Spanish provinces other than Galicia, where a vestigial Suevic kingdom still had a century of existence left to it, restored the political unity of the regions to the north and to the south of the Pyrenees. However, this was to be short-lived. In 507 in the battle of Vouillé the Visigoths were overwhelmed by the

[22] Tranoy, *Hydace*, 173—5, 178, vol. I, pp. 154—6.
[23] Collins, *Early Medieval Spain*, p. 24.

Franks, and in the aftermath lost most of their territory in Gaul. The only exception was the Mediterranean coastal region of Septimania. The hostilities engendered by this encounter in 507 did not abate throughout the course of the ensuing century, and a number of Frankish assaults were launched upon the remaining Visigothic enclave north of the Pyrenees, and also across the mountains into the valley of the Ebro. The most substantial of these occured in 542, when the Frankish kings Childebert and Chlotar attempted, without success, to take Zaragoza.[24] As none of the major towns of the Mediterranean littoral of Tarraconensis is mentioned in connection with this expedition, it is probable that the Franks came over the western Pyrenees. Visigothic forces were able to block their egress, and the Frankish kings were eventually forced to buy their way out.

The state of hostilities that existed between the two kingdoms had significant consequences for the Basque regions. For the first time this became a frontier area between two rival powers, one of which was frequently on the offensive, and on occasion this could result in campaigning in the western Pyrenees, as in 542, when the Visigothic general Theudisclus blocked the passes against the Frankish retreat from Zaragoza. Although documentary records for this period are few, and archaeology has remained silent, such circumstances are likely to have been reflected in the establishment of additional defences and garrisons on both sides of the mountains, though with little of the organization and sophistication of the previous Roman military presence in the area. The position of the Basques was thus a new one. If never fully integrated into the Roman system, they had at least been encapsulated by it; but in the sixth century they found themselves the inhabitants of a frontier zone between rival powers, a situation that presented them with both new opportunities and new difficulties.

According to Gregory of Tours, in the year 581 the Frankish dux Bladast led an army into Vasconia, only to have the greater part of it destroyed.[25] In itself this might seem to be no more

[24] Isidore, *Historia Gothorum*, 41, C. Rodríguez Alonso (ed.), *Las Historias de los Godos, Vandalos y Suevos de Isidoro de Sevilla* (León, 1975), pp. 240—1; also Gregory of Tours, *Decem Libri Historiarum*, III.29, eds B. Krusch and W. Levison, *Monumenta Germaniae Historica, Scriptores Rerum Merovingicarum* (alt. edn Hanover, 1951), vol. I, ii.

[25] Gregory, *Libri Historiarum*, VI.12.

than another of the attempted ravagings the region had been
subjected to over the previous century and a half, but another
episode recorded by Gregory suggests that expeditions such as
that of Bladast were this time of a pre-emptive or punitive
nature. In 587 the Vascones are reported to have raided the
plains of southern Aquitaine, destroying crops and vines, burning
houses and carrying off captives, together with herds of animals.[26]
A Dux Austrovald failed in various attempts to bring them to
heel. This is the first record of Basque depredations of this kind
and, although very brief and generalized, it contains a number
of suggestive details. Firstly, it is possible that the arable
produce was carried back into the mountains; secondly, herds
were taken; and thirdly, so too were human captives. What use
had the Basques for the last of these? The mountainous Basque
regions did not, and indeed could not, support a slave economy.
In the Pyrenean heartlands of sixth-century Vasconia the pastoral
mode of production did not require slave labour, nor could a
slave population be maintained and overseen. Some of the
captives were no doubt ransomable, but only a very small core
of wealthy ones. The only other way whereby captives could be
of value to the Basques was as objects of trade.[27] Franks or
Frankish subjects once inside the Visigothic kingdom had no
legal standing or protection. Thus anyone taken from the north
of the Pyrenees could be sold into slavery in the south with
impunity. A slave class certainly existed in Visigothic Spain,
whose economy was to some degree dependent upon it, and,
although such a slave society could have been in part self-
perpetuating, it will also have required additional renewal from
outside sources.[28] In this period the Basques were uniquely
placed between the two mutually hostile kingdoms to provide
such a service. It is also conceivable that they operated their
trade in both directions.

The seizure of crops and herds, as referred to by Gregory, is
also noteworthy. Such a resort to violence in place of exchange
may have several causes. That they took livestock back into the

---

[26] Ibid., IX.7.

[27] On slavery in the early Middle Ages see C. Verlinden, *L'esclavage dans l'Europe
médiévale I: Péninsule Ibérique—France* (Bruges, 1955).

[28] P. D. King, *Law and Society in the Visigothic Kingdom* (Cambridge, 1972),
pp. 159—89.

mountains is suggestive of mere acquisitiveness, but they may have been able to dispose of a larger surplus in market exchanges to the south of the mountains. Obviously possession of herds constituted the measure of wealth for Basque society, and thus their augmentation by whatever means was a socially desirable end in its own right. But unlike other societies, such as early medieval Ireland, in which social status could be quantified by livestock, that of the Basques looks to have been less stratified. There is no evidence for any form of aristocracy. Furthermore the capacity of their lands to maintain livestock, especially over the winter months, was limited. It is also inherently likely that the Basques were in this instance responding to or taking advantage of disturbed conditions in southern Aquitaine, not least the brief usurpation of power in that region by Gondovald (584—5), and his forcible suppression by the Frankish king Guntramn.[29]

It is difficult to be precise about the areas particularly affected by the Basque raids in the 580s (see map 12). Some deductions can be made from points of detail in Gregory's accounts. That Bladast attempted to campaign in Vasconia, and that the raiders of 587 were specifically said to have come from the mountains, seem to indicate that the Basques had not yet extended their territories beyond the northern fringes of the Pyrenees. Bladast was a dux in the service of King Chilperic (561—84) and then a supporter of Gondovald, and his sphere of activity seems to have been in Aquitaine. On the other hand Austrovald was probably a count of Toulouse until 587, when he succeeded Desiderius as dux in the same region. He was twice involved in unsuccessful Frankish attempts to take Carcassonne from the Visigoths.[30] Such indications that he was normally active in the eastern Pyrenean regions might suggest that the Basque raids of 587 had affected the areas under his control, perhaps across the headwaters of the Adour into the territory of the modern *département* of Gers.

That the Basques had still not expanded their settlement to the north of the Pyrenees, and were taking their loot and captives

[29] M. Rouche, *L'Aquitaine des Wisigoths aux Arabes, 418—781* (Paris, 1979), pp. 66—77.

[30] Gregory, *Libri Historarum*, VIII.45 and IX.31, Krusch and Levison, vol. I, pp. 411, 450.

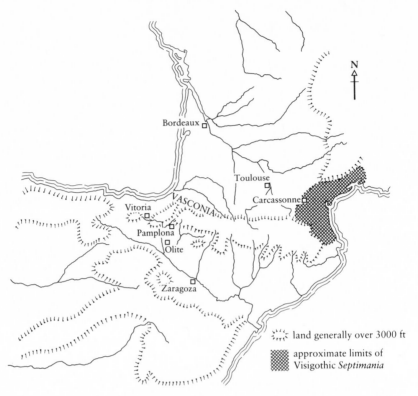

Map 12   Franks and Visigoths in the late sixth century

back into the mountains, would seem to counter the suggestion
that it was at this time that they were being driven into Frankish
territories in increasing numbers as the result of military activity
by the Visigothic kings directed against their homelands in and
to the south of the Pyrenees.[31] One such period of campaigning
had recently come to an end. In 573 the Visigothic king Leovigild
(569—86) initiated a series of annual expeditions that made him
the master of virtually the whole of the north of the peninsula.
The location of some of his wars, known only from annalistic
entries in the *Chronicle* of John of Biclar (*c.* 600), is not always
clear, but none of them appears to have brought him into the
Basque regions. In his entries for 578 John of Biclar records that

[31] A. Barbero and M. Vigil, *Sobre los orígenes sociales de la Reconquista* (Barcelona,
1974), pp. 52—8.

'King Leovigild, having rendered extinct all tyrants [usurpers], and with all of the invaders of Spain defeated, sought his rest among his own people.'[32] This may suggest that in the 570s at least the Basques were not regarded as a menace to the re-emergent order of the Visigothic kingdom.

By 581, the year of Bladast's defeat, such a view had altered. Despite a revolt in the south of the peninsula in 580 by his son Hermenigild, that had deprived him of control over all of the province of Baetica and the south of Lusitania, Leovigild launched an expedition northwards into Vasconia. As John of Biclar records it: 'King Leovigild occupied part of Vasconia, and he founded the town which is named Victoriacum.'[33] It was only in the following year that he began to gather forces to put an end to his son's 'tyranny' in the south. What prompted the expedition of 581 is not recorded, any more than is the degree of opposition with which it was met. Nor indeed is it certain where the new foundation of Victoriacum was situated. It is often assumed to be identical to that of the present city of Vitoria-Gasteiz in Alava, but this has not been confirmed archaeologically; the first appearance of Vitoria in historical records is in the foundation *fueros* granted by King Sancho the Wise in 1181, in which it is given the *new* name of 'Victory', and its previous one is said to have been the Basque one of Gasteiz (salt-market?).[34] Thus the situation of Leovigild's Victoriacum remains mysterious and, unlike his other urban foundation, Reccopolis in the centre of the peninsula, it has left no further trace of itself as mint site or bishopric.[35] So its very survival in the later Visigothic period is uncertain. In such circumstances it is impossible to say what Leovigild's purposes may have been, though John of Biclar's use of the word *occupare*, as evidenced by his use of it in other contexts in his work, certainly indicates that the king had brought a part of Vasconia under royal control.

Another contemporary account, that of Isidore in his *Historia*

---

[32] *Chonicon*, s.a. II Tiberii Imperatoris, J. Campos (ed.), *Juan de Biclaro Obispo de Gerona, su vida y su obra* (Madrid, 1960), p. 88.

[33] Ibid., s.a. V Tiberii, p. 90.

[34] Text in G. Martínez Díez, *Alava Medieval* (2 vols, Vitoria, 1974), vol. I, pp. 223–6.

[35] On Reccopolis see K. Raddatz, 'Studien zur Reccopolis 1: Die archäologischen Befunde', *Madrider Mitteilungen*, 5 (1964), pp. 213–33.

Gothorum or *History of the Goths* written *c*. 626, adds to this impression of the need for periodic royal campaigning and of the aim of imposing firm government upon the region. For Leovigild's campaigns Isidore is not an independent witness, in that here he relied upon John's *Chronicle*, but for the period after 590 he wrote from his own knowledge or on the basis of sources otherwise lost to us. For the brief reign of King Gundemar (610—12) he records that 'he ravaged the lands of the Vascones in one expedition', as well as directing another against the Byzantine forces occupying the coastal strip in the south-east of the peninsula.[36] The Basque campaign probably occurred in 611. Gundemar's successor but one, Suinthila (621—31), is also recorded by Isidore as initiating his rule with an expedition against the Vascones:[37]

At the beginning of his reign he also led an expedition aimed against the raids of the Vascones who were attacking the province of Tarraco; these mountain-roaming peoples were so struck by dread at his coming that, as if recognizing the rights due to him, they quickly gave up their weapons, stretched out their hands in entreaty, and as suppliants bent their necks before him; they then gave hostages and founded the city of Olite with income from the Goths and their own toil, promising to obey his rule and authority and to perform whatever would be commanded them.

The extensive and flattering character of this account can hardly be unrelated to the fact that Isidore was writing in the reign of Suinthila, and may have presented the *History* to him. It is as lacking in precision as the previous references to the campaigns of Leovigild and Gundemar, but it does make it clear that the royal activity was stirred by Basque raiding. Further-more, unlike the case of Victoriacum, there should be an almost certain location for Suinthila's Ologicus, the Latin name attested to in many late medieval documents for the modern town of Olite in Navarre, and site of a former royal residence.[38] Although there exists a hiatus in the records between the Visigothic foundation and the later flourishing of the town as royal palace and administrative centre, and the connection

[36] Isidore, *Historia Gothorum*, 59, p. 270; G. Donini and G. B. Ford (trs), *Isidore of Seville's History of the Goths, Vandals, and Suevi* (Leiden, 1970), p. 27.

[37] Isidore, *Historia Gothorum*, 63, pp. 276—8; Donini and Ford, *Isidore*, p. 29.

[38] J. del Burgo, *Olite* (León, 1978), pp. 11—15.

The Roman walls of Olite (Ologicus)

cannot be corroborated archaeologically, there seems little reason to doubt the identification. In itself this is a useful piece of information. Olite is situated on the southern edge of the Basque region, in open country on the northern slope of the Ebro valley, and directly on the route between Pamplona and the river. It thus does not qualify as a part of the mountainous core of the Basque country, and is indeed in those parts previously most affected by Celt-Iberian and Roman settlement. It is now far to the south of the area of contemporary Basque speech. It would seem highly unlikely that Suinthila's town was populated by inhabitants forcibly removed from the mountains. The fact of the foundation of Olite would rather suggest that a population of Vascones was then established in that area of the upper Ebro. Thus it is possible to suspect that some movement of population had occurred which had brought significant numbers of pastoralist tribesmen further into the Ebro valley than they had been allowed under Roman rule, cutting communication between Pamplona, and conceivably also Calahorra, and the major settlements such as Zaragoza lower down the river.

It was to contain the effects of this occupation of these

agrarian lands, probably largely owned by town dwellers and certainly regarded as part of the wider *territorium* of the *civitates* (the principal urban settlements), by unassimilated and possibly still pagan mountain tribes, that the Visigoths launched their expeditions into these regions. Their solution was only in part military, bringing the Vascones into some form of submission to their political authority, but it is clear that there can have been no possibility of just driving them back whence they had come. Thus, following Roman precedents, attempts were also made to assimilate them into more acceptable patterns of social and economic activity by founding towns for them.[39] This would have involved not so much building houses and forcing residence in them as a redistribution of lands, which would be linked to the new settlements that served as government and market centres as well as points of cultural irradiation. That neither Victoriacum nor Ologicus became major towns in the Visigothic period is perhaps not surprising. For one thing this method of containing the Basques might not have been very effective, but as well their principal functions were related to the surrounding countryside, where the new population of pastoralists turned farmers was established. It is quite unrealistic to imagine the temporarily cowed Basques just being herded into towns, as there was nothing for them to do there. A town thus conceived would fulfil no function, nor could it survive a single winter. It is surely more realistic to envisage the Basques as having been forcibly settled on the land by Leovigild and Suinthila, with the new towns created as the necessary centres for exchange and control.

In talking of Basque raiding in this period it is important not to give the impression of large and organized bodies of men, tribal armies as it were, threatening the physical existence of the urban settlements of the region. Basque social organization does not look to have been complex enough to create such a force. Indeed the very word 'tribe' is misleading in this context, in itself implying the existence of a unified structure and a focus of authority. There are no indications whatsoever of any form of Basque ruler at this period above the level of the heads of the extended families. As will be seen, all higher forms of political

[39] J. Orlandis, *Historia social y económica de la España visigoda* (Madrid, 1975), pp. 60—72.

organization had to be imposed upon them from the outside as a means of control in the course of succeeding centuries. In the late sixth and early seventh centuries the geographical extension of the large Basque family units into the settled areas was sufficient in itself to create serious instability, without our needing to envisage the existence of a more complex social order. Conflicts over land use in the valleys will have occurred between pastoralists and farmers, and, free from the fear of reprisals, Basque groups would be able to threaten all but the largest settlements, effectively isolating their victims in the towns and rendering travel between them exceedingly hazardous.

Royal action to the south of the Pyrenees, concentrated in the period *c.* 580—625, was intended to counter such a large-scale breakdown of order, but it may also have been prompted by the growth of Frankish activity in the Basque areas north of the mountains, which was leading to the creation of a real frontier between the two kingdoms. Evidence from the Frankish side also helps to confirm a view that in this period the Basques were presenting a new threat to the government of the settled lowland zones, at the expense of which they were expanding their own areas of occupation. At the same time the Franks, frequently in conflict with the Visigoths in the eastern Pyrenees, had additional incentives to become concerned with the western areas as well. The Burgundian-Frankish chronicle known as the *Chronicle of Fredegar* contains a number of references to the 'Wascones', which enables the history of the doings of the Basques north of the mountains to be followed in the course of the seventh century, if only in outline. In 602 *Fredegar* records: 'In the same year Theudebert and Theuderic sent an army against the Wascones and with God's help defeated them, subjected them to their overlordship and made them pay tribute. They appointed a duke (*dux*) named Genialis, who ruled them well.'[40] No further references to them appear in *Fredegar* before 625, but an earlier entry relevant to the Visigothic king Sisebut may contain a hint of important developments. This is included out of chronological order, being placed between events occurring in 607 and 608, though actually relating to the years 612—21. In recording Sisebut's

---

[40] J. M. Wallace-Hadrill (ed. and tr.), *The Fourth Book of the Chronicle of Fredegar*, 21 (London, 1960), p. 14.

accession *Fredegar* also gives a précis of the achievements of his reign, including that 'He . . . won Cantabria, previously held by the Franks, for the Gothic kingdom. A duke named Francio had conquered Cantabria in the days of the Franks and [it] had long paid tribute to the Frankish kings.'[41] This baffling statement, typical in its ambiguity of much of this chronicle, has been treated with some scepticism.[42] Classically conceived, Cantabria is that area of the centre of the northern edge of the Iberian peninsula that lies to the west of the Basque regions. A Frankish conquest here would have had to have involved conquest of or passage through the latter as well, but there is no reference to any such occurrence in *Fredegar* or elsewhere. However, there exists a measure of looseness about the use of the name of Cantabria. Although this is still controversial, it has been argued from the eighteenth century onwards that it could also be applied to certain parts of the upper Ebro valley, notably the Rioja.[43] This argument is based upon the *Vita Sancti Aemiliani* (*Life of St Aemilian*), written *c.* 630 by Bishop Braulio of Zaragoza.[44] This life of a Riojan hermit makes several references to Cantabria and to a senate of Cantabria, a body known from John of Biclar to have been eliminated by Leovigild in 574. Aemilian had personal dealings with some of the senators, but seems never to have left his Riojan hermitage. Modern Cantabrian historians strongly resist the argument that where he lived was therefore Cantabria, not least as this would deprive them of valuable sources for the history of their own region.[45] Some form of compromise may be possible. Certainly the Cantabri lived close enough to the Frankish kingdoms to be linked with the Vascones in the depredations of the latter. A poem of Venantius Fortunatus is dedicated to a Count Galactorius, who is praised for his defence of Aquitaine against both Cantabri and Vascones. If the argument that Cantabria is the same as the Rioja be distrusted — and it is quite possible that the Rioja was under the rule of the mysterious 'senate of Cantabria' without it

[41] Ibid., IV.33, p. 21.

[42] Ibid., IV.33, p. 21, n. 3.

[43] Enrique Flórez, *La Cantabria* (1768), ed. with commentary by R. Teja and J. M. Iglesias-Gil (Santander, 1981).

[44] Collins, 'The Basques in Aquitaine and Navarre', pp. 8—9.

[45] For example, J. González Echegaray, 'Algunos aspectos menos conocidos de la polémica sobre límites de Cantabria', *Estudios Vízcainos*, 9/10 (1974), pp. 23—43.

having to be so entitled or the sole area of their authority — then it is conceivable that the Frankish sources are referring to the Biscay coastal regions after all. It is even worthy of thought that the area of the later provinces of Guipúzcoa and Vizcaya, formerly the territories of the Varduli and Autrigones, is being indicated.

Thus if *Fredegar* is not to be dismissed out of hand — something for which there is little justification — it may be that in his own elliptical way the chronicler is telling his readers that the Frankish kings Theudebert and Theuderic brought these coastal regions under their control in 602, perhaps through the activity of a Dux Francio, and imposed a Dux Genial, of doubtless Frankish origin, on the population, but subsequently, soon after 612, this area was conquered by the Visigothic king Sisebut. *Fredegar*'s next reference to the Basques provides some additional information on their distribution. For the year 626 the chronicler records that 'Palladius and his son Sidoc, bishops of Eauze, were charged by Duke Aighyna with having been implicated in the rebellion of the Wascones. They were sent into exile.'[46] It is rather tiresome that no previous reference is made to any such rebellion, but the mention of the bishops is helpful. It would seem to establish the presence of the Basques within the area of the diocese of Eauze; for otherwise the accusation would be incomprehensible. Thus a Basque presence beyond the fringes of the mountains and not far west of Toulouse had been established by 626. This is the same area that they had been raiding for livestock and captives in 587.

It is both difficult and imperative to know what region the author of this part of the *Chronicle of Fredegar* is signifying in his references to Wasconia and the Wascones. Was there yet a substantial enough Basque presence beyond the Adour to suggest the existence of a 'French' Vasconia, ancestor to the later Gascony, or is he writing of the lands of the Vascones as defined by the Roman geographers, straddling the Pyrenees, but not extending into the old province of Novempopulana? A certain ambiguity may have existed not only in his mind but also in those of his contemporaries. The limited nature of government and settlement in these frontier areas must have

---

[46] Wallace-Hadrill, *Fredegar*, IV.54, p. 45.

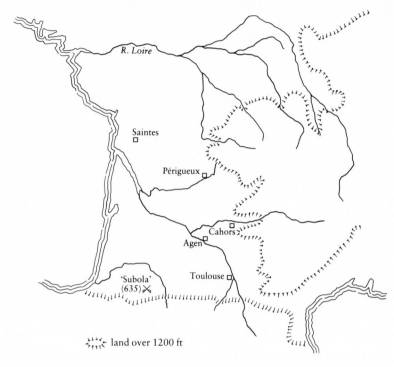

Map 13   The kingdom of Charibert II (629—632)

made precise delineation hard to achieve and unnecessary. However, it looks as if the *Fredegar* chronicler was using a more or less classical definition. For the year 628 (*recte* 629) he described the arrangements for the division of the Frankish kingdoms after the death of Chlotar II. The dominant heir Dagobert I made a provision for his half-witted brother Charibert, and thus 'on good advice made over to his brother Charibert the territories and cities between the Loire and the Spanish frontier [*limes Spaniae*] in the general area of Wasconia and the Pyrenees. . . . The territories were Toulouse, Cahors, Agen, Perigueux, Saintes and whatever lay between there and the Pyrenees.'[47] It is clear from this that the *limes Spaniae* is placed in Vasconia and the Pyrenees, i.e. it divides those political and

[47] Ibid., IV.57, p. 47.

geographical units into Frankish and Visigothic parts (see map 13).

The chronicler relates of Charibert that 'in the third year of his reign his army subjugated the whole of Wasconia, and thus somewhat extended his kingdom.'[48] This probably occurred in 631. The previous reference has made it certain that Charibert already controlled some of Vasconia, the part up to the *limes Spaniae*, but if he now took all of it this must imply that part which lay across the Pyrenees. That this took place in 631 is not fortuitous. In that year the Visigothic noble Sisenand revolted, and with the support (paid for in gold) of the other Frankish king, Dagobert, overthrew Suinthila and seized power in Spain. Charibert's extension of his authority across the Pyrenees was either a concerted part of the greater campaign, or the taking of an opportunity presented by the turbulent conditions within the peninsula. His fortune was short-lived in that he died the following year. His brother Dagobert had his heir removed and took over the kingdom himself, including Vasconia, as the chronicler explicitly states.[49] That the mountain regions are thus indicated is clear from the account of the Basque revolt that Dagobert had to face in 635 and the steps he took to crush it: a large army was sent from Burgundy under the *referendarius* Chadoind, divided into ten columns.

The whole of Wasconia was overrun by the Burgundian host, and the Basques, ready for war, emerged from their mountain fastnesses. But when battle had been joined and they saw they were going to be beaten, the Basques turned to flight, as their way was, and sought refuge in the Pyrenean gorges, where they hid in the heights among inaccessible rocks.[50]

One of the Frankish columns did not do so well. Duke Arnebert and the nobles with him were massacred in the valley of Subola, probably the Haute Soule, in the vicinity of Tardets-Sorholus. The sheer scale of this operation is impressive. It is rare to find more than one or two dukes operating together on a campaign, but a combination of ten of them is unprecedented. The fate of Arnebert would suggest that they operated in

[48] Ibid., IV.57, p. 48.
[49] Ibid., IV.67, p. 56.
[50] Ibid., IV.78, p. 65.

separate columns, sweeping through the Pyrenean valleys. This was the most systematic attempt to impose order on the Basques since the beginning of the Roman period, and was part of a wider move by Dagobert I to cow troublesome peoples on the frontiers of Francia. The threat of sending the same great army on into Brittany led to the immediate submission of the Breton ruler Judicael. The Basques also submitted to the king when faced with the harrying of their valleys by the Burgundian army, and the Saxon dux Aighyna was appointed or reinstated over them. The *seniores* of the Basques came with Aighyna to submit in person to Dagobert at Clichy in 636, but the chronicler makes it clear that this proved short-lived: 'But this oath they kept in their usual manner, as events were to prove.'[51] Unfortunately, he never reveals what those events were.

The nature of the operations undertaken to bring the Basques to heel indicates something of the scale of the problem they presented. The chronicler refers to them as rebels, but this is an over-legalistic view, deriving from the submissions they or some of them were forced to make to Theudebert and Theuderic in 602 and to Charibert in 631. It is a reasonable assumption that, despite the latter, the Basques were presenting another serious threat to the Frankish position in southern Aquitaine by 635, requiring the substantial military action undertaken by Dagobert to bring them to heel. That this threat took the form of a spreading of their settlement across the Adour and out from the fringes of the Pyrenees into the plains of Aquitaine is supported by some further evidence. An anonymous Italian geographical writer of the seventh century known as the Ravenna Cosmographer applied the term 'Vasconia' to the whole extent of the lands between the Loire and the Pyrenees.[52] This by itself may seem to be the mistaken interpretation of a none too closely placed observer, but the first continuator of the *Chronicle of Fredegar*, writing in the very early eighth century, made an identical association. In reporting the return to power of the mayor of the palace Ebroin and the massacre of his opponents, he records that the survivors 'escaped by flight across the Loire

---

[51] Ibid., IV.78, p. 67.
[52] J. Schnetz (ed.), *Ravennatis Anonymi Cosmographia*, IV.40—1 (Leipzig, 1940), pp. 77—8.

into Gascony.'[53] This usage then becomes standard for the eighth-century entries. Thus an important change of perspective has occurred. The original *Fredegar* chroniclers wrote of Vasconia more or less as their Roman predecessors had defined it, but by the end of the seventh century there existed a new Vasconia that could include all lands south of the Loire. Such a transformation must have resulted from a major shift in population, with the Basques, hitherto not encountered north of the Adour, coming to form a dominant element over a greatly increased area, and this in spite of the scale of the military activity directed against them in 635, which seemed to have pushed them back into the mountains. But, as with the campaign of the Visigothic king Suinthila *c.* 625, it clearly proved impossible to dislodge them from their new territories.

Although the spread of the Basque presence is more clearly demonstrated on the Frankish side of the Pyrenees, the limited effectiveness of military action in containing them is more obvious on the Visigothic. In spite of Leovigild and Suinthila's campaigns and new settlements, references to Basque raids and the threat to urban populations in the Ebro valley continue to appear throughout the seventh century. From 642 comes the epitaph of a Visigothic noble called Oppila, killed by the Vascones.[54] In 654 they are reported as active in the area of Zaragoza in a letter of the bishop of that city.[55] In 673 the first undertaking of King Wamba was to launch an expedition against them, from which he was called by the revolt of Count Paul in Narbonne.[56] Likewise Roderic, the last of the Visigothic kings, had to abandon a campaign against the Vascones in 711, to march to meet the Arab invasion that resulted in his defeat and the overthrow of the kingdom.[57] Thus the Basque problem was far from settled when the Visigothic period in Spanish

[53] Wallace-Hadrill, *Fredegar*, Continuations 2, p. 82.

[54] J. Vives (ed.), *Inscripciones Cristianas de la España Romana y Visigoda*, 2nd edn (Barcelona, 1969), no. 287, pp. 90—1.

[55] Taio, Bishop of Zaragoza, *Epistula ad Quiricum Barcinonensem*, in *Patrologia Latina*, 80 (Paris, 1863), c. 727.

[56] Julian of Toledo, *Historia Wambae*, 9, ed. T. Mommsen, reprinted in *Corpus Christianorum*, 115 (Turnholt, 1976), p. 224.

[57] Al-Makkari, *History of the Mohammedan Dynasties in Spain*, IV.2, tr. P. de Gayangos (2 vols, London, 1840—3), p. 268.

history came to an end — any more than it was on the Frankish side after Dagobert's campaign in 635.

It is obvious that the problems the Basques presented to the Visigothic and Frankish rulers were on a scale quite unlike anything found in the previous Roman period. Up to *c.* AD 500, townsmen and mountain dwellers alike could think of themselves and be called Vascones. By the mid seventh century the latter were the most dangerous opponents the inhabitants of the urban settlements of the upper and middle Ebro valley had to face. Had the Basques been as much of a threat and as little a part of the established socio-economic order in the Roman period as they were in the sixth and seventh centuries, the imperial military presence could hardly have been maintained on the very limited scale that it was. Clearly there are new features in the conditions in the later period that have severely strained relationships between town and country and between mountain and plain. That this was affected by a growth in population on the part of the mountain-dwelling people can be no more than a guess, but they do start to spread themselves down the Ebro and northwards into Aquitaine, affecting the economic and social order of those areas in an initially very violent way. In the process they gave birth to a new region that took its name from theirs. By *c.* 700 Gascony (from Latin Wasconia) certainly existed, and as an entity separate from the older Basque heartlands of the western Pyrenees.

4

Gascony and Pamplona

The emergence of Gascony

It is paradoxical that the Basques appear to flourish best in conditions of greatest adversity. In the seventh century such an impression is probably due to a confusion of cause and effect. The unusually concentrated military efforts directed against them by both Frankish and Visigothic kingdoms resulted from the prior success of the Basques in spreading themselves into new areas, in part assisted by the mutual hostility of their two powerful neighbours. The causes of this infiltration of new territory by the Basques can only be hypothetical. As their Pyrenean heartlands did not become denuded of population, it may be suspected that the necessary migration resulted from a substantial rise in the number of the inhabitants of the mountains, leading to a spilling over into the plains. It might on the other hand be questioned whether or not a quite different process was at work. This would be not so much a movement of population out of the Pyrenees as a spread of Basque cultural influence by diffusion. In other words significant elements amongst the inhabitants of the surrounding lowland zones became, as the result of changes that can only be guessed at, more open than hitherto to adopt features of the social and economic organization and even the language of their Basque neighbours. Such a view is probably far-fetched, but very little is known of the rural population of the upper Ebro and southern Aquitaine, who may have been more open to cultural transformation in this period than any other. Both the impress of the attenuated higher culture of the Romanized towns and the vestiges of any Celtic or other indigenous pre-Roman survivals were particularly weak in these centuries of transition between the end of the empire and the emergence of its dwarf Carolingian successor.

Leaving such (doubtless wild) speculations aside, there is one feature of traditional Basque social organization that may help to explain how the necessary reserves of manpower came into existence and enabled the Basques to spread themselves over areas at least as large again as their original homelands in the western Pyrenees. This is the strongly observed Basque tradition of non-partible inheritance. As far back as such practices can be traced, it is clear that family property holdings were not broken up for division amongst multiple heirs; instead they would be passed intact to one heir. In recent times this would normally be on the basis of primogeniture in strict patrilineal descent, but this could have been done matrilineally in the early Middle Ages.[1] At the same time the stress placed upon the extended family meant that younger sons were not deprived of a position in the household or of maintenance, and could also set up subordinate homesteads of their own. In modern times this has often involved turning the herders' shelters in the high mountain summer pastures into residences for such detachments from the main family unit.[2] However, if such younger sons and other subordinate relatives wished to build up resources of their own it had to be by their own independent efforts away from the family holdings and the main house, itself the symbol of continuity and focus of family identity.[3] Such a system cannot but have been controlled by the geographical conditions of the western Pyrenean regions, in which usable land is finite, and where subdivision of property would rapidly have rendered the divided holdings too small to provide subsistence.

In the Roman period it is possible that much of the reserve of manpower thus created and looking for opportunities beyond the Basque homelands was absorbed by recruitment into the

---

[1] J. Caro Baroja, *Los Vascos*, 4th edn (Madrid, 1971), pp. 207—22; M. Lafourcade, 'Le particularisme juridique', in *Être Basque*, ed. J. Haritschelhar (Toulouse, 1983), especially pp. 177—83; M. Segalen, *Love and Power in the Peasant Family*, English translation (Basil Blackwell, Oxford, 1983), pp. 69—72.

[2] D. A. Gómez-Ibañez, *The Western Pyrenees* (Oxford, 1975), p. 35.

[3] Caro Baroja, *Los Vascos*, pp. 110—23; *Etxea ou la maison basque* (Laaburu, 1979).

army — not necessarily just the auxiliary units of local origin. This the succeeding centuries could not provide. A resort to migration and the obtaining by force of the resources necessary to build up new family units in areas contiguous with and detached from the old homelands may have been the result, which it was beyond the capacities of the successor states to Rome to contain. The limits of the northward flow of the Basques, into a region easier to penetrate than those south of the Pyrenees, is hard to determine. The sources previously referred to certainly envisaged the river Loire as marking the furthest limits of the new Vasconia, which it is probably convenient if not accurate now to call Gascony.[4] But there are few detailed references that would place Basques so far north, and no place-name evidence to support the idea of so substantial an extension. On the other hand there are good grounds for believing in a major Basque presence to the south of the river Garonne. If an expansion of Basque settlement thence towards the Loire ever occurred, it must have been short-lived.

The nature of the Basque presence is hard to depict. There is no settlement archaeology that can detect their presence, let alone describe the nature of their dwellings and material culture. Their impact upon the towns of the region may have been slight, but again the evidence for town life in Aquitaine at this time is almost non-existent. It consists of little more than the signatures of bishops on the *acta* of various ecclesiastical councils held in the course of the seventh century, which suggest that the settlements from which their sees took their names retained at least nominal existence. Of the handful of bishoprics dotted along the northern fringes of the Pyrenees, continuity may have been preserved in most, but records are scarce. Bayonne, if it is to be identified with the Roman fort of Lapurdum, is last heard of in the early-fifth-century *Notitia Dignitatum*, but does not re-emerge into history until the very end of the tenth century, by which point it has become the site of a bishopric, though probably of recent creation.[5] Whether any form of settlement existed between these two times is entirely unknown. The last bishop of Eauze is recorded in 673—5, but his see may well have survived into the ninth century,

[4] See above, p. 96.
[5] *Gallia Christiana*, vol. I, ed. D. Sammarthani (Paris, 1715), cc. 1309—11.

when it was formally merged with that of Auch, probably as the result of Viking raids.[6] Continuity in Auch itself is equally unsusceptible of proof, in that after 673—5 the next bishop whose existence is known is recorded posthumously in charters of 836 and 838.[7] An even wider gap, between 585 and 898, exists in the case of Dax.[8] Tarbes, with a hiatus in the records between 585 and 879, is virtually identical, and Oleron and Lescar, last known in attestations in 673—5, seem to have had no Carolingian bishops at all, or at least none that has left a record.[9] Even Bordeaux has no known eighth-century bishop (see map 14).[10]

The problem is twofold. Episcopal continuity may have existed in all or any of these cities, but even so this would be but slight evidence of the nature of the settlements themselves and the life led in them in these centuries. Not much help in this respect can be gained from looking across the Pyrenees to the towns of the upper Ebro in the period after 711. Victoriacum and Ologicus disappear from view entirely. The history of Calahorra is by no means clear, but conditions in the area in general were very different as a result of the Arab conquest and the establishment of a number of garrisons and fortresses in the region, notably at Tudela, which preserved forms of urban life.[11] This could also be true of Pamplona. It is thus impossible to be categoric about the decline of towns in southern Aquitaine in the seventh and eighth centuries, let alone about the role the Basques may have played in it. One obvious factor that would have had a bearing is the degree of the Christianization of the Basques at this time, which would have affected their relations both with urban populations and with the bishops, who were the leaders of local society. To say that the evidence is small will hardly be surprising, but one source of information is a chapter in the *Life* of the missionary bishop Amandus, written soon

---

[6] L. Duchesne, *Les Fastes épiscopaux de l'Ancienne Gaule*, 2nd edn (3 vols, Paris, 1910), vol. II, pp. 91—5.

[7] Ibid., pp. 96—7.

[8] Ibid., p. 97.

[9] Ibid., pp. 101—2.

[10] Ibid., p. 62.

[11] *Crónica del Moro Rasis*, eds D. Catalán and M. Soledad de Andrés (Madrid, 1975), p. 53 for Tudela.

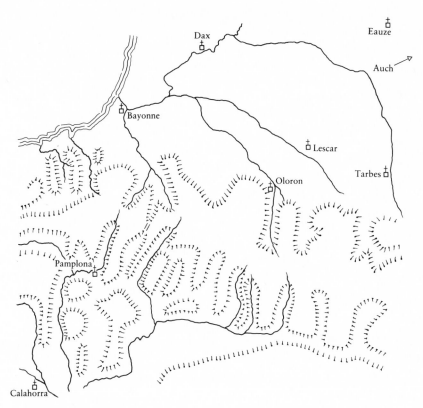

Map 14   Bishoprics of the western Pyrenees in the early Middle Ages

after his death (*c.* 684) by his disciple Baudemond.[12] In this it is recorded how Amandus, at an early stage in his career and soon after leaving the court of King Dagobert I, ventured amongst the Basques in an effort to convert them. It would seem from Baudemond's description that this took him into the Pyrenees.

It has been claimed that Amandus's work initiated the mass conversion of the Basques, hitherto resistant to Christianity, but Baudemond records only opposition and failure.[13] No success whatsoever is attributed to Amandus's mission, and if others

---

[12] *Vita Sancti Amandi Episcope Traiectensis*, ch. 20, ed. B. Krusch, *Monumenta Germaniae Historica, Scriptores Rerum Merovingicarum* (Berlin, 1910), vol. V, pp. 443—4.

[13] A. Barbero and M. Vigil, *Sobre los orígenes sociales de la Reconquista* (Madrid, 1974), p. 94 and n. 154.

followed on his work they have left no account of themselves. After the failure of his preaching, and with only the satisfaction of seeing one particularly abusive Basque opponent struck dead in a fit of demonic possession, Amandus crossed the mountains and, descending to an unnamed town, was there received by its bishop and entertained. The point of the inclusion of this story was that the bishop was able to retain a relic of his guest in the form of the water he had washed his hands in, which was later used to heal a blind man. The fact that Amandus crossed the Pyrenees to reach this unspecified see might suggest that it was Pamplona. If, as has been suggested in the previous chapter, Charibert and then Dagobert had extended their rule over all of the classical Vasconia, then Pamplona would at this time have been under Frankish rule — a view abetted by the fact that no bishops of Pamplona are recorded as attending any of the 'national' or provincial councils of the Church in Spain between 589 and 681.[14] But however much Amandus may have impressed his episcopal colleague, he seems to have made no headway with the Basques and moved on to more fruitful fields of evangelizing on the north-eastern frontiers of Francia. As for the Basques, it is reasonable to assume they retained their paganism untroubled for the rest of the century.

The emergence of Gascony is thus thoroughly shrouded in mist. Beyond the fact that such a region did come into being in the course of the seventh century, little can be said of it. The state of urban settlements is uncertain, as is episcopal continuity, and the extent and nature of the Basque presence itself is hard to determine. No purely Basque settlements have been identified, and place-name evidence is currently so ambiguous in its significance as to be effectively useless. Although Basque elements in Gascon place-names have been detected, their status is debatable, and it has even been argued that they derive from a much earlier pre-Roman Aquitanian language that has Basque affinities.[15] Alternatively, they may be evidence of a previously

---

[14] J. Vives (ed.), *Concilios Visigóticos* (Barcelona—Madrid, 1963), pp. 407 and 434. For possible archaeological evidence of a Frankish presence see M. A. Mezquíriz de Catalán, *Pamplona Romana* (Pamplona, 1973), pp. 17—18.

[15] J. Seguy, 'La colonisation romaine et préromaine en Gascogne et en Aragon', in his *Studien zur romanischen Namenkunde* (Munich, 1956), pp. 103—13; J. Bernard and J. Ruffié, 'Hématologie et culture: le peuplement de l'Europe de l'ouest', *Annales — Économies, Sociétés, Civilisations*, 31 (1976), p. 667 and map.

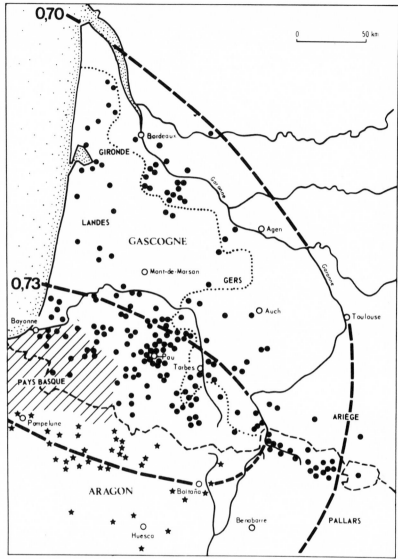

- ● Place-names ending in -os, -osse, -ons, -ost, -oz
- ★ Place-names ending in -ues, -ueste
- •••• Limit of area containing place-names ending in -anum and -acum

Map 15   Place-name suffixes: -os, -ous, -ues, -ost, -oz, -ués, -ueste

wider diffusion of a Basque-speaking population in southern Aquitaine in the period prior to the Roman conquest. This intriguing possibility would thus make of the sixth and seventh-century developments a Basque recolonization of an area in which they had been culturally dominant half a millennium earlier (see map 15).

The Carolingians in Aquitaine

Some indications from eighth-century evidence may throw some light on these problems, or provide materials for an interpretation. From the continuations of the *Chronicle of Fredegar* it is possible to learn something of the role the Basques played in the troubled politics of Francia in the first half of that century. In 718 the Neustrian or western Frankish magnates, trying to break the hold established by the Arnulfing mayors of the palace over all of the component kingdoms of Francia, appealed for aid to Duke Eudo, the *de facto* independent ruler of Aquitaine. He in turn raised an army of Basques — *hoste Vasconum commota* — but in the outcome failed to support the Neustrians and came to terms instead with the Arnulfing Charles Martel.[16] The next reference comes from nearly 30 years later in 742, after Charles Martel had in practice imposed his own authority on Aquitaine. In that year, following his death, 'the Gascons [Wascones] of Aquitaine rose in rebellion under Duke Chunoald, son of the late Eudo.'[17] To this the new Frankish rulers, Charles's sons Pippin and Carloman, countered with an invasion of Aquitaine in the region of Bourges and Loches. According to the chronicler they there overwhelmed 'the Romans'. In 745 the two mayors of the palace 'once more made an expedition to the Loire; for the Gascons were provoking them.'[18] Finally, there are plentiful references to Vascones in the accounts of the campaigns of Pippin, now first king of the Arnulfing or Carolingian dynasty, against Waiofar, last inde-

---

[16] J. M. Wallace-Hadrill (ed. and tr.), *The Fourth Book of the Chronicle of Fredegar*, Continuations 10 (London, 1960), p. 89.

[17] Ibid., Continuations 25, p. 98.

[18] Ibid., Continuations 28, p. 100.

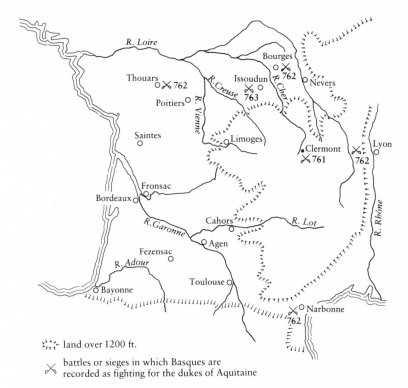

R. Loire

Bourges
○ ✕ 762

Thouars
○ ✕ 762

Issoudun
✕ ○
763

R. Creuse

R. Cher

Nevers

Poitiers ○

R. Vienne

Lyon

Saintes ○

Limoges

● Clermont
✕ 761

✕ ○ Lyon
762

R. Rhône

Fronsac
○

Bordeaux ○

R. Garonne

Cahors
○

R. Lot

○ Agen

Fezensac
○

R. Adour

Toulouse ○

○ Bayonne

✕ ○ Narbonne
762

⟩ᵗ⟨ land over 1200 ft.

✕ battles or sieges in which Basques are
✕ recorded as fighting for the dukes of Aquitaine

Map 16   The duchy of Aquitaine and the Rhône valley in the eighth century

pendent duke of Aquitaine, between 760 and 768 (see map 16).

In 761 Pippin overran the Auvergne and captured its count, then an ally of Waiofar, in the course of which 'many Gascons were taken and slain'.[19] In 762 he captured Bourges and its count. Here too Basques were found: 'Count Chunibert and such Gascons as he found there had to swear fealty to him and to remain in his company.' Also in 762 one of Waiofar's relatives, a Count Mantio, failed in a surprise attack upon some of Pippin's supporters in the vicinity of Narbonne. Here too Mantio is described as being accompanied by 'a crowd of Gascons'. In the same year Count Chilping of the Auvergne raided the district of Lyon with a mixture of Arvernians and

[19] Ibid., Continuations 42, p. 111.

Gascons.[20] In 763 Pippin struck at the heartlands of Aquitaine, to destroy the vineyards:[21]

At this point Waiofar came to meet King Pippin with a big army and a host of those Gascons who live beyond the Garonne and were formerly called Vaceti. But straight away all the Gascons followed their usual practice and not a man of them but turned tail: and very many of them were killed there by the Franks.

In 766 Pippin launched a major invasion of Aquitaine and marched from north to south, as far as Agen in the shadow of the Pyrenees: 'The Gascons and the magnates of Aquitaine now saw they had no option but to come to him: many there swore oaths to him and became his men.'[22] Lastly, in 768, Pippin came from Bourges to the Garonne, 'where the Gascons who live beyond the Garonne came to his presence. They gave hostages and swore evermore to remain loyal to the king and to his sons, Charles and Carloman.'[23]

There are a number of features of note in these accounts. Firstly, whenever fighting is recorded those said to be doing it on the part of Aquitaine are the Vascones; moreover, they are found to be operating in areas, such as the Auvergne, Narbonne and Lyon, well outside the limits of the greatest possible extent of their zones of settlement. Secondly, a distinction is made on two occasions between Vascones in general and those Vascones living beyond (in other words south of) the river Garonne, who are said formerly to have been called the Vaceti. This name is probably a corruption of Vaccaei, a term last encountered in the seventh-century *De Laude Pampilone*, and a synonym for or possibly a tribal subdivision of the Vascones. Does this imply that the 'Vascones living beyond the Garonne' were the Basques proper, and that references to Vascones not qualified by such a geographical limitation indicate just Aquitanians in general? This is unlikely. For one thing it would seem strange for the general name for the inhabitants of Aquitaine to have been drawn from one localized and culturally backward element of the population, especially when alternatives clearly existed. One of these appears in the continuations to *Fredegar* and is the term

[20] Ibid., Continuations 43—5, pp. 112—14.
[21] Ibid., Continuations 47, p. 115.
[22] Ibid., Continuations 48, p. 116.
[23] Ibid., Continuations 51, p. 119.

'the Romans'. This may sound mildly eccentric and only features once in the chronicle, but its use is confirmed by charter and other evidence that shows that the civilian urban population of Aquitaine, especially in the north, did regard and describe themselves as the Romans, even after several centuries of coexistence with the Franks.[24] In addition, it is clear from the passage relating to the campaign of 766 that the author regarded the Vascones and the magnates of Aquitaine not only as separate entities but also as two equal elements in the political equation, and both came to submit to Pippin at Agen.

The impression given by the continuations of *Fredegar* strengthens that presented, however hesitantly, by place-name evidence, which is that to the south of the Garonne the Basques constituted the major or possibly the sole recognizable body of the population. On the other hand, between the Garonne and the Loire there was clearly a significant but not preponderant Basque presence. This, however, may have been largely military in character. Vascones appear to be synonymous with Aquitanian armies, and are found helping to hold Bourges and Clermont against the Frankish king. They are removed by the victorious Pippin, suggesting that they were not part of the established population of the two cities, and they were taken into his service and accompanied him in what can only have been a military capacity. It is thus hard to resist the conclusion that the rulers of Aquitaine, whose main interests and base of authority lay between the rivers Loire and Garonne, recruited Basques in large numbers to provide the stuff of their armies.[25]

Such an interpretation is supported by the accounts of the next chronicler whose work is relevant to this region, and who, overlapping with the last continuation of *Fredegar*, brings to a conclusion the history of the Frankish kings' campaigns in Aquitaine and the extinction of the independence of its duchy. This is the author (followed by a reviser) of the first section of the *Royal Frankish Annals*, a palatine chronicle probably composed and kept up to date at Aachen from *c*. 794 onwards. The annalist introduces a clearer geographical distinction into

[24] M. Rouche, 'Les survivances antiques dans trois cartulaires du Sud-Ouest de la France aux X et XI siècles', *Cahiers de Civilisation Medievale*, 23 (1980), pp. 93—108.
[25] M. Rouche, *L'Aquitaine des Wisigoths aux Arabes 418—781* (Paris, 1979), pp. 111—32.

what appeared as a much vaguer definition in the work of the last continuator of *Fredegar*. He records that in 769 Hunald, probably the son of the Aquitanian duke Waiofar, murdered in 768, tried to get both Aquitaine and Vasconia to renew the war against the Franks, now ruled by Pippin's son Charles.[26] The regional distinction between Aquitaine and Vasconia or Gascony is further clarified by the additional note that when Charles invaded the former, Hunald was forced to flee for refuge to the latter. It is clearly stated by the annalist that Angoulême, which fell to Charles and is only 80 miles north of the Garonne, was a city of Aquitaine, whilst the fugitive Hunald was seized in the fortress of Fronsac, just south of the river, on the orders of the duke of Gascony. That the Garonne marked the frontier between the two regions is thus further made probable.[27]

This episode also introduces on to the historical scene one Lupus, *dux Vasconum* or duke of the Gascons, one of whose few recorded acts is his handing over to the Frankish king of the fugitive Hunald and his wife when threatened with retaliatory action should he fail to surrender the fugitives. Brief, ignoble and prudent as Duke Lupus's appearance in history may be, it gives rise to various questions. Was he a Basque himself, or, like the only known previous *duces Vasconum* Genialis and Aighyna, of Frankish or other origin? Was he indeed, like his two seventh-century predecessors, a Frankish royal nominee? The evidence is unclear, and it is impossible to know if there had existed an unbroken line of such dukes from the time Genialis was first imposed upon the Basques in 602. As for his origins, although Lupus is not a Basque name, it could be a Latinizing of the Basque *otso* (wolf). It would seem unlikely, in view of the almost continuous warfare of the 750s and 760s, that Lupus was a royal nominee in the way his seventh-century predecessors clearly had been; though it is conceivable that he had only been appointed after Pippin's final victory in 768. The lack of references to earlier eighth-century dukes may be just the product of ignorance on the part of the chroniclers or it may

[26] *Annales Regni Francorum/Annales q.d. Einhardi*, ed. F. Kurze, *Monumenta Germaniae Historica* (hereafter *MGH*), *Scriptores Rerum Germanicarum* (Hanover, 1895), pp. 28—31.
[27] Ibid., pp. 29—30.

indicate that the office was only reintroduced with the Frankish triumph over the rulers of Aquitaine in the 760s.

There is one deduction that can be made *ex silentio*, and that is that the Basques of Gascony are likely to have been Christians by this stage. The continuators of *Fredegar* and the first compilers of the *Royal Frankish Annals* were certainly no admirers of the Basques, and make patent their feelings that the Vascones, whose doings they occasionally chronicled, were perfidious, unreliable and militarily inept. Such denunciations constituted a standard feature of Frankish historiography in the depicting of hostile peoples from the time of Gregory of Tours onwards. In view of this such authors are unlikely to have omitted the charge of paganism, a formidably damning accusation, if they could decently have levelled it against the Basques and the Aquitanian dukes who employed them. It may be suggested that the chroniclers were unaware of the existence of Basque paganism, but as the Vascones are to be found as far afield as Bourges and Clermont, fighting side by side with the unquestionably Christian Aquitanians, and as some were subsequently taken into Frankish royal service, such ignorance must be considered unlikely. Thus it seems eminently reasonable to believe that in the period between the failure of Amandus's mission *c.* 630—40 and the Basque involvement in the wars between the Franks and the Aquitanians in the 760s, the Basques, in their newly created region of Gascony at least, had accepted Christianity in significant numbers. Precisely how and when remain mysterious.

The eastwards extension of the newly emerged Gascony is not easy to delimit. References in the last continuator of *Fredegar* certainly indicate a Basque presence in the Agenais, a view corroborated by the seventh-century mentions of their activity in that area.[28] Information is too sparse to enable a precise frontier line to be drawn, but it must have lain to the west of Toulouse. The relatively rapid disappearance of the Basque language from most of the 'greater Gascony' north of the Adour and south of the Garonne, between the seventh and twelfth centuries, makes it impossible to use such later sources

---

[28] Wallace-Hadrill, *Fredegar*, Continuations 48, p. 116.

as monastic cartularies, full of information on local societies and conditions, to plot the distribution of Basque-speaking populations in this region and to suggest the limits of their original settlement. The Basque element seems thus to have been relatively quickly assimilated after the initial period of expansion in most parts of eighth-century Gascony. By the eleventh century the eastern frontier of Basque Gascony was probably marked by the upper reaches of the river Adour, representing a substantial shrinking from its probable position 300 years before. This also indicates one of the methodological problems to be faced by historians of the Basques north of the Pyrenees: in certain periods the area of distinctively Basque settlement and linguistic dominance is coterminous with a region recognized by outsiders as Vasconia-Gascony, but progressively the political and regional definition becomes divorced from the cultural reality that first gave rise to it. In the eighth century, Vasconia-Gascony and the lands of the Basques north of the Pyrenees are probably one and the same thing. By the eleventh and twelfth centuries this is far from true, and moreover Gascony is starting to develop an identity quite detached from that of the Basque region proper, between the Adour and the Pyrenees.[29] At the very least this raises considerable problems of terminology, and the use of the term 'Gascony' rather than a more pedantic 'Vasconia' inevitably creates problems of definition as well as difficulties in respect of modern regional 'nationalisms' of south-west France.

The Arab expeditions

It is particularly regrettable that what was probably the most significant period in the history of the Basques north of the Pyrenees, in which their territorial and cultural impact was at its greatest and when they were receptive to so many outside influences, not least that of Christianity, should be so veiled from our sight. The seventh and eighth centuries in Gascony lie hidden behind the occasional and generally hostile notices of

[29] For evidence of the linguistic divide on the Adour by the early twelfth century see the travel guide in the *Codex Calixtinus*, J. Vielliard (ed.), *Le guide du pélerin de Saint-Jacques de Compostelle* (Macon, 1938), pp. 18, 20.

two or three Frankish chroniclers. However, parallel developments south of the Pyrenees may shed some additional light, or
at least suggest that some of the interpretations advanced here
seem equally appropriate to both the southern and the northern
divisions of Vasconia. Indeed, it is likely that events which were
directly affecting the regions south of the mountains, notably
the Arab conquest of most of the peninsula and the ensuing
threat of further expansion by Arab and Berber forces into parts
of Francia, had a controlling impact on developments to the
north of the Pyrenees. It is clear that the Arab expedition into
Aquitaine in 732 had a direct effect upon the immediate future
of the duchy, though not so much because of the actual
outcome of the battle of Poitiers as is often assumed.[30] Despite
the eloquence of Gibbon's statement there was really little
chance that further Arab advance into western Europe could
have been sustained and that 'perhaps the interpretation of the
Koran would now be taught in the schools of Oxford.'[31]
Rather, the significant effect was the drawing of the Arnulfing
mayors of the palace and later the kings of that line into the
affairs of Aquitaine, with the consequence that 30 years later
the independence of the duchy was to be extinguished.[32]

The Arab pressure from the south — for some of the expeditions
certainly came through the passes across the western Pyrenees —
and the military needs of the dukes of Aquitaine in defending
themselves, not only against periodic Islamic invaders but
increasingly against the aspirations of the Frankish monarchy,
were twin forces of change working on the Basques north of the
mountains. Whatever may be attributed to differences of per-
ception on the part of individual chroniclers, and little as we
know of the origins of the ducal line, it does seem clear that by
770 a defined area known as Gascony (Wasconia) had come
into being south of the Garonne, that this was under the rule of
a duke (*dux*), and that its population was Christian enough for
hostile chroniclers not to remark otherwise. These all represent
substantial steps on the part of a people hitherto confined to the
Pyrenean regions proper, lacking any form of more complex

[30] J. Deviosse, *Charles Martel* (Paris, 1978), pp. 159—78.
[31] E. Gibbon, *The Decline and Fall of the Roman Empire*, ch. 52, ed. J. B. Bury (7
vols, London, 1898), vol. VI, p. 15.
[32] *Chronicon Moissiacense*, s.a. DCCXXXIV et al., ed. G. H. Pertz, *MGH, Scriptores*
(Hanover, 1826), vol. I, p. 291 for continuing Arab aggression in Provence.

political organization, and resistant to the spread of Christianity. On the last point it is interesting to note that any identification of resistance to Christian mission with opposition to Frankish and royal aggression, which may have looked closely related in the 640s, was rejected in the course of the next 100 years. What relationship did any of this have to developments south of the Pyrenees?

The last of the Visigothic kings was recorded as campaigning against the Vascones before being called to face the Arab invasion in 711. The extent of Basque-controlled territory in the north of Spain at this time is hard to calculate. Certainly their presence did not prevent various bishops of Pamplona, or rather their representatives, from making their way to attend councils held in Toledo in the final decades of the existence of the Visigothic kingdom. Bishop Atila of Pamplona was represented by a deacon called Vincomalus at XIII Toledo in 683, and Bishop Marcianus was deputized for by probably the same deacon at XVI Toledo in 693, the last general council of the Visigothic Church of which the signatures to the *acta* have survived.[33] It cannot be known whether the absence of the bishops' own persons on both occasions was due to the coincidence of ill-health or to conditions in the Basque regions being so troubled that they did not dare entrust themselves to the roads. It is likely that the rural areas colonized by the Basques in the Pyrenees and upper Ebro valley had increased in size, and that the last Visigothic kings were attempting to contain their depredations over a region that extended from at least the valley of the river Aragón to the borders of Cantabria, in the vicinity of modern Santander. It is impossible to be more specific as no additional information is available to throw any light on Basque social organization at this time, or the degree to which, if at all, Frankish influence was making itself felt south of the Pyrenees in the late seventh century. Nothing is heard of Basque leaders of any sort, or of the Visigothic kings trying to impose their own officials, counts or dukes on the region. However, it is a reasonable assumption that the periodic campaigning by the kings must have begun to make some impact on Basque society, in that a greater degree of social

[33] Vives, *Concilios*, pp. 434, 521.

organization and co-operation will have been required to put up the effective resistance to control and assimilation that was clearly demonstrated.

The overthrow of the Visigothic kingdom in 711 creates, for the eighth century at least, fresh problems of evidence, just at the time when that for events and conditions north of the Pyrenees is becoming relatively plentiful. Contemporary historiography was virtually a non-existent art in the late Visigothic period, with the unique exception of Julian of Toledo's *Historia Wambae*, an account of the opening year of the reign of King Wamba (i.e. 672—3). The Arab conquest and the breaking of the political unity of the peninsula that had been created by the Visigoths led not only to the emergence of new and more numerous states within Spain but also to considerable regional variation within the corpus of the evidence relating to the different parts, as well as, through the Arabs, the introduction of an entirely new historiographical tradition.[34] Thus sources for the history of Al-Andalus, or Arab-ruled Spain, become really quite substantial, but present formidable technical and interpretational problems. The Christian kingdom of the Asturias, that came into being *c.* 720 and rose to dominance over the whole north-west corner of the peninsula, produced a tradition of brief but informative chronicle writing, though not before the late ninth century, which can also be complemented by the survival of a substantial body of legal and administrative documents.[35] Even Catalonia after its conquest by the Franks in 801, although historiographically barren before the very late tenth century, is enormously rich in charters. However, readers now inured to authorial laments on the lack of evidence will not be surprised to learn that the Basque regions of the western Pyrenees and upper Ebro have provided us with no chronicle sources at all and very little of anything else over a period extending from the fall of the Visigothic monarchy to the turn of the millennium. Once more knowledge has to be gleaned from the pitiful scraps that outsiders have provided in their all too brief notices of events in these regions. Few of these come up to the standard of utility as a source for the northern doings

---

[34] R. Collins, *Early Medieval Spain: Unity in Diversity, 400—1000* (London and Basingstoke, 1983), pp. 146—9.
[35] J. E. Casariego, *Historias asturianas de hace mas de mil años* (Oviedo, 1983).

of the Basques of the *Chronicle of Fredegar* and its continuations.

Although the Visigothic monarchy was subverted at a stroke and in a single battle, the effective conquest of the peninsula took somewhat longer to complete. The main southern and central areas submitted to Arab armies relatively quickly, but towns in the west and the north remained initially little affected. The principal urban centres of Catalonia only surrendered during the period of rule of the second Arab governor, Abd al-Azīz ibn Mūsa (714—16), at which time Pamplona is also said to have submitted. This is not a question of protracted armed resistance: it just took that long for the Arabs to reach these areas and make the necessary formal arrangements for the towns' submissions and their future government. At this level and in the general state of communications in the early Middle Ages, the Iberian peninsula was a rather large area to take over. There is a reference, admittedly lacking in detail and found in a later and non-historical source, to a formal treaty being made between the inhabitants of Pamplona and the commander of the Arab forces.[36] Such agreements feature frequently in the early period of the Arab conquests throughout the Mediterranean, and generally involve a concession by the conquerors of the rights of the conquered to maintain their own religion and local self-government in return for the regular payment of certain capitation and land taxes and a promise to refrain from further resistance.[37] As the alternative offered was destruction of the town and enslavement of the population, it is not surprising that many such bargains were struck. In Spain the text of one of these treaties, between Abd al-Azīz ibn Mūsa and a certain Theodemir, governor of seven small towns in the south-east of the peninsula, has been preserved.[38] No trace of the text of the Pamplona agreement survives, but there are no good reasons for doubting that such an arrangement was made or that it followed the standard pattern for such treaties.

[36] For the conquest see *Ajbar Machmua*, ed. and tr. E. Lafuente y Alcántara (Madrid, 1867), p. 38; for the reference to a treaty see E. Lévi-Provençal, *Histoire de l'Espagne Musulmane* (3 vols, Paris—Leiden, 1950), vol. I, p. 30, n. 1.

[37] Al-Balādhuri, *Futūh al-Buldān*, P. Hitti (tr.), *The Origins of the Islamic State* (Beirut, 1966), pp. 187, 223, 246—7, 249, 271—5, 338—40 for other examples of such treaties.

[38] The text of the Theodemir treaty: F. Simonet, *Historia de los Mozárabes* (Madrid, 1867), pp. 797—8.

The very fact of the making of such an accord is in itself of greater significance than the details of its lost but doubtless standardized contents. For it shows that Pamplona was still, by the end of the Visigothic period, an urban settlement sufficiently flourishing to have had the potential to resist the Arab armies and therefore deemed capable of a measure of future self-government. It was able to survive the collapse of Visigothic royal rule and a hiatus of three or four years before the new masters of the peninsula made their appearance at its gates. If its security had been dependent upon the actions of the former royal armies in restraining the incursions of the Basques, then it is possible its citizens openly welcomed the new military presence of the Arabs and their Berber mercenaries.

Conditions in the western Pyrenees during the first half of the eighth century are in several respects reminiscent of those of the early fifth. Once more this became a region through which armies passed. At this time they were all going northwards, in the raids on southern Aquitaine led by successive governors of Al-Andalus.[39] The series culminated in the major offensive of 732 and the defeat of the Arab forces at the battle of Poitiers. In itself this did not put an end to such forays across the Pyrenees, but they were turned instead to the routes around the eastern end of the mountains into Provence. Civil wars between Arab factions and between the Arabs and the Berbers in the 740s and 750s finally put an end to such transmontane aggression.[40] It is noteworthy that the expeditions into southern Aquitaine are not recorded as having encountered any Basque hostility south of the Pyrenees. The Basques there were not capable of or interested in barring the passage of an army, although on the other side of the mountains they were providing part or much of the increasingly strained defence that Duke Eudo of Aquitaine was putting up to such raids. The Basques in Spain, though, did not at this stage present any serious problems for the new Arab order in the peninsula, and it is conceivable that Pamplona may have enjoyed a brief period of flourishing at this time as the launching point from which the expeditions across the Pyrenees took their departure, and perhaps as a centre of assembly.[41]

[39] Lévi-Provençal, *L'Espagne Musulmane*, vol. I, pp. 53—65.
[40] Ibid., vol. I, pp. 41—51.
[41] Ibid., vol. I, p. 60 for the assembling of the expedition of 732 at Pamplona.

The pass of Roncesvalles, legendary site of Roland's death

Roncesvalles

The ending of the period of possible Arab expansion and frequent campaigning across the mountains around the year 750 may thus have introduced a period of stagnation, and we also then hear for the first time of clashes between Basques and

Arab armies. This was also marked by a phase of considerable internal disruption within the peninsula as a whole. In 755 the last of the governors of Al-Andalus, Yūsuf al-Fihri, launched an expedition into the north of Spain to suppress a revolt by Yemeni Arabs, supported by dissident Berbers, in the region of Zaragoza and the valley of the Aragón. This petered out at his approach and he was able to detach some of his forces to proceed towards Pamplona, where Basque raids had been reported.[42] This Arab army was defeated by the Basques, and the governor was unable to come to its assistance, for at this point Abd ar-Raḥmān landed from Africa, and Yūsuf had to hurry south to face, albeit unsuccessfully, the revolt and the subsequent establishment of the Umayyad amirate in Al-Andalus. Thus by 755 the Basques were again threatening the towns of the upper Ebro, and could take on and defeat Arab forces sent against them, at least on their own terrain. This is unlikely to have been a matter of pitched battles on the open plains, and should rather be interpreted as large-scale guerrilla activity in the valleys and mountain passes, whose physical difficulties were to their advantage, and whose hidden lines of communications, such as the crest paths, could be used to concentrate their forces unperceived by their opponents, as well as providing them with the means for easy 'hit and run' attacks on a slow-moving enemy. Such actions do presuppose a measure of co-operation between family groups, and between the populations of different valleys.

Perhaps the most striking testimony to the Basques' ability to act together to inflict military humiliation on the forces of their powerful neighbours comes in their massacre of the rearguard of Charlemagne's army in the pass of Roncesvalles in the summer of 778, the only major defeat suffered by the Frankish ruler in the course of a long career of campaigning and conquest.[43] The whole episode of Charlemagne's intervention in the peninsula in that year and his abortive campaign in the Ebro valley is a somewhat controversial one, in that both the Latin and the Arabic sources agree neither amongst themselves

---

[42] Ibid., vol. I, pp. 53, 95—104; *Ajbar Machmua*, Lafuente, p. 77 for the despatch of forces against the Basques.

[43] For the events of 778 and modern discussions of them see J. M. Lacarra, *La expedición de Carlomagno a Zaragoza y su derrota en Roncesvalles* (Pamplona, 1981).

nor with each other on matters of dating, motives, the personnel of the participants and the details of what actually occurred. Thus Arab accounts tend to place the expedition in 779 or 780, whilst the Frankish ones put it firmly in 778. As the latter were effectively contemporary with the events described, their reliability in this respect is beyond doubt, but they give little explanation of what Charlemagne's purposes were. The view of the *Annals of Metz* (*c.* 805) that his intention was to succour the Christian communities of the Ebro valley has little to recommend it when the course of his actions is noticed, and more satisfactory reference can be made here to the Arab sources.[44] It looks as if the Frankish ruler took advantage of the current turmoil in the Ebro valley, where one of a number of rebels against Abd ar-Raḥmān I had established himself in Zaragoza.[45] When faced by the possibility of seige by the amir's forces, he appealed to Charlemagne for help. Whatever the pretext, it must have suited the Frankish king's interests to intervene south of the Pyrenees, and after the successful capture of Narbonne and the relative pacification of Gascony, the idea of a Frankish march in the mountain area, something later to be achieved on a more limited scale, may have been his aim in 778. If so it proved abortive for, despite initial success in occupying Pamplona, Charlemagne found Zaragoza held against him and his erstwhile ally overthrown, and so he was forced to retreat. In the process he had the walls of Pamplona, so proudly described in the *De Laude Pampilone*, demolished — in all probability to prevent the city being held against him should he return, as he may have planned.[46] In withdrawing across the Pyrenees to Francia his forces were ambushed and the detached rearguard massacred. The episode is briefly described in the revised version of the near contemporary *Royal Frankish Annals*,[47] and an even fuller account is given in Einhard's *Vita Karoli Magni*, written in the early 830s:[48]

[44] *Annales Mettenses Priores*, s.a. 778, ed. B. de Simson, *MGH, Scriptores Rerum Germanicarum* (Hanover and Leipzig, 1905), vol. X, pp. 66—7.

[45] Ibn al-Athīr, *Annales du Maghreb et de l'Espagne*, tr. E. Fagnan (Algiers, 1901), p. 128.

[46] *Annales q.d. Einhardi*, Kurze, p. 51.

[47] Ibid., pp. 51, 53.

[48] Einhard, *Vita Karoli Magni Imperatoris*, 9, L. Halphen (ed.), *Eginhard, Vie de Charlemagne* (Paris, 1967), pp. 28—30, L. Thorpe (tr.), *Two Lives of Charlemagne* (Harmondsworth, 1969), pp. 64—5.

While he was in the Pyrenean mountain range itself, he was given a taste of Basque treachery. Dense forests, which stretch in all directions, make this a spot most suitable for setting ambushes. At the moment when Charlemagne's army was stretched out in a long column of march, as the nature of the local defiles forced it to be, these Basques, who had set their ambush at the very top of one of the mountains, came rushing down on the last part of the baggage train and the troops who were marching in support of the rearguard and so protecting the army which had gone on ahead. The Basques forced them down to the valley beneath, joined battle with them and killed them to the last man. They then snatched up the baggage, and, protected as they were by the cover of darkness, which was just beginning to fall, scattered in all directions without losing a moment. In this feat the Basques were helped by the lightness of their arms and by the nature of the terrain in which the battle was fought. On the other hand the heavy nature of their own equipment and the unevenness of the ground completely hampered the Franks in their resistance to the Basques. In this battle died Eggihard, who was in charge of the King's table, Anshelm, the Count of the Palace and Roland, Lord of the Breton Marches, along with a great number of others. What is more this assault could not be avenged there and then, for, once it was over, the enemy dispersed in such a way that no one knew where or among which people they could be found.

Attempts have been made to minimize the Basque role in this affair, and to suggest that the principal participants were Spanish *muwallads* (non-Arab converts to Islam) directed by the family of Charlemagne's former ally the Zaragozan rebel Sulayman, whom certain sources, not very reliably, record as being taken as a prisoner into Francia.[49] None of these is very convincing, and there seems no grounds for doubting the Frankish accounts, so close in time to the events described. A number of features in Einhard's version are particularly interesting. His reference to Basque treachery (*perfidia*) suggests that the Basques, in Frankish eyes at least, owed some form of allegiance to their king. This is certainly true of those in Gascony, whose leader, the Duke Lupus, had 'submitted himself and the province over which he ruled to Charlemagne's suzerainty', probably in 769.[50] Although the southern frontiers

[49] R. Moreau, 'Les assaillants de Roncevaux ont-ils été des Basques ou des Arabes?', *Bulletin de la Société des Sciences, Lettres et Arts de Bayonne*, 128 (1972), pp. 123—7.
[50] Einhard, *Vita Karoli Magni, 5*, Halphen, p. 18, Thorpe, p. 60.

The twelfth-century chapel of the Holy Spirit at Roncesvalles

of Lupus's domain may have been hazy, it is by no means certain that they reached as far down as the pass of Roncesvalles, and there are no references to the Basques in the area of Pamplona having made a formal submission to Charlemagne, though this may have occurred earlier in 778. Thus it is possible that those Basques who ambushed the rearguard had come from Gascony.[51] From Einhard's description they may not have been immediately local to the valley of Roncesvalles. It is also conceivable that a number of different communities co-operated in this venture.

The description of the Basques as being lightly armed is hardly surprising, but it is interesting to note that Einhard has the Basques driving the rearguard back into the valley and there engaging the Franks in open battle. This was not just an ambuscade with primitive mountaineers rolling down rocks on to the heads of their defenceless victims. The fact that the rearguard could be thus detached and annihilated without the

[51] R. d'Abadal i de Vinyals, 'La expedición de Carlomagno a Zaragoza: el hecho historico, su caracter y su significación', in *Colloquios de Roncesvalles* (Zaragoza—Pamplona, 1956), pp. 39—71.

main body of the army being aware of what was going on, let alone being able to do anything about it, also suggests a high level of incompetence on the part of the Frankish commanders, and the seriousness of the defeat is indicated by the names of the Franks who fell in the fray. Both Eggihard, the seneschal, whose surviving epitaph provides a date for the battle as occurring on 15 August, and Anselm, the count of the palace, were important palatine nobles, and the unavenged killing of such men was an additional source of humiliation.[52] It is extraordinary to find this débâcle transformed by the eleventh century into a scene of heroic fiction in the epic poem *Chanson de Roland*, a work that entirely ignores the Basque role in the original in the interests of turning the conflict into one between Christians and Muslims.[53]

Rebellion in Pamplona

Any further interest Charlemagne may have had in vengeance or in reasserting his presence in the Ebro valley was dampened yet more by the Saxon revolt of 778. Together with other concerns, this prevented him renewing Frankish involvement in the Pyrenean regions for nearly a quarter of a century. Pamplona reverted to Muslim rule, which by the end of the century was being exercised by a governor appointed by the amir and drawn from the ranks of the *muwallad* family of the Banu Qasi, the supposed descendants of a Visigothic count Cassius, said to have come to terms with the Arabs in the aftermath of the conquest of 711.[54] Certainly the family claiming such ancestry was able to make itself the dominant local power in the middle and upper Ebro for most of the ninth century. Their rise is also inextricably linked to the emergence of the tiny Christian kingdom of Pamplona.

The beginnings of this process seem to be linked to stirrings within the city against the rule of the governor Mu'tarrif ibn

[52] E. Dümmler (ed.), *MGH Poetae Aevi Carolini* (Berlin, 1881), vol. I, p. 109.

[53] R. Fawtier, *La Chanson de Roland, Étude Historique* (Paris, 1933).

[54] Collins, *Early Medieval Spain*, pp. 190—2; for an alternative approach that takes the family tradition at face value, see C. Sánchez-Albornoz, 'La conquista de España por los musulmanes: sometimiento de los vascones', in his *Orígenes y Destino de Navarra* (Barcelona, 1984), pp. 33—43.

Mūsa, and in 799 an uprising resulted in his murder.[55] Leadership in Pamplona appears to have been in the hands of a certain Velasco, whose name is of Basque origin.[56] How constituted and for how long his power lasted is not clear, but in 802 the inhabitants of Pamplona provided some independent support for the revolt of Fortún ibn Mūsa, leader of the Banu Qasi and probably the brother of Mu'tarrif ibn Mūsa, which was centred on Tudela. This was rapidly suppressed by the forces of the amir of Córdoba Hisham I and, although the power of the Banu Qasi was far from broken by this episode, Pamplona was brought back into allegiance to the Umayyad ruler. At the same period the Franks were resuming their interest in establishing a march to the south of the Pyrenees, and a major step in this direction had been achieved by their conquest of Barcelona in 801, carried out by Louis the king of Aquitaine, under the aegis of his father Charlemagne.[57] Further expansion along the Mediterranean coast was, however, effectively blocked by the end of the decade when Louis failed to take and hold Tarragona and Tortosa (808—10). In the meantime another Frankish expedition had crossed the Pyrenees at the western end, and in 806 Pamplona was captured. For the author of the *Royal Frankish Annals* this was a matter of bringing the 'Vascones and Navarri' back to their former allegiance — hardly a fair judgement when Charlemagne had quitted the area so ignominiously in 778, leaving Pamplona defenceless to resist a second subjection to Córdoba even if it had wished to.[58] But in Frankish eyes this region had become part of their territory, more specifically part of the subordinate kingdom of Aquitaine created in 781.

What the nature of Frankish rule in the area was like in the years following 806 is uncertain. There are no indications that a marcher county was established with its centre at Pamplona, though this may have occurred. The only conceivable administrative alternative would have been the extension over the

[55] Ibn al-Athīr, *Annales du Maghreb*, pp. 164—5.

[56] For quite different interpretations of these complex and poorly documented events, see C. Sánchez-Albornoz, 'Problemas de la Historia Navarra del siglo IX, *Cuadernos de Historia de España*, 25/26 (1957), pp. 5—82, and also J. Pérez de Urbel, 'Lo viejo y lo nuevo sobre el origen del reino de Pamplona', *Al-Andalus*, 19 (1954), pp. 1—42.

[57] J. M. Salrach, *El procés de formació nacional de Catalunya*, 2nd edn (2 vols, Barcelona, 1981), vol. I, pp. 9—26.

[58] *Annales Regni Francorum*, Kurze, p. 122.

region of the authority of the none too reliable duke of Gascony. A military and administrative district does seem to have been set up in the valley of the Aragón under a Count Aznar, son of Galindo, a Basque of unknown origin.[59] Unlike the Frankish march in Catalonia, that created in the Basque regions failed to survive, and its inhabitants demonstrated no loyalty towards their new and short-lived overlords.[60] Partly this may have been a problem of communications: Aquitaine, let alone French Vasconia or Gascony, had not easily accepted the rule of the Frankish monarchs, which had little to offer them. This is in distinction to Catalonia, where the new settlements had to rely initially on military support from beyond the mountains to defend themselves against the attacks of regional *muwallad* lords and the Berber garrison of Tarragona. On the other hand, in the upper Ebro valley the inhabitants of Pamplona at least had established a good working relationship with the dominant Muslim power in the area. Frankish protection and the ideal of pan-Christian solidarity had no appeal (see map 17).

Nor were the Basques north of the Pyrenees entirely easy under the closer allegiance to the Frankish crown that had resulted from the submission to Charlemagne in 796. Two episodes from the period *c.* 778 to 801 that relate to the Basques in Gascony, recorded only in the near contemporary *Life of Louis the Pious*, depend for their interpretation on previously formulated models for Basque social organization and behaviour. In themselves the reports of the two incidents are too brief and unelaborated to be self-explanatory. Around the year 789 a *Dux* of Toulouse called Chorso was outwitted and 'bound by the chains of oaths' by a certain Adeleric. But for the text's clear designation of him as *Wasco*, the latter's Germanic name (cf. Athalaric) would have concealed from us his Basque identity. An attempt to bring him to book for this mysterious outrage against the representative of public authority at a general assembly of the Aquitanian kingdom held in Septimania came to nothing, but the following summer Charlemagne summoned

[59] 'Genera comitum Aragonensium', in J. M. Lacarra (ed.), 'Textos navarros del Códice de Roda', *Estudios de Edad Média de la Corona de Aragón*, vol. I (1945), pp. 240—5.
[60] R. Collins, 'Charles the Bald and Wifred the Hairy' in *Charles the Bald: Court and Kingdom*, eds M. T. Gibson and J. Nelson (Oxford, 1981), pp. 169—89.

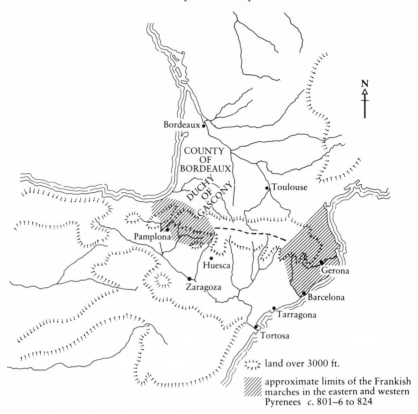

Map 17   The Frankish marches c. 806—824

Adeleric to Worms and sent him into perpetual exile, doubtless the result of some form of hearing, and at the same time dismissed Chorso, apparently thereby giving much pleasure to the Basques. The second incident occurred in 801 just prior to the Frankish campaign against Barcelona. Count Burgundio of Fezensac having died, King Louis replaced him by a certain Liutard, but this appointment led to an outburst of Basque resentment against the new count's followers, some of whom were burnt to death. These disturbances were suppressed and appropriate punishments inflicted.[61]

[61] 'Astronomer', *Vita Hludovici Imperatoris*, ch. 5 and 13, ed. R. Rau, *Quellen zur karolingischen Reichsgeschichte* I (Darmstadt, 1974), pp. 264/6, 272/4; for an alternative interpretation see P. Wolff, 'L'Aquitaine et ses marges' in H. Beumann ed. *Karl der Grosse: Leben und Nachleben*, vol. I (Aachen, 1965), pp. 269—306.

Adeleric was clearly no mere bandit. He went to Worms in answer to a royal summons. It is possible that he should be linked to the dynasty of Lupus the *Dux Vasconum*. In regions such as the Agenais, where their territories marched together, rivalry and conflicts of authority between the Basque duke and his colleague based in Toulouse can hardly have been avoided. Alternatively, if Adeleric is not seen as a representative of the ducal line in such a region, it is possible to envisage him as some form of *condottiere* in the service of Chorso. It is highly unlikely that the use of Basque mercenaries in Aquitaine terminated abruptly with the events of 768, especially when the intensified frontier problems created by Charlemagne's expedition of 778 are taken into account. The Pyrenees themselves, rather than the northern and eastern margins of Aquitaine, became the focus of defensive requirements against a belligerent and recently provoked neighbour. Perhaps also the obscure disturbances in 801 around Fedensac reflect the objections of a military following mishandled or dispossessed by the new incumbent of the comital office. The presence of the Basque duke Lupus Sancho on the ensuing campaign against Barcelona shows that no wider Basque—Frankish conflict was involved.

In 816 the Basques 'across the Garonne and around the Pyrenees' rebelled because the new Frankish ruler, the Emperor Louis the Pious (814—40), had removed their Duke Sigiwin 'because of his boundless arrogance and wicked ways.' What this actually means, and what the relationship was between this Sigiwin and the last duke known to us, Lupus of 769, is not clear. It has been argued that the name Sigiwin is a Latinate corruption of the Basque name Jimeno, and that, fleeing from the emperor to the south of the Pyrenees, this Sigiwin-Jimeno became the ancestor of the second ruling dynasty of the kingdom of Pamplona, the Jiménez.[62] However, the grounds for such an argument are flimsy in the extreme, and Sigiwin looks instead to be a perfectly acceptable Frankish name. This may also suggest that the Carolingians had resumed the practice of their Merovingian predecessors of appointing Franks to hold the office of duke of Gascony, which was their own creation in

---

[62] *Annales Regni Francorum*, Kurze, p. 144, tr. B. W. Scholz, *Carolingian Chronicles* (Ann Arbor, 1970), p. 100. M. Ilarri Zabala, *La tierra natal de Iñigo Arista* (Bilbao, 1980), pp. 9—18 disposes of the Jimeno argument.

any case. It is possible that the office was held concomitantly with that of count of Bordeaux.

It is probably in the context of the suppression of this revolt that Louis the Pious crossed the Pyrenees and (as the anonymous author of his biography, generally known as 'the Astronomer', puts it) 'settled matters' in Pamplona. This followed on from his receiving of the submission of Basque rebels at Dax.[63] The author also records that Louis, on his return, took precautions against the danger of ambush, perhaps in the pass of Roncesvalles, by seizing hostages. The Basque regions were thus clearly not pacified, though the emperor's activity in Pamplona suggests some form of administration was being developed. It would be interesting to know what kind of hostage was needed to secure Louis's safe conduct. The next Frankish commanders to enter the region were less far-sighted. In 824 the *Royal Frankish Annals* record that Counts Aeblus and Aznar, the latter in all probability the count of Aragón, led an army to Pamplona, only to have it ambushed and massacred on the return march. Count Aeblus was sent as a present to the Umayyad ruler in Córdoba, but Aznar 'as a relative of his captors' was released.[64] This episode marked the end of Frankish rule in Pamplona, and in all probability the initiation of the independent kingdom that was to succeed it.

Despite reports of rebellions and of frequent opposition to the central authority of the Carolingian kings, the duchy of Gascony or Vasconia Citerior ('hither' Gascony) did not go the way of its southern counterpart, the Basque region across the Pyrenees, which in the kingdom of Pamplona established a political independence that was not only in practice but also formally divorced from Frankish royal power. The ninth-century dukes of Gascony make all too infrequent appearances in contemporary sources, and their precise relationships one with another and with the first holder of the office in Carolingian times, the Duke Lupus of 769 and 778, are far from clear. A Duke Lupus Sancho 'of the Vascones' was one of the leaders of King Louis of Aquitaine's successful expedition against Barcelona in 801, and as such makes two brief appearances in the later

---

[63] 'Astronomer', *Vita Ludowici Imperatoris*, 18, ed. R. Rau, *Quellen zur karolingischen Reichsgeschichte* (Darmstadt, 1974) vol. I, pp. 282—4.

[64] *Annales Regni Francorum*, Kurze, p. 166, Scholz, p. 117.

poetic account of the campaign that forms a part of Ermoldus's panegyric on the Emperor Louis.[65] Of particular interest here is the poet's reference to Lupus Sancho as having been the *nutritus* of Charlemagne, a term possibly implying that he had been brought up in the Carolingian ruler's court. This in itself might be an indication of the increased significance of the western Pyrenean regions in Frankish eyes after 769. However, after the references relating to the events of 801, Lupus Sancho does not reappear, and by 816 another duke, by the name of Sigiwin (I), is recorded. In that year he was removed from office, and the rebellion 'beyond the Garonne' that this caused was effectively crushed.[66]

Sigiwin's successor as duke may have been Lupus Centulli, who in 819 was defeated in a battle by the counts of Toulouse and the Auvergne and was condemned for treason by the Emperor Louis on the accusation of the victors. His brother Garsand (García?) was reported to have been killed in the fray. The *Royal Frankish Annals* do not record his fate, nor do they specifically name him as a duke, but his ability to conduct a war against the two Aquitanian counts makes the attribution of such an office to him reasonable. Louis the Pious's son Pippin I, king of Aquitaine, led an army into Gascony later in the year and pacified the province.[67]

Silence descends for the next few years, but the court-centred *Annals of St Bertins* report under the year 836 that 'Aznar, count of Vasconia Citerior, who a few years previously had revolted against Pippin, died a horrible death, and his brother Sancho Sánchez took over the same region, with Pippin opposing him.'[68] This Aznar and his revolt against King Pippin, his immediate overlord below the emperor, cannot be securely located, though his successor Sancho is probably to be identified with the Sancho duke of Gascony active in the period *c.* 848— 52. If that be so, his initial tenure of power may have been short-lived, as by 839 a Count Sigiwin (II) is recorded as having been installed in Bordeaux. He probably also held the title of *dux Vasconum*, as a Duke Sigiwin is reported as being defeated

[65] Ermold le Noir, *Poéme sur Louis le Pieux*, ed. E. Faral (Paris, 1964), lines 164—71, 310, 313; pp. 16—18, 28.
[66] *Annales Regni Francorum*, Kurze, s.a. 816, p. 144.
[67] Ibid., s.a. 819, pp. 150, 151—2.
[68] *Annales de Saint-Bertin*, eds F. Grat et al. (Paris, 1964), s.a. 836, p. 20.

A possible genealogy of the first line of the dukes of Gascony c. 769—864

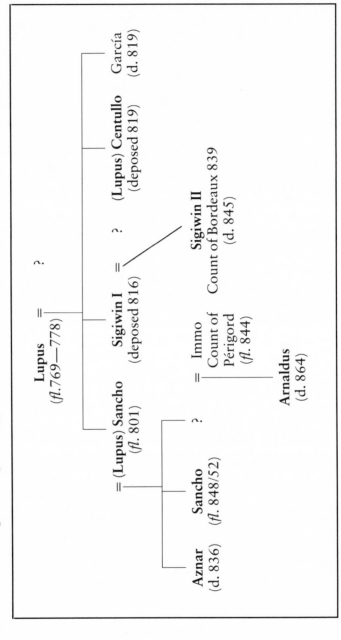

and killed by the Vikings in a contemporary letter by Lupus, abbot of Ferrières.[69] By 848 Sancho Sánchez had reappeared as duke of Gascony, and in the troubled period of Charles the Bald of west Francia's war against his nephew Pippin II of Aquitaine he played off the two opponents against each other before eventually surrendering the fugitive Pippin to Charles in 852.[70] Although less well documented, this looks like a repeat of the dealings of Duke Lupus of Gascony with Hunald of Aquitaine and Charlemagne in 769.

Finally, and apparently as the last member of this first line of dukes, an account of the translation of the relics of St Fausta records the death in 864 of the *dux Vasconum* Arnaldus, nephew and successor to Sancho.[71] This Arnaldus was the son of Count Immo of Périgord and Angoulême (d. *c.* 844), and he certainly enjoyed no hereditary right to his father's offices, which went to unrelated royal appointees.[72] The duchy of Gascony, though, seems to have come to him by virtue of his family relationships, and this may help to confirm the impression of a hereditary tenure existing as much in the case of the first line of dukes as it clearly did for the second, which came to power by 887 if not in 864. A hypothetical reconstruction of a genealogy that would link all of the early holders of the office and which does not stretch chronological credibility too far might be something like that shown.

According to the *Translatio Sanctae Faustae*, which records the translation of the relics of St Fausta from her church at Fezensac to the rebuilt monastery of Solignac near Limoges, Viking depredations in the regions of Bordeaux and Saintes were not only frequent in the middle of the ninth century but also resisted on several occasions by Duke Arnald who took the field against them, though with apparently small long-term effect.[73] One of his predecessors, Sigiwin II, had been killed by them in the aftermath of a defeat. Following the general pattern traceable throughout western Europe in general, Viking activity reached a peak in the middle years of the ninth century, after

[69] Servatus Lupus, *Epistulae*, ed. P. K. Marshall (Leipzig, 1984), ep. 30·4, p. 42.

[70] *Annales de Saint-Bertin*, Grat et al., s.a. 852, p. 64.

[71] *Translatio Sanctae Faustae*, in *Acta Sanctorum*, Jan., vol. I (1643), cc. 1091—2.

[72] J. Boussard (ed.), *Historia Pontificum et Comitum Engolismensium* (Paris, 1957), pp. 6—7.

[73] *Translatio Sanctae Faustae*, c.1091.

which came something of a lull before they resumed in strength again in the second half of the tenth century. By the latter period the dukes of Gascony at least were better able to deal with this mobile sea-borne threat, and in 982 a decisive victory by Duke William Sancho put a term to recorded Viking incursions in the territory of the duchy, which then went on to enjoy a period of monastic restoration and new foundation.[74] No such successes are recorded for the earlier period, and it has even been suggested that Bordeaux was virtually abandoned in the middle of the ninth century as a result of the Viking attacks along the Atlantic coast. However, such long-established urban sites apart — and these were virtually all on the northern fringes of the region — it is unlikely that the duchy of Gascony was a major target of Viking raiding, not least because it contained so few towns and monasteries, the prime sites for plundering. Viking slave raiding should not be discounted, and both the Adour and the Garonne provided easy routes of access for the deep and quick water-borne penetration of defenceless countryside that the Scandinavians favoured.[75] However, the sand dunes of the Landes and the valleys of the Pyrenees constituted territory less amenable to Viking tactics and tastes. In general, the phase of Viking raiding, together with the rapid decline of the authority of the Carolingians and with it the political cohesion of Francia, especially after the death of Charles the Bald in 877, probably affected the Basques of Gascony mostly in terms of what was thereby prevented from happening. Thus the social and cultural impact of the region's increasing absorption into a Frankish or more particularly Aquitanian political orbit was postponed and ultimately lessened in consequence. Not until the late tenth century does this begin to be reversed.

---

[74] See the foundation charter of Saint-Sever: *Gallia Christiana*, vol. I: *Instrumenta ad Ecclesiam Adurnensem*, 1, p. 181.

[75] See in general J. M. Wallace-Hadrill, 'The Vikings in Francia', in his *Early Medieval History* (Oxford, 1975), pp. 217—36.

5

The Kingdom and the Duchy

That the evidence for the development of the tiny Pyrenean realm of Pamplona is both confused and fragmentary will probably occasion little surprise. The same is true of virtually every aspect of Basque history and society before the late Middle Ages, when for the first time their records start to proliferate. However, it is particularly frustrating that, just as in the comparable case of the appearance of the duchy of Gascony, the first significant and recognizable political institution to take shape amongst the Basques south of the Pyrenees should be so obscure in its origins and in the history of its formative period. The principal problem is the lack of indigenous sources of information. Unlike the Frankish monarchy, the Umayyad amirate or even the tiny Christian realm in the Asturias, the kingdom of Pamplona produced no chronicle writing of any sort before the later Middle Ages.[1] Its administrative records only begin to appear at the end of the tenth century and then only in small numbers, and they are bedevilled by forgeries. The only early texts are in the form of an elaborate set of genealogical records of the ruling dynasty and its affinities, to which have become attached various miscellaneous items, such as the *De Laude Pampilone* and the verses composed to celebrate the marriage of a certain Leodegunda, daughter of Ordoño, to one of the kings, whose identity and therefore the date of the poem

[1] Notably the two fifteenth-century compositions: *Crónica de Garci López de Roncesvalles*, ed. C. Orcastegui Gros (Pamplona, 1977), and *La crónica de los Reyes de Navarra del Principe de Viana*, ed. Orcastegui (Pamplona, 1978), both of which have brief but fanciful accounts of the kingdom's early history.

remains unknown.[2] Even the genealogical materials are of
limited use, for they are brief, and incomplete in respect of the
period before 905. As a result the history of the whole of the
first century of the kingdom's existence has to be reconstructed
on the basis of the very occasional notices of Frankish and Arab
chroniclers, which are by no means mutually consistent. Judge-
ments have to be made at all points as to where to place the
weight of credence between contradictory accounts. In consequence, for a subject so remote and specialized, the early history
of the kingdom of Pamplona has generated a remarkable
amount of scholarly controversy, and hardly any two interpretations can be found to agree.[3] As well as for its own intrinsic
interest, the subject is an important one in the longer term.
From the tiny kingdom of the ninth and tenth centuries was to
emerge the Navarrese monarchy, which was able to maintain an
independent existence until the early sixteenth century, and on
occasion play a crucial role in the wider political history of the
Iberian peninsula and of France in the Middle Ages.

The three monarchies

It is not just a matter of pedantry to talk of this kingdom in the
ninth and tenth centuries as being that of Pamplona rather than
Navarre. For one thing that is how its rulers entitled themselves.
The indigenous documents, few as they are, make no mention
of 'Navarre' or 'Navarrese' before the eleventh century. On the
other hand periodic Frankish references to 'the Navarri' indicate
that the name was in use even as early as the beginning of the
ninth century.[4] The appearance of this term presents problems,

[2] J. M. Lacarra (ed.), 'Textos navarros del Códice de Roda', *Estudios de Edad Media
de la Corona de Aragón*, vol. I (1945), pp. 272—5.

[3] See, among others, C. Sánchez-Albornoz, 'Problemas de la Historia Navarra del
siglo IX', *Cuadernos de la Historia de España*, 25/26 (1957), pp. 5—82, reprinted in his
Vascos y Navarros en su primera historia, 2nd edn (Madrid, 1976), pp. 267—342; J. M.
Lacarra, *Historia Política del Reino de Navarra* (3 vols, Pamplona, 1972—3), especially
vol. I, pp. 1—202; C. Clavería, *Historia del reino de Navarra* (Pamplona, 1971), largely
reproduced as vol. 4 of the *Historia General del País Vasco*, ed. J. Caro Baroja (Bilbao,
1980).

[4] *Annales Regni Francorum*, ed. F. Kurze, MGH, *Scriptores Rerum Germanicarum*
(Hanover, 1895), pp. 50 and 122; Einhard, *Vita Karoli Magni Imperatonis*, 15, L.
Halphen (ed.), *Eginhard, Vie de Charlemagne* (Paris, 1967), p. 44; *Fragmentum
Chronici Fontanellensis*, ed. G. Pertz, MGH, *Scriptores* (Hanover, 1829), vol. II, p. 302.

not uncomplicated by modern connotations of the differences between the Navarrese and the inhabitants of the three Basque provinces of Alava, Guipúzcoa and Vizcaya. With the contraction of the the Basque-speaking area of Navarre many of the inhabitants of that province are anxious to stress their separateness from the Vascongadas in political, cultural and historical terms. Therefore distinctions in early medieval terminology can take on contemporary significance. For the author of the *Royal Frankish Annals* the Wascones and the Navarri were separable peoples, as he makes clear in the entry relating to the events of 778, and in a subsequent one for 806 he makes a further distinction between the Navarri and the Pampilonenses, the inhabitants of Pamplona.[5] The politico-geographical problems created by these differentiations are made no easier by the ethnographic labels found in the works of Arab writers who refer to these regions. There appears to be no equivalent in their terminology for the Navarrese, and the Baskunis, clearly a transliteration of Vascones, are placed in Pamplona and adjacent regions, whilst another body of people, the Sirtaniyyun, a name confusingly similar to that of the Frankish county of Cerdanya in the eastern Pyrenees, seem to appear in the Aragón valley.[6] There is also a clear distinction in the Arab historians' works between the Baskunis and the Basques of Gascony.

The problem of the Sirtaniyyun, for whom no Latin reference can be found, could be resolved by believing that they were not an ethnic group but rather a political one, and that the name, like that of the Banu Qasi, was that of a dynasty rather than of a people.[7] This is a possible but by no means certain explanation. At least it is clear that the Arabs saw no distinction between Navarrese and Basques to correspond with that made in the Frankish sources. It has been seen how, from their very earliest appearances in historical records, differences were held to have existed between Basques living across the Pyrenean watershed on the shores of the Bay of Biscay and those living to the south of the mountains; this manifested itself until at least *c.* AD 500 in differences in tribal name. Although the earlier forms, if any, of

[5] *Annales Regni Francorum*, Kurze, pp. 50 and 122.

[6] *Ajbar Machmua*, ed. and tr. E. Lafuente y Alcántara (Madrid, 1867), p. 105; compare Ibn al-Athīr, *Annales du Maghreb et de l'Espagne*, tr. E. Fagnan (Algiers, 1901), p. 129.

[7] See below, p. 159 and n. 54.

The centre of Pamplona. The city is situated on a cliff overlooking the Rio Arga

the name Navarri cannot now be recognized, this looks like a manifestation of the same phenomenon. None of the documents of the ninth and tenth centuries ever names the people over whom the kings ruling from Pamplona held sway, but there seems good reason to believe, on the basis of the Frankish accounts, that some of them called themselves Navarri, or the Navarrese. Their kings did not refer to themselves in this period by any form of racial title, as the Visigothic rulers had or as the Frankish ones currently did. Instead they were always referred to in relation to their seat of government, in other words as 'ruling in Pamplona', or in the later tenth century as 'ruling in Pamplona and in Nájera'.[8] It is conceivable that this practice,

[8] For example, *Cartulario de Albelda*, ed. A. Ubieto Arteta (Zaragoza, 1981), docs 6 (931), 7 (933), 11 (945), 24 (958) etc.; for Nájera see I. Rodríguez de Lama (ed.), *Colección diplomática medieval de la Rioja* (3 vols, Logroño, 1976), doc. 2 (972).

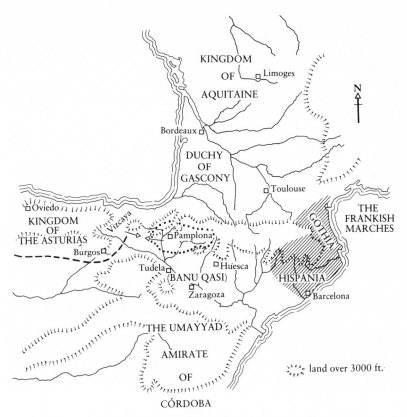

Map 18   The kingdom of Pamplona and its neighbours c. 840—850

paralleled in the Asturian kingdom, arose from their exercising their authority over more than just a Navarrese population. At least there was insufficient a sense of racial unity for such a title as *rex Vasconum*, or king of the Basques, to have any meaning.

Nor for that matter were the kings of Pamplona in any position to impose their rule on all of the Basques. To the north of the Pyrenees an independent authority existed in the persons of the dukes of Gascony, whose allegiance was directed, if anywhere, towards the Frankish kings. Even to the south of the mountains certain Basque-occupied regions were beyond their sphere of influence (see map 18). It is clear that a county of Vizcaya, subordinate to the ruler in Pamplona, at least on occasion, had come into existence by the end of the tenth century, but there is no knowledge of it in the ninth, and Guipúzcoa does not feature in any records before the early eleventh century. Alava, on the other hand, is more fully accounted for, and has a history at this time quite distinct from the rest of the Basque regions in that it had become part of the kingdom of the Asturias. This small realm had come into existence *c.* 722 (traditionally in 718) as the result of a successful revolt by the Asturians against the recently established Arab governor of the region.[9] Its first king, Pelagius (d. 737), probably a Visigothic noble, subsequently married his daughter to the son of a Duke Peter of Cantabria. The premature death, after a brief reign (737—9), of Pelagius's son Fafila led to this son-in-law succeeding to the Asturian throne as Alfonso I. The process of the expansion of this kingdom perched in the mountains in the north of the peninsula is obscure, recorded in only two brief chronicles written in the late ninth century. From these it is clear that a substantial population of Basques was under the rule of the Asturian kings by the middle of the eighth century, as the account of the reign of Alfonso I's son Fruela the Cruel (757—68) in the *Chronicle of Alfonso III* reports his suppression of a revolt on the part of the Vascones, and his subsequent marriage to one of them by the name of Munia. Basques are also reported to have supported the unsuccessful bid of the short-lived king Nepotian (842) to hold his throne against the Galician rebel Ramiro I, and Ramiro's son Ordoño I (850—66) suppressed a Basque revolt in the course of his reign.[10]

How the Asturian kings came to have Basque subjects is not clear, any more than is their precise location. Alava had to all appearances lost any traces of former Basque occupancy in the course of the late Iron Age and the succeeding Roman period, but the unquestionable Basque imprint on the area in the medieval centuries may well be attributed to their expansion into the plains around the later city of Vitoria and into the eastern fringes of Castille in the time of the Visigothic kingdom. Thus the north and the east of Alava, and also the westerly parts of Vizcaya, look to be the likely areas of Basque occupation

---

[9] C. Sánchez-Albornoz, *Los orígenes de la nación española* (3 vols, Oviedo, 1972—5), vol. II, pp. 7—135.

[10] *Chronicle of Alfonso III*, J. Prelog (ed.), *Die Chronik Alfons III* (Frankfurt, Bern and Cirencester, 1980), pp. 40—1, 52.

brought under Asturian rule. Some Basque territory may have formed part of the murky duchy of Cantabria from an earlier period, for as no military activity in these directions is recorded of either Pelagius or Fafila, it is a reasonable supposition that some or all of these parts had been under the rule of the Duke Peter and were then joined to the Asturian kingdom by the accession of his son Alfonso. This again raises the controverted issue of the geographical location of Cantabria in early medieval sources. Whatever may be thought of the argument involving the *Life of St Aemilian*, there does seem a possibility that the Rioja could have at least been included in a definition of the region of Cantabria. Thus even allowing that the traditional Cantabria, roughly equivalent to the modern province of Santander, was the heart of the older region, it is possible to envisage it extending both further eastwards to include some of the coastal parts of Vizcaya, and also southwards around the headwaters of the Ebro. The Rioja proper was firmly under Arab rule until the early tenth century, when for the first time both the kingdom of Pamplona and the Asturian—Leonese monarchy began to extend themselves in that direction. In the case of the latter, this was probably undertaken from longer-established holdings further up the Ebro.

Thus it is clear that by *c.* 850 the Basques were ruled, if nominally, by the representatives of three separate, and on occasion mutually hostile, monarchies. There may also have been some areas of their occupancy that were still entirely untouched by outside political control, principally in Guipúzcoa and some of the less accessible Pyrenean valleys, though such an argument depends on the silence of scanty sources. No sense of a common Basque identity seems to have existed as a counterweight to this political diversity. The *Royal Frankish Annals* record that the army sent by the Franks to Pamplona in 824, and then massacred in the Pyrenees, was largely made up of Basques, obviously from Gascony.[11] Count Aznar was released because he was consanguineous to his captors, whoever they may have been, but Basques appear to have fought one another in the interests of alien kings. Similarly, Basque contingents from north of the Pyrenees came to attack the kingdom of

---

[11] *Annales Regni Francorum*, Kurze, p. 166.

Pamplona in 862 as allies of King Ordoño I of the Asturias.[12] Regional and cultural variations may have counted for more than points of similarity in language that made outsiders often class them all together as Vascones.

The Iñíguez kings

Whilst it is obvious that the Asturian and Frankish monarchies were alien in terms of language, law and culture to their Basque subjects, the case of Pamplona is more complex. Can this be regarded as a Basque kingdom, the first self-generated political institution of the Basques? However, the very notion of kingship seems an anachronism in the context of Basque society. No indigenous Basque word for it and its institutions exist: they are all Latin borrowings. Nor, on the other hand, would the inhabitants of Pamplona have easily identified themselves as Basques. They had stopped thinking in such terms by the Visigothic period at the latest, and in the *Royal Frankish Annals* the distinction between Navarri and Pampilonenses is a clear one. Contact with Arab civilization and with Islam had a profound effect upon the middle Ebro valley in the eighth century, as evidenced by the rise of the *muwallad* or indigenous convert family of the Banu Qasi in Tudela and other fortresses of the region. Although there is no evidence of any form of Muslim population in Pamplona, the city was open to a broad range of influence through its contacts with the Ebro valley. Pamplona and Tudela were directly linked by the Ebro and the valley of the Arga. The hinterland of the city, though, looks to have been firmly Basque; the existence of Basque toponyms and the survival until relatively recently of the Basque language in the region between Pamplona and the Ebro, as far south as Olite, makes it hard to deny that this was a kingdom the bulk of whose population must be classed as Basque in cultural and linguistic terms. Alien as the institution might be, and more culturally diverse as was its centre of government, in this respect Pamplona can legitimately be called a Basque kingdom, as was its first ruling dynasty.

[12] *Chronicle of Alfonso III*, Prelog, pp. 56—63.

The records of this line of kings are too few for any agreement to exist as to their length of reigns or even their exact numbers. The founder of the line and of the kingdom is almost certainly Iñigo Arista, probably identifiable with the 'Yannaqo ibn Wanniqo' of Arab accounts.[13] If so, this suggests that his father's name was also Iñigo, and a reference in the fragmentary historical work of Ibn Hayyān puts his death in 858.[14] His reign probably began *c.* 824, with the successful overthrow of Frankish hegemony. There are problems of genealogy here that also affect the *muwallad* family of the Banu Qasi, allies and relatives by marriage of the line of Iñigo. According to the fragments of the work of the Arab historian al-'Udri, Iñigo ibn Iñigo's sister was married to Mūsa ibn Fortún; the latter, however, is held to have died in 802.[15] This seems rather remote from the period of Iñigo's own activity, though not impossibly so. It also seems to involve a relationship between the two families at a surprisingly early stage, but this has been used to provide complex explanations for the supposed involvement of the Iñigo family in the obscure events of 802—3, when the Banu Qasi rebelled against the Umayyads in alliance with the inhabitants of Pamplona. This has necessitated bringing the start of Iñigo Arista's ascendancy to *c.* 803 — again requiring a stretching of the timescale if it be accepted that he died in 858.[16] The difficulties thus created stem from a rather wilful refusal to accept al-'Udri's words at face value. He makes it clear that it was Fortún ibn Mūsa who died in 802, and it was Mūsa ibn Fortún who married the sister of Iñigo.[17] The editorial 'correction' that reversed the names resulted from an unwillingness to doubt the Banu Qasi's own genealogical myth that their line stemmed from a Visigothic count Cassius, extant *c.* 711, whose son was called Fortún. The genealogy of the two families is shown here as reconstructed on the basis of al-'Udri's uncorrected account, and supplemented

---

[13] F. de la Granja (tr.), 'La Marca Superior en la obra de al-'Udri', *Estudios de Edad Media de la Corona de Aragón*, vol. VIII (1967), chs 27 and 30, pp. 468—9, 470.

[14] E. Lévi-Provençal and A. García Gallo (tr.) 'Textos inéditos del *Muqtabis* de Ibn Hayyan sobre los orígenes del reino de Pamplona', *Al-Andalus*, 19 (1954), pp. 295—315.

[15] Al-'Udri 20, de la Granja, 'La Marca Superior', p. 465; Lacarra, 'Textos navarros', p. 229 and n. 1.

[16] See especially Sánchez-Albornoz, 'Problemas de la Historia Navarra'.

[17] de la Granja, 'La Marca Superior', p. 465, note to ch. 20 of the text. Unemended, Mūsa ibn Mūsa's grandfather (Fortún) thus dies in 802.

The Banu Qasi and the dynasty of Iñigo Arista

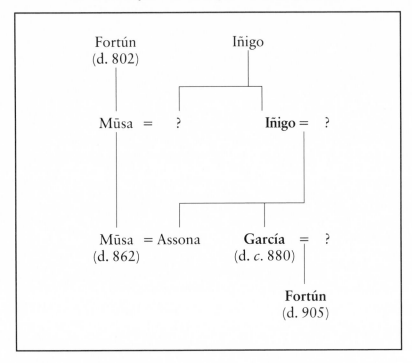

with information taken from the Navarrese genealogical texts; it is perfectly consistent within itself and makes better sense than the alternative. It removes the need to find a role for Iñigo Arista around 803, and makes more credible a commencement of his reign in the aftermath of the Frankish collapse in 824. The close interrelationship of the two families is notable, with a marriage of cousins taking place with the wedding of Mūsa ibn Mūsa to Assona daughter of Iñigo. It also affected family naming practices, as witnessed by the taking over of the name of Fortún from the line of Mūsa as the name of the last king of the line of Iñigo.

The second king of the dynasty was Iñigo's son García, whose political fortunes were less felicitous than those of his father. In 861 he was captured by Vikings and obliged to pay a substantial ransom to secure his release.[18] How this occurred is not certain: the view that the Vikings had sailed up the Ebro is unlikely to be correct, as a penetration so far inland is contrary to their normal practices, and it is unlikely in the extreme that their passage would have left no mark on the other major settlements of the valley, notably Zaragoza. It has to be assumed that either they came over the mountains from the Bay of Biscay, again out of keeping with their penchant for advancing along waterways, or that García was captured at some point far removed from Pamplona. Alliances with the leaders of the Banu Qasi, Mūsa ibn Mūsa (d. 862) and Lubb ibn Mūsa (d. 875), resulted in disastrous defeats at the hands of Umayyad armies in 860 and 872, in the course of one of which his son and heir Fortún was captured and taken off to Córdoba.[19] It is possible too that the king had a brother called Fortún who was killed in an earlier battle, though his existence may be no more than the product of confusion in the Arab sources concerning the capture of the prince Fortún. The latter remained in Córdoba until *c.* 880, after his father's death, when he was released and returned as the last of his line to rule in Pamplona (*c.* 880—905). At some point it is also necessary to include the reign of a King García son of Jimeno, thus clearly not a patrilineal descendant of any of the Iñigo line.[20] It is usually assumed that he ruled as some form of stop-gap between the death of García Iñiguez and the liberation of the latter's son from captivity in Córdoba.[21] His relationship to the dynasty remains uncertain, but he may have been linked to the lineage that succeeded them in 905, and could be the father of the first of those kings, Sancho Garcés I. The accompanying genealogy shows the links between the counts of Aragón and the kings of Pamplona *c.* 824—994.

The problems of making sense of the history of Pamplona in the ninth century are by no means simplified by the existence of a small number of dated charters, purporting to be the royal

[18] E. Lévi-Provençal, *Histoire de l'Espagne musulmane* (3 vols, Leiden, 1950), vol. I, p. 311.

[19] Ibid., vol. I, p. 323.

[20] 'Ordo numerum regnum Pampilonensium', in Lacarra, 'Textos navarros', p. 234. For a forged charter in the name of this king, see *Cartulario de San Juan de la Peña*, ed. A. Ubieto Arteta (2 vols, Valencia, 1962), doc. 3 (828).

[21] A. Ubieto Arteta, 'La dinastía Jimena', *Saitabi*, 10 (1960), pp. 65—79.

The counts of Aragón and the kings of Pamplona c. 824—994

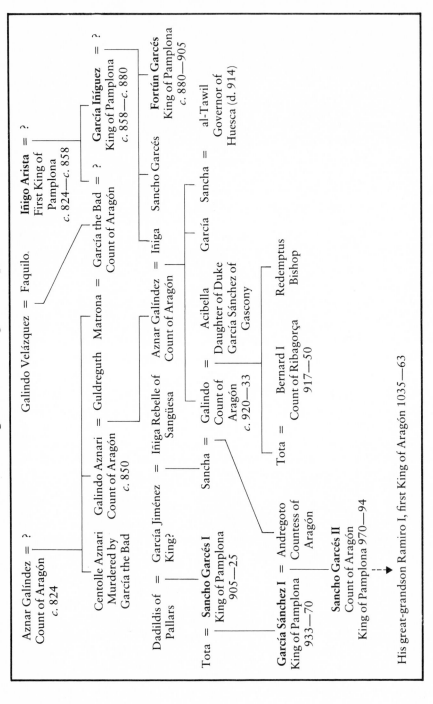

acts of the kings. These used to be taken at face value, but more recent critical scrutiny has shown that not a single one of them is authentic.[22] Perhaps the only genuine instrument in which one of the Iñiguez kings features comes from the mid tenth century and merely reports the actions of King Fortún Garcés in respect of the earliest stages of the settlement of a long-standing boundary dispute.[23] Indeed there are good reasons for suspecting that formal diplomatic was unknown in the kingdom of Pamplona in the ninth century, and that it was only introduced as the result of external influences in the course of the succeeding century.[24] Thus there never could have been a charter of the kings of the Iñiguez line. This is not to suggest that the kingdom was culturally unsophisticated. In a number of respects it proved itself to be quite the opposite.

Crown and church

A number of monasteries existed within the orbit of the kingdom that between them were the possessors of considerable literary treasures. These are revealed in the accounts of the visit to Pamplona by the Cordoban priest Eulogius, which probably took place in 848. Both in a letter that he wrote on his return to Córdoba to his host, Bishop Wiliesind of Pamplona, and in the section of the *Life of Eulogius* written after his death in 859 by his friend Alvar that relates to his travels, there are references to the visits he paid to monasteries in the vicinity of Pamplona, when prevented from continuing his journey across the Pyrenees as he had first intended.[25] The monasteries in question can generally be identified and they correspond with ones of whom much later history is known. They include both Leire and Siresa. More mysterious and yet more important in terms of its

[22] J. Goñi Gaztambide, *Catálogo del Becerro antiguo y del Becerro menor de Leyre* (Pamplona, 1963), p. 3.

[23] *Cartulario de San Juan de la Peña*, Ubieto, doc. 14 (928).

[24] R. Collins, 'Visigothic law and regional custom in early medieval Spanish dispute settlement', in W. Davies and P. Fouracre (eds), *The Settlement of Disputes in Early Medieval Europe* (Cambridge, 1986), pp. 85—104.

[25] Eulogius, *Epistula*, III, and Alvar, *Vita Eulogii*, 9, both ed. J. Gil, *Corpus Scriptorum Muzarabicorum* (2 vols, Madrid, 1973), vol. II, pp. 497—503, vol. I, pp. 335—6; see also C. Sánchez-Albornoz, 'La epistola de San Eulogio y el *Muqtabis* de Ibn Hayyan', *Principe de Viana*, 19 (1958), pp. 265—6.

Leire: the monastery of San Salvador, founded in the ninth century

manuscript treasures is the monastery 'of St Zacharias'. It was here, as Alvar's account indicates, that Eulogius found a corpus of texts that he then brought back with him to Córdoba, where they had previously been unavailable. They included Augustine's *City of God*, Vergil's *Aeneid*, the *Satires* of Juvenal and Horace, the *Fables* of Avienus, Aldhelm's *Aenigmata* and the curious *opuscula depincta* of the early-fourth-century poet Optatus Porphyrianus, together with a corpus of hymns. On the basis of these texts a mild revival of poetic composition took place in Córdoba under Eulogius's direction, and the manuscripts themselves continued to exert an influence throughout the rest of the century, not least in the Asturian kingdom, where some of them, or copies derived from them, arrived in 882.[26] The listing made by Alvar may not have been comprehensive, and it is

[26] R. Collins, 'Poetry in ninth-century Spain', *Papers of the Liverpool Latin Seminar*, 4 (1983), pp. 181—95.

A carving from Alava, probably of the tenth century, depicting an abbot

arguable that at least one other work by Aldhelm was also brought back to Córdoba from Pamplona by Eulogius.[27]

Although some have claimed that the home of these manuscripts must have been either Siresa or Leire — and there are

[27] Ibid., 186—7.

supporters of both — it does seem certain that St Zacharias was the monastery in which Eulogius found the texts, and that this house is quite distinct from both the other two.[28] The description of its location given in Eulogius's letter to Wiliesind confirms this impression: it was 'sited at the roots of the Pyrenean mountains, in the gateway to Gaul, whence the river Arga flowing from the east in rapid course, irrigating Seburim and Pamplona, waters all of Cantabria.'[29] This could not refer to Siresa, situated in Aragón, high up in the valley of the Subordán, nor could it apply to Leire in the valley of the Aragón, which does not flow to Pamplona and could not be considered as a 'gateway to France'. On the other hand, Pamplona is situated on the river Arga, whose valley provides access to the pass of Roncesvalles, and it is likely that the Seburim of Eulogius's letter is to be identified with the modern Zubiri, also sited on the Arga. The reference to Cantabria is, incidentally, useful evidence of the very broad geographical definition of the term in the ninth century: the Arga runs into the Ebro south of Calahorra, in other words in the Rioja. In general, although the precise site of St Zacharias is lost, and nothing is known of its further history, there seems no reason to doubt the reality of its existence (see map 19).

This mysterious house, which provided the manuscripts that were to have so profound an effect upon the Latinate culture of Mozarabic Córdoba, must in turn have received its literary treasures from some other source, but what this was it is impossible to determine.[30] There are, however, some general but clear indications that there existed a mutually beneficial relationship and intellectual interchange between the monasteries of the western Pyrenees and some of those of northern Aquitaine. Thus, for example, there seems to have been some degree of filiation between the text of Aldhelm's *Aenigmata* contained in the St Zacharias manuscript, which like the rest of the corpus

[28] M. C. Díaz y Díaz, *Libros y librerías en la Rioja altomedieval* (Logroño, 1979), p. 231 seems to favour Leire; E. P. Colbert, *The Martyrs of Cordoba* (Washington, 1962), pp. 186—92 prefers Siresa; J. Goñi Gaztambide, *Historia de los obispos de Pamplona* (2 vols, Pamplona, 1979), vol. I, pp. 67—71 rightly insists upon its independence of both.

[29] Eulogius, *Epistula*, III.2, Gil, p. 498.

[30] Collins, 'Poetry in ninth-century Spain', pp. 191—2 is too confident that the transmission was from Spain into France.

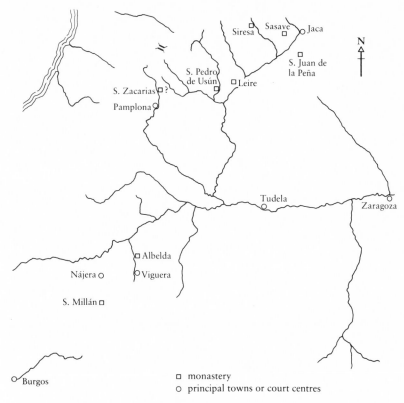

Map 19   Early monastic sites in the kingdom of Pamplona

found by Eulogius is now lost, and a later and extant manuscript of the work coming from the Abbey of St Martial at Limoges.[31] Medieval library lists from the latter also give other indications that some of its holdings were of Spanish derivation. A twelfth-century Limoges list includes *Ildefonsus Duos* and *Itinerarium Egerie Abbatisse*.[32] Both of these refer to Spanish texts. The former may indicate either two separate works or one work in two books — in both cases indicating that the widely disseminated *De Perpetua Virginitate Beatae Mariae Semper Virginis*, which is in three books, is not the work being referred to, or not

[31] Ibid., pp. 190—1.
[32] T. Gottleib, *Über mittelalterliche Bibliotheken* (Leipzig, 1890), nos 314 and 315; H. Duplès-Agier, *Chroniques de Saint Martial de Limoges* (Paris, 1874), pp. 323—7.

exclusively. It is more likely that what are being listed are the related texts, in one book apiece, the *De Cognitione Baptismi* and the *De Itinere Deserti* of Ildefonsus (Bishop of Toledo 657—67).[33] These two works are not otherwise recorded as having circulated outside Spain. Equally rare is the *Itinerarium* or travel narrative of the Spanish aristocratic lady pilgrim Egeria, both in its original form and in its condensed retelling by the late-seventh-century hermit Varleius of Bierzo.[34] A *Liber Baruc* in the same list, if implying a copy of the Latin version of the *Apocalypse of Baruch*, might also indicate a text of Spanish provenance.[35] Obviously these and other such texts might have arrived at a later date than the ninth century, as St Martial at Limoges became increasingly linked to the peninsula through the growth of the pilgrimage route to Santiago, but the manuscript connection between the Limoges Aldhelm and that known to have existed in the kingdom of Pamplona in 848 is telling. In addition there were tenth-century manuscripts in the Spanish 'Visigothic script' that reached the Abbey of St Martial of Limoges, and if scholars have generally looked for a place of origin for these further westwards, in the kingdom of León, this may be largely due to an unnecessarily pessimistic view of the intellectual resources of the kingdom of Pamplona, which the existence of the Eulogius corpus indicates to have been rich in manuscripts as early as the mid ninth century.[36] As for evidence of a flow in the opposite direction, from Aquitaine into Navarre, the Eulogius manuscripts may themselves provide it, though this cannot be proved one way or the other. Certainly, at the other end of the Pyrenees, Frankish control of the Spanish march in the first half of the ninth century had a profound effect on the libraries, the liturgy, the monastic practices and the script of Catalonia. Relations between the Franks and the Basques in the march in the western Pyrenees were never so cordial and the exercise of authority was much more short-lived, but some

[33] V. Blanco and J. Campos (eds), *San Ildefonso de Toledo* (Madrid, 1971), pp. 236—436; the two texts can be united to form a single work in two books.

[34] The *Itinerarium* is edited by P. Maraval, *Égérie, Journal de voyage* (Paris, 1982), *Sources Chrétiennes*, vol. 296, to which is appended the *Epistola* of Valerius, ed. M. C. Díaz y Díaz.

[35] M. R. James, 'Learning and literature till the death of Bede', in *The Cambridge Medieval History III: Germany and the Western Empire* (Cambridge, 1922), p. 494.

[36] A. Mundó, 'El codice parisinus latin 2036 y sus anadiduras hispanicas', *Hispania Sacra*, 5 (1952), pp. 67—78.

intellectual impact might be anticipated. Northern Aquitaine was itself a major centre of learning, but one of which all too little is now known and which is grossly under-represented in the corpus of surviving manuscripts.[37]

Obviously, such discussion of monasteries and their intellectual resources leads back once more to the question of the conversion of the Basques to Christianity. It must be admitted that all of those monasteries whose existence in the ninth century can be proved were situated on the eastern fringes of the Basque regions. One of them at least — Leire — may have owed its development to the patronage of the royal dynasty of Pamplona. An account of the translation to Leire of the relics of the two martyrs Nunilo and Alodis from Huesca, where they had been executed *c.* 842, which is preserved in two tenth-century manuscripts, records that the monastery had been founded by Oneca, the wife of King Iñigo Arista.[38] Both he and Queen Oneca, together with their grandson King Fortún Garcés, are held to have been buried there. The account of the translation has had doubt cast upon it on the grounds that its dating of the martyrdom to 842 and of the translation itself to 851 would contradict the implications on dating of Eulogius's contemporary description of the martyrdom.[39] Inexact as it may be on such points of detail, the early date of the manuscripts of the *Translatio* requires us to give it considerable credence. It represents at the very least what the monks of Leire thought about their foundation no more than 100 years later, and their claim to have a royal pantheon, not least that of a by then dispossessed royal dynasty, is not likely to have been fabricated.

Monasticism in general, though, looks from the limited evidence available, which consists of little more than the *Translatio* and the writings of or concerning Eulogius, to have been confined to the vicinity of Pamplona and the valley of the river Aragón and its tributaries. The latter area was probably more developed by reason of its greater proximity to the Ebro with its urban centres and entrenched Christian traditions. However, if it is correct to believe that, as the character of the

[37] M. Rouche, *L'Aquitaine des Wisigoths aux Arabes 418—781* (Paris, 1979), pp. 387—422.

[38] *Translatio Sanctorum Nunilonis et Alodiae*, in *Acta Sanctorum Mense Octubris*, vol. IX, pp. 645—6.

[39] E. P. Colbert, *The Martyrs of Cordoba* (Washington, 1962), p. 224.

earliest documents indicates, the writing of charters did not develop in the western Pyrenees before the second half of the tenth century, the very class of evidence that provides the unique proof of the existence and development of monastic houses in the rest of the peninsula under Christian rule is just unavailable for the Basque regions. Thus it is theoretically possible that monasteries did exist in northern and western Navarre and in Guipúzcoa and Vizcaya. The line of argument that sees Christianity only taking root in the Basque territories when the proliferation of documents establishes the existence of numerous monasteries is thus undermined.[40] Moreover, evidence on monastic institutions from the Basque areas to the north of the Pyrenees suggests that such an approach to the problem of the conversion is misguided. The Frankish monastic census of 817 recorded a small number of monasteries as existing in Gascony: Saramon, Simorre, Pesan, Fagito and St Sabinus.[41] All of these were located on the eastern extremities of ninth-century Gascony, in areas adjacent to Toulouse. However, as has been suggested, there is little reason to doubt that the Basques living north of the Pyrenees were fundamentally Christianized by the middle of the eighth century. The number and placing of monasteries thus does not seem to be a sure indicator of the progress of Christianity in Basque society.

If this type of argument be abandoned, it becomes all the harder to pin down the period in which the Basques to the south of the mountains were effectively Christianized. The late Visigothic period represents one distinct possibility in this respect. As in the case of the Basques of Gascony the argument *ex silentio* is a reasonably strong one: no source ever describes them as being pagans, and certainly by the ninth century this is a rather surprising omission if that is what they still were. Furthermore, there is some useful archaeological evidence for the Christian penetration of Basque-occupied zones in the seventh century. This comes in the form of cave churches and hermitages, which have been found in significant numbers in both the provinces of Santander and Alava, and the style of carving employed in some of them has led to a general date in the

[40] See above, p. 59.
[41] *Constitutio de Servitio Monasteriorum*, in J. P. Migne (ed.), *Patrologia Latina*, 97 (Paris, 1862), cc. 437—8.

A cave church, probably of late sixth- or seventh-century date, at Laño, Condado de Treviño, Alava

later Visigothic period being attributed to them all.[42] The monastic ambience in which such habitations would have fitted is also clearly related to that described in such literary texts as the *Life of St Aemilian* (*c.* 630) and the 'autobiographical' writings of the hermit Valerius of Bierzo (*fl. c.* 680). It is also reasonable to suspect that it was at this kind of level, and perhaps through the charismatic influence of locally established holy men, that Christianity began to penetrate Basque society, in a way little influenced by and unmeasurable in terms of formal ecclesiastical structures and institutions.[43] There seems to have been no amplification of the diocesan arrangement of these parts in the seventh century, and in the one that followed there was substantial dislocation.

The ecclesiastical organization of the southern Basque regions suffered some considerable upheaval as the result of the Arab

[42] Santander: J. González Echegaray, *Los Cántabros* (Madrid, 1966), pp. 236—7. Alava: Latxaga, *Iglesias rupuestres visigóticas en Alava* (Bilbao, 1976).

[43] A. Barbero and M. Vigil, *Sobre los orígenes sociales de la Reconquista* (Barcelona, 1974), pp. 188—90.

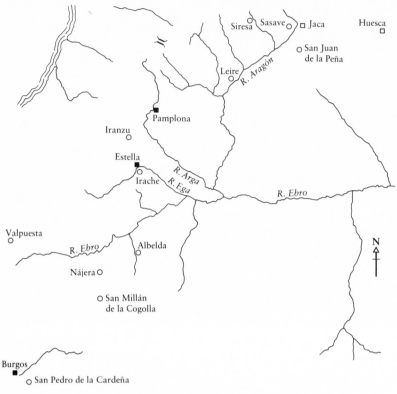

Map 20   Monasteries of Navarre and the Rioja in the ninth to eleventh centuries

conquest. Whether there was episcopal continuity preserved in Pamplona after 711 is entirely uncertain. Evidence of any sort is so scarce that bishops only make the slightest and most occasional of impressions in the sources. The consecration of a monastery church of San Pedro de Usún in the valley of Romanzado by a Bishop Opilano in 829 is the first reference to a bishop of Pamplona since 693.[44] The new monastery was some 5 km north-west of the site of Leire. After Opilano, Eulogius's friend Bishop Wiliesind is the next to feature, and after him only one other ninth-century bishop of Pamplona is known, in the person of a certain Jimeno, *c.* 880—90.[45] Even in

[44] J. Goñi Gaztambide, *Historia de los obispos de Pamplona*, vol. I, pp. 63—4.
[45] Ibid., vol. I, pp. 79—80.

the tenth century there are a number of problematic gaps, and an unbroken episcopal succession can only be recorded from 1005 on. Other sees lack even the possibility of continuity (see map 20). On the fringes of the Basque regions, neither Huesca nor Calahorra survived the Arab conquest. The former began its eventual return to its original site as a 'bishopric in exile' established in the monastery of Sasave in the mountains north-west of Jaca, though even so not until the early tenth century.[46] It was transferred to Jaca in 1063, and finally returned to Huesca in 1097.[47] There was no institutional continuity between the Visigothic see of Huesca and its eventual replacement at Sasave. Calahorra, which did not return to Christian rule until 1045, remained equally devoid of a resident bishop after 711. Nominal bishops of Calahorra may have continued to be consecrated and to have carried out their functions in the eastern extremities of the Asturian kingdom, in other words amongst the Basque subjects of that monarchy. In the reign of Alfonso II of the Asturias (791—842) both a Bishop Theodemir and a Bishop Recared of Calahorra feature amongst the signatories of royal charters.[48] The last of these is dated 812, and the two texts in which they appear may both be interpolated, if not total fabrications. It has been claimed that Armentia, outside the city of Vitoria in Alava, became the centre of the transferred see of Calahorra, but there is no contemporary evidence for this.[49] Likewise, it is generally believed that a new diocese was created in Alava in 804, based on the monastery of Valpuesta.[50] The two documents that record this foundation are, however, both highly suspicious, and it is notable that no further charters relating to the abbey survive from the whole of the ninth century. That such a monastery and episcopal see existed in 911 is sure, but its supposed previous history needs to be regarded with considerable scepticism. There are no grounds for believing that a bishopric was functioning at Bayonne, later to be the

[46] A. Ubieto Arteta, 'Las diócesis navarro-aragonesas durante los siglos IX y X', *Pirineos*, 10 (1954), pp. 179—99.

[47] A. Durán Gudiol (ed.), *Colección Diplomática de la Catedral de Huesca* (2 vols, Zaragoza, 1965), docs 27 (1063) and 64 (1097).

[48] *España Sagrada*, 33, ed. M. Risco (Madrid, 1781), pp. 173—7.

[49] A. E. de Mañaricua, *Obispados en Alava, Guipúzcoa y Vizcaya hasta la erección de la diócesis de Vitoria* (Vitoria, 1964) for discussion of these sees.

[50] L. Barrau-Dihigo (ed.), 'Chartes de l'Eglise de Valpuesta', *Revue Hispanique*, 7 (1900), docs 1 and 2 (both of 804).

Armentia: church of San Andrés (c.1181). Armentia is the site of a Roman town and the possible birthplace of the poet Prudentius

episcopal see for much of Guipúzcoa, before *c.* 980, and the evidential problems concerning the survival of the other dioceses of the northern edge of the Pyrenees have already been discussed.

Overall ecclesiastical organization in the Basque regions was clearly in a rudimentary state in the ninth century, and evidence for monasticism is limited and localized. Regrettably, material remains cannot help to balance the bleak picture drawn from the scanty historical sources. The earliest extant churches in the Basque regions cannot be dated earlier than the tenth century, with the exception of the cave churches of Alava. Against all of this is the fact that conversion does not feature as a problem in the texts relating to these areas, and Basque paganism, whatever forms it took, has left no traces of itself. The question of the Christianizing of the Basques has to remain an open one, in that no evidence exists to give a clear answer one way or another. For that matter an element of ambiguity may have existed at the time, for with the evident weaknesses of the structure of the church in the Basque regions in the eighth, ninth and early tenth centuries, it is hard to imagine how the religious life of the population was made to follow the norms of Christian practice standard in other parts of western Europe. Even if the Frankish impact on Pamplona had been sufficient to influence the local customs of its church, other Basque areas, notably in Alava, remained outside the Frankish cultural orbit. In those regions the liturgy and customs of the Visigothic church will have continued to be employed, just as Carolingian norms and their Rome-derived liturgy were applied in Gascony. The position in the kingdom of Pamplona remains uncertain at this time.[51] It cannot have failed to draw upon the traditions of the Visigothic past, but these may have been modified by a Frankish presence, however short-lived, that manifested itself at the time when the greatest period of ecclesiastical renewal was taking place in Francia itself. Thus in matters of church custom and liturgy the Basques were as divided as they were politically. At the same time conditions made it difficult for ecclesiastical oversight to make itself felt effectively in all areas of Basque occupation, and it is conceivable, if not provable, that pockets of heathenism survived. If the hold of Christianity was not total in the Basque regions south of the Pyrenees, this cannot have been the case in Pamplona, its hinterland, and the valley of the river Aragón. The latter area in particular is notable for the number of its monasteries that can trace their foundation back to the ninth century.

Aragón and Pamplona

A county was created in the region of the upper Aragón by the Franks as part of their ultimately unsuccessful bid to create a march in the western Pyrenees, perhaps at the time of Louis the Pious's visit to Pamplona in 813. Its first count was Aznar, probably to be identified with the man who was defeated together with Count Aeblus in the second battle of Roncesvalles

[51] It is conceivable that the fragments of a tenth- or eleventh-century Breviary, Cambridge University Library Add. MS 5905, comes from Navarre; the text is related to that of a group of southern French breviaries, and with Mozarabic 'symptoms'; its musical notation is Aquitanian, whilst its script and decoration is Visigothic.

in 824. Further information concerning him is found in the Navarrese genealogies, which, unusually, provide a brief narrative of an episode in his career.[52] This records how, as the result of some ill-judged mockery, Aznar's son Centolle was murdered by his own brother-in-law García, who then seized power in the county from Aznar himself. This García, known from his deeds as *el malo* or 'the Bad', then repudiated Aznar's daughter and married instead a daughter of Iñigo Arista, king of Pamplona, to whom he made formal submission (see the genealogy of Aragón and Pamplona presented earlier). A possible context for such a coup would be the aftermath of Aznar's defeat in 824, when both his own and Frankish power were in eclipse.

García may have had some claim to rule in his own right if his father, who can be identified from the genealogies as Galindi Belascotenes, is the same man as the Basque leader called Ibn Balaskut in Arabic sources, and who was forced to submit to the Umayyad amir Abd ar-Raḥmān I in 781.[53] A son of García is probably the Ibn Garsiya al-Sirtan reported by al-'Udri to have been the ally of Iñigo Arista *c.* 842—3.[54] The dispossessed count Aznar is said by the genealogies to have taken refuge with Charlemagne (d. 814), though this is chronologically impossible, and to have been invested instead with the counties of Cerdanya and Urgell in the Frankish march in the eastern Pyrenees. The same source records that his surviving son Galindo Asnari was subsequently able to recover his father's county of Aragón, thus dispossessing García the Bad or his heirs. It might be thought that here the genealogies are supported by charter evidence, as an Aragonese count Galindo features as signatory to a number of documents in the period 833—58, though in nearly all cases these texts must be adjudged to be spurious.[55] However, his existence and his return to power in Aragón need not necessarily be doubted. Nor was his restoration indicative of a change of political direction as far as the county was concerned. Its Frankish connections were not resumed, and Galindo's son

[52] Lacarra 'Textos navarros', section 19, p. 241.

[53] Ibid., p. 241 for Galindo; *Ajbar Machmua*, Lafuente, p. 105 for Ibn Velasco; see also Lévi-Provençal, *Histoire de l'Espagne Musulmane*, vol. I, p. 126, n. 1.

[54] Al-'Udri 30, de la Granja, 'La Marca Superior', p. 470.

[55] *Cartulario de San Juan de la Peña*, Ubieto, docs 2 (828), 3 (828), 5 (*c.* 850). No. 3 is certainly false; the editor is prepared to accept no. 2, but this is far too optimistic; no. 5 is probably reliable.

Aznar married Oneca the daughter of King García Iñíguez of Pamplona. A line of counts repetitively named Galindo and Aznar ruled the county for the next 100 years under the aegis of the kings of Pamplona until one of the latter, Sancho Garcés II (970—94), inherited both kingdom and county. A more thorough institutional absorption of the one by the other occurred in the reign of his grandson Sancho the Great (1004—35).

It might be questioned to what extent the Aragón valley could still be considered as a Basque area at this time. Its lower reaches, extending down to its confluence with the Ebro just south of Calahorra, had been in the hands of Muslim rulers since the Arab conquest, as had both Huesca and Jaca, the principal towns of its eastern end. The valley of its tributary, the Cidacos, provided the most direct line of communication between Pamplona and the stronghold of the Banu Qasi at Tudela. In general quite a cultural mix must have existed in the region by the end of the ninth century. However, there seems little reason to doubt the existence of a Basque-speaking rural population, barely encountered as it may be in our sources, not only along virtually the whole extent of the Cidacos valley but also throughout most of that of the Aragón as well. The easternmost frontiers of Pyrenean Vasconia are not easily defined with precision. Even in the time of Strabo it looks as if not all of the upper Aragón may have been included within the territory of the Vascones, and Huesca, the ancient Osca, was certainly a centre of Celt-Iberian cultural irradiation. But even at the end of the first millennium AD there still existed in some of the remoter valleys of the central Pyrenees local societies that displayed features of a social organization clearly non-Indo-European in origin and akin to that traditionally associated with the Basques.

A particularly interesting source for this is a document called the *Benasque Roll*, now preserved in the Archivo Historico Nacional in Madrid.[56] It is a form of cartulary in that, apart from one possible original sewn on to its opening, it is a copy in the form of a roll of a long set of documents, 70 in number, probably written in the twelfth century but recording original charters dated in the late tenth and the eleventh centuries, consisting mainly of deeds of sale. All of these texts relate to the

[56] Archivo Historico Nacional, Madrid, Sección de Códices 1048B: *Cartulario de Obarra*.

landholdings of a lady called Sanza and her two consecutive husbands in the valley of Benasque. The preservation of this remarkable set of records, unique in Spain for its period in containing so many texts relating to the property and activities of one small landholder, is the result of the estate being bequeathed to the Aragonese monastery of Obarra, where they were later enrolled and preserved in the archive. For present purposes perhaps the most interesting feature of these materials is the use of matronymics by the inhabitants of the Benasque valley who appear in the documents, particularly the priests who enscribed the texts.[57] Virtually all the persons named in the roll, the exceptions always being outsiders, were known by the name of their mothers. That this indicates a matrilineal pattern of inheritance is a reasonable surmise, which is supported by the overall role of Sanza herself in the documents and in her legal rights over the property that these indicate. Similar naming practices can be detected in one or two charters from equally remote regions on the western fringes of Catalonia, and they stand in clear distinction to the general use of patronymics in all documents from relatively more cosmopolitan areas such as the Aragón valley. These few texts seem to be the last indications of ancient social practices then on the verge of extinction. Whether they had been more widespread at a slightly earlier time cannot be determined, because of the lack of this kind of evidence in the western Pyrenees before the tenth century, and also because in other adjacent areas where a charter tradition was longer established the practice of including patronymics or any other form of surname was only introduced in the tenth century itself. However, patrilineal primogeniture looks to have been the norm in the royal and comital dynasties, and the older practices are likely to have died out in the towns centuries earlier, probably under Roman influence.

To speak of a royal line in the ninth-century kingdom of Pamplona begs certain questions. As has been suggested, the

---

[57] For example, the priest Oriolus son of Adulina in doc. 13, Centullo son of Nina in doc. 30, Oriollus son of Bella in doc. 34, Raimundus son of Onecha in doc. 36, the priest Ato son of Sancha in doc. 58, etc. However, it is important to note that faint traces of the use of matronymics and the matrilineal inheritance practices they imply have survived from other parts of early medieval Europe and amongst populations not associated with a pre-Indo-European descent; see D. Herlihy, *Medieval Households* (Cambridge, Mass., 1985), p. 47 and n. 123—5.

institution of monarchy had no antecedents in Basque society, and may therefore be considered as a cultural borrowing. Admitting that little may be known of the exact geographical extent of the kingdom at this time, it must be wondered upon what the authority of Iñigo Arista and his successors was based. Why were they accepted as having the power that they claimed in a society generally so localized and fragmentary in the distribution of its social units? Nothing is known of the earlier status of the family of Iñigo, and the absence of charters makes it impossible even to guess at the distribution of their land-holdings. Even Leire, the likely pantheon of the kings, was founded by relatives by marriage of the royal line. What was the basis of royal wealth? It is no easy task to create a monarchy. Firm economic and social roots are necessary to make it workable and acceptable. In the contemporary Asturian kingdom the pre-existing status and probably also the landed possessions of both Pelagius and, perhaps more significantly, Duke Peter of Cantabria provided the necessary starting point, but by the end of the eighth century an ideology, which also manifested itself in art and ceremonial, had been developed to justify and give authority to the monarchy in terms of its claimed continuity with the Visigothic kingdom that had once exercised power over the whole peninsula.[58] As direct heirs of the Visigothic kings the Asturian rulers could claim the rights and prerogatives of their predecessors. The monarchs of Pamplona had no such past to look back to. Their sole recognizable assets in the ninth century would appear to have been possession of the city of Pamplona, and a close family relationship and alliance with the powerful Banu Qasi, lords of Tudela and often of Zaragoza. Indeed the two dynasties look like Christian and Muslim mirror images of one another as local potentates with defined regional interests, possession of strongholds, and a military following whose needs dictated policy.[59] Both were dynasties of adventurers: the Banu Qasi justified themselves by recourse to a mythical Visigothic count Cassius, but the past of the Iñíguez is hidden.

---

[58] Sánchez-Albornoz, *Orígenes de la nacion espanola*, vol. II, pp. 623—39.
[59] C. Sánchez-Albornoz, 'El tercer rey de España', *Cuadernos de Historia de España*, 49/50 (1969), pp. 5—49 for the career of Mūsa ibn Mūsa, the greatest of the Banu Qasi.

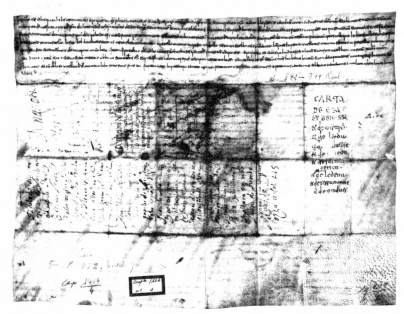

An early forgery (top) and its reverse side (below) from the collection of documents concerned with the monastery of Leire. It purports to record a series of grants made by successive kings from the time of Iñigo Arista (842) to that of García Sánchez I (944)

Control over Pamplona, however achieved, gave Iñigo and his heirs some automatic hold over its interland, but it is hard to believe that this extended far into the mountains north of the city. Likewise control from Pamplona of the western access routes of the Aragón valley made that region a natural dependency. To the south, though, the power and the family relationship with the Banu Qasi blocked the most natural route of expansion from Pamplona. How a monarchy could be created on such a basis of a single city, a single bishopric and a tiny extent of territory, with no clear historical antecedents, is hard to envisage. Some expertise was obviously required. For instance, how were the kings consecrated and by whom? There are indications that the abbots of the monasteries, already seen to be the centres of cultural sophistication in the region, played a role in government by meeting together in council — perhaps a version in miniature of the Toledan assemblies of the Visigothic church.[60] It is likely to have been from the resources of these houses that the intellectual materials were drawn to create and nurture the extraordinary idea of the tiny Pyrenean monarchy. To this should be added the probability of the continuing urban vitality of Pamplona, the centre of the kingdom, which had had to look after itself on its own resources since the fall of the Visigothic kingdom, if not longer, and from whose strong sense of identity that of the realm was derived. The Frankish recognition *c.* 800 that the Pampilonenses constituted a recognizable group separate from others is an important indicator of the citizens' self-awareness. Coupled with the ambitions of the Iñiguez, the combination produced a monarchy in microcosm, but on slender foundations.

Castille and the Jiménez dynasty

The Jiménez, the dynasty that replaced the line of Iñigo in 905, were more fortunately circumstanced and perhaps more adept at taking advantage of their opportunities. They could also build on their predecessors' work. How Fortún Garcés came to be the last of the Iñiguez kings is not known. According to the

[60] For example, the group of abbots and other clerics who were available at one time to act as witnesses for the resolution of the boundary dispute recorded in *Cartulario de San Juan de la Peña*, Ubieto, doc. 14 (928). For a similar gathering in 997, see A. J. Martín Duque (ed.), *Documentación Medieval de Leire* (Pamplona, 1983), doc. 13.

The second line of the kings of Pamplona and the counts of Castille

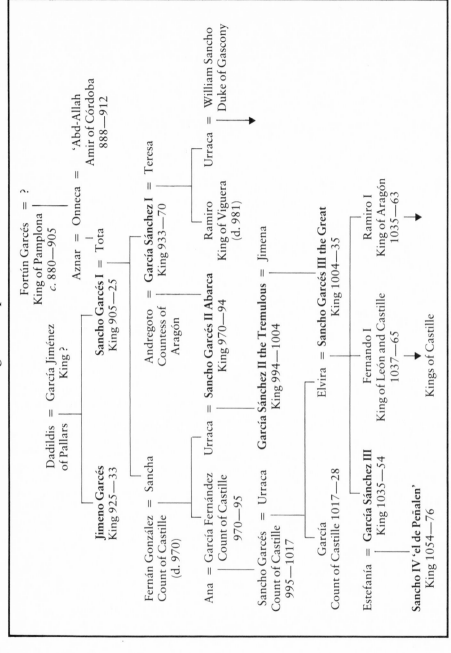

Navarrese genealogies he had four sons.[61] They may all have predeceased him, but he may have fallen victim to a coup. In later tradition he was known as Fortún the Monk and was held to have abdicated and retired into monastic life at Leire. The origins of the new dynasty that commenced with Sancho Garcés I (905—25) are disputed, as is their relationship to the Iñíguez line.[62] They might be the descendants of the shadowy King García Jiménez. Sancho Garcés I married his predecessor's granddaughter, a lady called Tota, who was later the effective ruler of the kingdom for much of the middle of the tenth century as regent for their son García (see accompanying genealogy). One piece of information in the genealogies may hint at the area of the family's power prior to its rise to the kingship: Sancho Garcés I's father had married the sister of Count Raymond of Pallars, on the western edge of Catalonia, and this could indicate that the family origins should be sought in the central Pyrenean regions.[63]

It would not be appropriate here to consider the subsequent history of the kingdom of Pamplona or Navarre in detail and reign by reign. However, certain features and episodes can be discussed with profit where they have a bearing on the particular relationship of the monarchy with the Basque element in its population. It was in the final phase of the reign of Sancho Garcés I that the kingdom made its first significant move in expanding itself southwards, and thus out of areas largely or even exclusively populated by Basque speakers. This was into the region of the Rioja, conceivably once an area of Basque occupation, but showing no evidence of continuity in this respect into the period after the Arab conquest. This expansion into territory previously dominated by the Banu Qasi was facilitated not only by the change of dynasty in Pamplona, but also by the virtual political extinction of the Banu Qasi themselves in 907, and a period of considerable internal weakness and instability in the Umayyad amirate in Córdoba.[64] This enabled Sancho Garcés in alliance with the Leonese monarch Ordoño II,

[61] Lacarra, 'Textos navarros', section 3, p. 230.

[62] Ubieto, 'La dinastía Jimena'; but see C. Sánchez-Albornoz, 'Otra vez los Jimenos de Navarra', *Cuadernos de Historia de España*, 33/34 (1961), pp. 314—26.

[63] Lacarra, 'Textos navarros', section 10, p. 234.

[64] Lévi-Provençal, *Histoire de l'Espagne Musulmane*, vol. I, pp. 329—97.

whose hold over Alava gave him interests in this direction, to make a major descent into the Ebro valley. Their initial thrust provoked an active response from Córdoba. The Amir Abd ar-Raḥmān III defeated the two kings in 923 and went on to sack Pamplona in the following year.[65] Little daunted, Sancho Garcés I resumed his offensive in the last year of his life, and took Nájera on the southern slope of the Ebro valley. This rapidly developed into an alternative capital for the monarchy and its preferred place of residence.

The growth of Navarrese interest in this newly acquired southern region was rapid, and monasteries such as San Millán de la Cogolla that were founded or restored in it became the beneficiaries of substantial royal patronage, and it is probable that Santesteban in the Rioja became the site of the pantheon of the new royal dynasty.[66] This geographical shift of the centre of balance in the kingdom, away from the areas of predominantly Basque population, also made of it a close neighbour of the developing frontier march of the kingdom of León in Castille. The latter's principal settlement of Burgos, founded in 884, was only some 80 km west of Nájera, and a period of weakness in the Leonese monarchy in the middle of the tenth century drew the counts of Castille increasingly into the political orbit of the Navarrese kings. Count Fernán González of Castille was the frequent ally, though not subject, of King García Sánchez of Pamplona-Nájera (931—70), and his daughter Urraca married the king's son and successor Sancho Garcés II (970—94).[67] All of this led both to an important revival of Christian intellectual culture in the Rioja and the monasteries of Castille, both of which may have benefited from the richness of Navarrese collections, and also, at a different social level, to substantial opportunities becoming available to Basques prepared to migrate to the new frontier areas.[68]

[65] A. Cañada Juste, *La campaña musulmana de Pamplona (año 924)* (Pamplona, 1976).

[66] A. Ubieto Arteta, 'Dónde estuvo el panteón de los primeros reyes pamploneses?', *Príncipe de Viana*, 19 (1958), pp. 267—77.

[67] For a detailed account see J. Pérez de Urbel, *Historia del Condado de Castilla* (3 vols, Madrid, 1945).

[68] For the MSS and monasteries of the region see Díaz y Díaz, *Libros y librerías*, especially pp. 27—164. Another major influence on these areas was that of the Mozarabic immigrants from Al-Andalus.

King Sancho Garcés II Abarca of Pamplona, flanked by his wife Urraca Fernández on the left and his brother Ramiro, king of Viguera, on the right, from the Codex Vigilano *of 976. Above them are portraits of the great royal legislators of the Visigothic kingdom, and below them are the three scribes of the manuscript*

The latter is a rather controversial question, in that it depends for its interpretation upon *a priori* assumptions concerning the extent of the prehistoric Basque settlement of the peninsula. If a widespread or even universal Basque occupation be accepted, along the lines suggested by the Vasco-Iberist linguistic argument, then it is possible to believe (as some do) that Basque settlements in the north of Castille, in the modern province of Burgos, represent continuity of occupation from pre-Roman times to the tenth century and beyond.[69] On the other hand a more modest view of the initial spread of the Basques makes it necessary to see them as new foundations of the period of the Christian reoccupation of these regions in the later ninth and the tenth centuries. Moreover, the evidence for the eclipse of Basque in Alava in the late Iron Age and Roman periods makes it hard to credit the survival of a Basque enclave further south and west in Castille.

That there were such Basque settlements in Castille in the tenth century is, fortunately, indisputable. The cartulary or *Becerro* of the important monastery of San Pedro de Cardeña, situated 10 km east of Burgos, records the foundation of one of them, called Villa Vascones, in 926.[70] This is now a deserted site between Cardeña and Burgos. Other documents in the same collection refer to it, and it is no surprise to find that all of its inhabitants who are named in the texts have such characteristic Basque names as Gazo Laztago, Galindo García, Fortún García, Belazo Manto and so on. Other Basque names appear frequently in the Cardeña records, including that of one of its abbots called Iñigo, and also in other Castillian charters.[71] A sizeable though not necessarily predominant Basque population in northern Castille in the tenth and eleventh centuries is indicated. This taken together with the crucial role played by Castille in the subsequent *reconquista* and the development of the modern Spanish state has enabled centralists in current political arguments to claim that Basque participation in such fundamental

---

[69] For Basque place-names in Castille see A. Herrero Alonso, *Voces de origen vasco en la geografía castellana* (Bilbao, 1977), and for the linguistic arguments, J. J.-B. Merino Urrutia, *La lengua vasca en la Rioja y Burgos*, 3rd edn (Logroño, 1978).

[70] L. Serrano (ed.), *Becerro gótico de San Pedro de Cardeña* (Valladolid, 1910), doc. 42.

[71] Ibid., docs 53, 54, 98, 100, 210, 211, 275 among others; L. Serrano (ed.), *Cartulario de San Pedro de Arlanza* (Madrid, 1925), docs 17, 18 among others; these are all tenth-century examples.

processes of national development being thus established deprives them of the right to demand autonomy on grounds of their cultural distinctiveness.[72]

What the particular contributions of the Basques to the repopulation of Castille and the forms of its ensuing social and legal organization might have been is not easy to tell, not least as the result of the lack of information of a comparative kind concerning the Basque regions proper. Certainly there were features of Castillian life that distinguished the region from its parent kingdom of León. For one thing its inhabitants generally enjoyed a much greater degree of personal freedom, and the earliest Spanish *fueros* or charters of immunity were granted by lords, such as its count, to settlers in Castille.[73] It is possible, though not proveable, that such distinctive features derived from Basque traditions. Certainly Castillian villages and small towns were largely self-governing under their own councils, however chosen, and these were involved in the adjudication in all legal cases involving the inhabitants, as well as representing and in a legal sense personifying the settlement in all negotiations that affected the whole body. Thus in 956 an agreement was reached and written down between the abbot and monks of Cardeña and named individuals constituting the *concilio* of Villa Vascones over the village's rights to water from the abbey's canal.[74] Such 'democratic' institutions do not have their counterparts in León and Galicia at this time, but are not dissimilar to the self-governing institutions found in Guipúzcoa and Vizcaya in later centuries, when the evidence for these provinces becomes fuller.

Guipúzcoa and Vizcaya were themselves being brought under measure of royal government at this time. A Momo, *comes Bizcahiensis*, appears in the Navarrese genealogies as the son-in-law of Sancho Garcés I, and is perhaps to be identified with the signatory of a document of 919; he died before 931.[75] The text in question is the record of the settlement of a legal dispute, contained in the cartulary of the abbey-see of Valpuesta, with a

---

[72] C. Sánchez-Albornoz, 'Trayectoria histórica de la nueva Vasconia', in his *Orígenes y destino de Navarra* (Barcelona, 1984), pp. 131—53.

[73] G. Martínez Díez, *Fueros locales en el territorio de la provincia de Burgos* (Burgos, 1982), pp. 11—24.

[74] Serrano, *Becerro de Cardeña*, doc. 54.

[75] Lacarra, 'Textos navarros', section 17, p. 238.

dating clause referring to one Monnio Vigilaz, count 'in Alava'.[76] If the two are identical, it would suggest that he held office over both Alava, which was longer developed, and the nucleus of the later province of Vizcaya. From the document of 919 it is clear that Monnio exercised authority over Alava in the name of the king of León. If he is also the Momo of the genealogies, the same must be true for Vizcaya. Contention and periodic conflict over the control of Alava and Vizcaya continued intermittently between the rulers of Pamplona and León, only finally achieving resolution in the late twelfth century. Of Guipúzcoa at this time there is still no word.

This period, which sees the first appearance of a count in Alava and probably Vizcaya, is marked by the proliferation of such office-holders in most parts of the Christian states of northern Spain; however, with the exception of Aragón, long established and of Frankish origin, this is not true of the Navarrese kingdom. Admittedly the charter evidence needed to detect the earliest appearance of such office-holders is lacking for these regions, and it is not even possible to detect the existence of a palatine or court nobility centred on Pamplona and Nájera. However when, in the first half of the eleventh century, the mists clear and the number of records starts to grow, what is revealed is the existence instead of a rather broader group of locally based potentates, not dignified by comital or vicecomital titles, as in León, Castille or France, but known as *seniores*.[77] This may in part reflect deliberate royal intentions to fragment provincial power rather than concentrate it in the hands of a more limited number of great office-holders, but it must also have been conditioned by the structure of Basque society, lacking any indigenous aristocracy of birth. The care taken to ensure the continuous tenure of family land, with little or no possibilities for intrusive lordship, together with the probably extremely limited resources of the monarchy, resulting from the particular circumstances and recentness of its creation, prevented the emergence of territorial lordships in most parts of the kingdom. It is notable that virtually all of the *seniores* are to

---

[76] Barrau-Dihigo, 'Chartes de l'Eglise de Valpuesta', doc. 12.

[77] Well illustrated in the signatory lists from a number of documents from Leire: Martín Duque, *Documentación medieval de Leire*, docs 15 (1014), 16 (1014), 17 (1015), 18 (1015), 23 (1032), 30 (1042), 31 (1042), 32 (1042), 33 (1043).

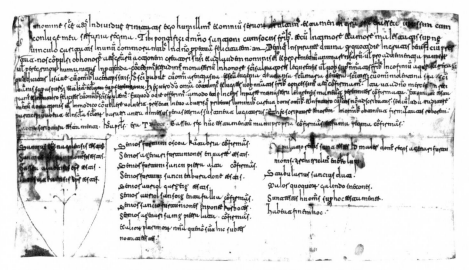

An early copy of a charter of King García III, 1052. Note the list of seniores
who witnessed the document

be found on the southern and western fringes of Navarre. This
was, of course, where the military needs were greatest, but it
also represented that part of the kingdom where the process of
conquest had given the monarchs the resources needed to create
marcher lordships. Although unrecorded, it is likely that such a
process began in the initial period of expansion in the tenth
century.

The duchy of Gascony

A somewhat different approach was adopted north of the
Pyrenees in the duchy of Gascony. After the brief chronicle
entry recording the removal of Duke Sigiwin in 816 evidential
darkness once again tends to descend upon Frankish Wasconia.
In the *Divisio Imperii* of 817 it was allotted, together with
Aquitaine, as part of the kingdom entrusted to the Emperor
Louis's son Pippin, but, for whatever reason, it receives no
specific mention in the revised *Divisio* of 831.[78] Thereafter, for

[78] *Divisio Imperii*, ed. A. Boretius, *MGH, Capitularia Regum Francorum* (Hanover,
1897), vol. I, no. 136.

The second line of the dukes of Gascony c. 864—1032

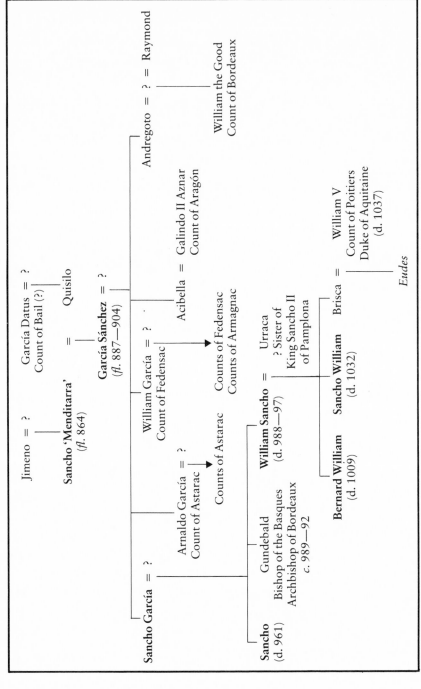

the next 200 years, much recourse has to be made to materials that are considerably later in date but which purport to recount the history of the region from the late ninth century onwards. These sources are in the form of monastic and cathedral cartularies, mostly written in the twelfth century. To add to the historian's problems, some of these are no longer extant, and it is necessary to use copies or extracts taken from them by antiquarians in the seventeenth and eighteenth centuries. Fortunately, this is not true of the one that is most valuable for immediate purposes, the twelfth-century Black Cartulary of the cathedral church of Auch, then archdiocese of most of Gascony.[79] The particular importance of this lies not only in a small number of early charters that it contains, but also in its record of the genealogies of the dukes of Gascony. To this can be added some additional or corroborative information from the handful of early charters preserved in other cartularies of the region, and from the genealogies composed at Nájera in Navarre in the tenth century.

On this basis a rough chronology and genealogy of the line of the hereditary dukes of Gascony can be drawn up as shown here. Of the origins of the family nothing is known for sure, though the foundation legend preserved in the Auch cartulary mesmerized historians of previous centuries. According to this a certain Jimeno García, third son of García Jimeno and Dadildis of Pallars, having been defeated by King Ordoño of the Asturias *c.* 850, was then made by his 'consul' (i.e. count) of Castille. This Jimeno had three sons: García became king of Pamplona; Roderic succeeded his father as count of Castille; and Sancho Jimeno 'Menditarra' (the Mountaineer) was summoned by the Basques north of the Pyrenees in 864 and was by them elected as duke. From him descended the ducal line that became extinct in 1032.[80] With the probable exception of the last statement, none of this is true. The story displays thematic similarities to the equally unhistorical foundation legend of the counts of Barcelona preserved in the *Gesta Comitum Barcinonensium*, which was elaborated in this same period of the late eleventh or early

[79] C. Lacave la Plagne Barris (ed.), *Cartulaires du Chapitre de l'Eglise Métropolitaine Sainte-Marie d'Auch* (Auch—Paris, 1899).
[80] Ibid., 'Cartulaire noire', doc. 2.

twelfth centuries.[81] There are some particularly interesting features: the Gascon legend displays knowledge of the Navarrese genealogies and a desire to relate the north Pyrenean ducal family to those of both the kings of Pamplona and the counts of Castille. The concern to seek an ultramontane origin for the ducal line, and implicitly to deny any role in the process to the Frankish kings, is also notable. The notion of election by the Basques is also stressed, though this is only in respect of the selection of the founder of the dynasty and not in the choosing of his successors. The name of Sancho Jimeno's unrelated predecessor, Arnaldus, may be a genuine historical memory but it would be unwise to rely upon it.

Ideologically fabricated and historically unsound as the foundation legend might be, the subsequent outline genealogy of the ducal family gives greater grounds for trust in that it can on occasion be corroborated from dated and reliable charters. Thus Sancho Jimeno's successor García Sánchez the Bent features in a document of 904, in which he is entitled, rather poetically, 'Comes et Marchio in limitibus Oceanis'.[82] The office of duke or *marchio* (warden of the march or marquess) was held concomitantly with that of count of Bordeaux by all of the ruling members of the family. Such offices and titles were all of Frankish royal creation, and there seems little reason to doubt that the first member of the line, Sancho Jimeno Menditarra, owed his place, as had his predecessors, to Frankish royal appointment. The conversion of the duchy and county into hereditary possessions of his family rather than offices held at pleasure at the probable time of his activity, that is to say c. 880, fits well into a wider pattern of such transformations carried out by act of royal policy at just this period. The creation of hereditary lines of counts in Carcassonne and Barcelona was effected at the very end of the reign of Charles the Bald (840—77).[83] Similar developments occurred elsewhere in the Frankish kingdoms both then and in the course of succeeding decades.

[81] R. Collins, 'Charles the Bald and Wifred the Hairy', in *Charles the Bald: Court and Kingdom*, eds M. T. Gibson and J. Nelson (Oxford, 1981), pp. 169—89, for a synopsis of the Catalan foundation legend.

[82] *Gallia Christiana*, vol. I, ed. D. Sammarthani (Paris, 1715), *Instrumenta Ecclesiae Ausciensis*, doc. 23, p. 170; he is probably also to be identified with the 'Garcie Sanz (regnante) in Gallias' of a document (somewhat suspicious) of 893: *Cartulario de San Juan de la Peña*, Ubieto, doc. 7.

[83] R. Collins, 'Charles the Bald and Wifred the Hairy', pp. 176—7.

The monastery of Saint Sever in south-west Gascony

Gascony was thus not out of step with other parts of Francia.

The successors of Sancho Menditarra are little more than names, but the genealogical and charter evidence does show that, from the third generation on, younger sons of the ducal line were appointed to newly created comital and vicecomital offices, which in turn they passed on to their own descendants.[84] In the course of the tenth century the family of the dukes seem to have created the aristocracy of Gascony single handed and exclusively from their own lineage. On what resources this was based it is hard to say. Each branch thus established required to be endowed with the landed basis necessary to support their new status. Gascony was potentially more urbanized than the Basque regions south of the Pyrenees, which at this time could

---

[84] The genealogies of the various lines are worked out in J. de Jaurgain, *La Vasconie* (2 vols, Pau, 1898—1902), vol. II, pp. 2—173.

boast of no settlement other than Pamplona worthy of being called a town. On the other hand, in Gascony there were town sites of considerable antiquity such as Dax and Bordeaux which, whatever diminution they had suffered in previous centuries, could still function as centres of population and of some economic activity. These became the focal points of the new counties and viscounties that took their names from them. It is also possible that some foundation of new settlements and reclamation of waste and virgin land may also have occurred. The movement of population then taking place south of the Pyrenees into the frontier areas of Castille could have had its parallel north of the mountains in intensified land use in Gascony.

Some of the new wealth thus created, at least for the leaders of society, manifested itself in increased patronage of the church. A steady and increasing flow of endowment of cathedral churches and monasteries gets under way in the later tenth century. The first major monastery in south-west Gascony was founded at Saint-Sever on the Adour by Duke William Sancho *c.* 982, and the same period saw the transformation of what may have been an itinerant bishopric amongst the montagnard Basques into a fixed see at Bayonne (*c.* 980) as well as the re-emergence of dioceses centred upon Agen, Bazas, Aire, Dax, Oloron, and Lescar. In the years *c.* 977—89 these were all held in plurality by Duke William Sancho's brother Gumbald, but on his translation to Bordeaux in 989 new incumbents were found for each.[85] Bayonne, the site of the former Roman fort of Lapurdum, may well have been abandoned for the previous half millennium, but it developed in the course of the next two centuries into a major city and trading port. Further east, the cartularies of Auch and of the monasteries of Pessan and Simorre show evidence of the increasing benevolence of the ducal family and its branches in the course of the tenth century; though some of the charters on which such a view is based have probably been interpolated. Duke William Sancho was responsible for the foundation of St Vincent de Luco in the diocese of

[85] St Sever charter: *Gallia Christiana*, vol. I, Sammarthani, *Instrumenta ad Ecclesiam Adurnensem*, doc. 1, pp. 181—2. On the foundation of Bayonne see P. Narbaitz, 'La cristianización del País Vasco francés', in *I Semana de Estudios de historia ecclesiástica del País Vasco* (Vitoria, 1981), pp. 43—68.

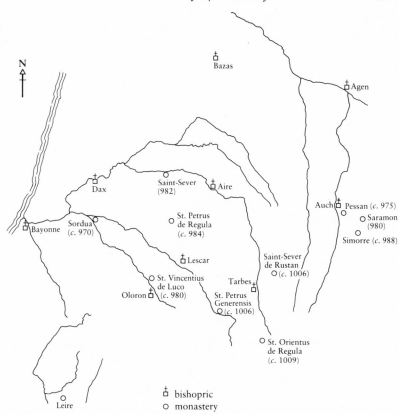

Map 21   Bishoprics and monasteries of southern Gascony in the late tenth century

Oloron (*c.* 980), whose first abbot was a member of his family, and the duke was also a patron of the monastery of Sordua in the diocese of Dax (*c.* 970). His relative Count William of Astarac carried out the restorations of Pessan (*c.* 975) and Simorre (*c.* 988).[86] The monastery of Saramon, apparently functioning in 817, was refounded in 980 by Oddo, son of Arnald count of Astarac of the ducal line.[87] There were also less

---

[86] Extracts from the lost cartularies of southern Gascony are preserved in L.-C. de Brugèles, *Chroniques ecclésiastiques du Diocèse d'Auch* (Toulouse, 1746): Cartulary of Pessan, pp. 34—9; Simorre, pp. 180—247. See also H. Stein, *Bibliographie génerale des Cartulaires français* (Paris, 1907).

[87] Copied from lost original in the monastery archives by de Brugèles, *Chroniques*, pp. 44—5.

An illumination from the Commentary on the Apocalypse *of Beatus of Liébana, illustrated in the Gascon monastery of Saint Sever c.1050—1070. This is the only MS of this work that was produced outside Spain*

socially exalted founders and benefactors, such as Bernard Luseus, who established the monastery of St Orientius *in suburbio* of the town of Auch.[88] This also indicates the growth of a section of Auch detached from the archiepiscopal *burgus*, the original nucleus of the city (see map 21).

Both south and north of the Pyrenees significant changes were clearly taking place as the first Christian millennium drew to its close. New political structures had come into being, the church was at last expanding its institutional hold on society, and in some areas at least urban life was starting to reassert itself. The last factor, especially in Gascony, may have marked the beginning of the slow contraction of the areas of the predominance of the Basque language, which probably reached its apogee in the eighth to tenth centuries, but whose gradual decline was to be more or less constant thereafter. Divergences of interest, culture and dialect had long existed amongst the various groupings of the Basques, and the developments of these centuries had done little to alter this; indeed the creation of a more rigid political framework for society and the making of frontiers only intensified them. However, for one brief and never to be repeated period all of the Basques were to be united under a single authority.

[88] Now lost; copied from the archives by ibid., pp. 47—8. The cult of St Orientius was a trans-Pyrenean one, linking the diocese of Auch to the Ebro valley; see *Gallia Christiana*, vol. I, cc. 973—4.

6

The Old and the New
in the Eleventh Century

The expansion of Navarre

The opening decades of the eleventh century saw the kingdom of Pamplona or Navarre achieve its greatest physical extension, in the process bringing the entire Basque-speaking population, not only south but also north of the Pyrenees, within its compass. This in itself was by no means the aim of the kings ruling in Pamplona and Nájera: the notion of a Basque state would be as anachronistic in this period as in the preceding centuries. Basque unity as far as outsiders was concerned was merely a function of their being the speakers of a common language, which was also markedly different to those in use in the areas contiguous to the western Pyrenees. For the Basques themselves, no sense of racial, linguistic or cultural unity seems to have existed that could prove itself greater than their own internal divisions and apparent looseness of social structure at anything beyond the level of the extended family. This internal divisiveness was intensified by political separations imposed upon them from without, but these were only accentuating features: the real divisions seem to have lain within Basque society. For this reason the emergence of a kingdom which in practice embraced all of them, ruled by a monarch of Basque origin who may well have been a speaker of their language, was not to have any impact on their self-awareness or aspirations. This expansion of the power and territorial limits of Navarre was achieved in the last years of Sancho Garcés III, known as the Great (1004—35), and it was not so much at the expense of

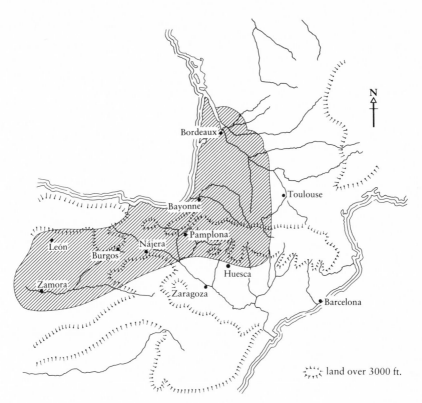

N

land over 3000 ft.

Map 22 The kingdom of Sancho the Great at its fullest extent c. 1032—1033

the remaining Muslim lords in the Ebro valley as at that of the kingdom's Christian neighbours (see map 22).[1] In the 1020s Sancho extended his authority across the Pyrenees, occupying recently restored Bayonne and the Basque lands at least south of the Adour if not the Garonne. The dukes of Gascony, who had become relatives by marriage of the Navarrese royal house in the late tenth century, were periodic attenders at his court, as on at least one occasion was Count Berengar Ramón I of Barcelona.[2] In the same period the Basque coastal regions of Vizcaya as well

[1] For the career of this monarch see in general J. Pérez de Urbel, *Sancho el Mayor de Navarra* (Pamplona, 1950).

[2] William Sancho II, duke of Gascony *c.* 961—97, married Urraca, daughter of García Sánchez I of Pamplona *c.* 972: J. de Jaurgain, *La Vasconie* (2 vols, Pau, 1898—1902), vol. II, pp. 11—12.

as Guipúzcoa passed from Leonese to Navarrese control, and the dynasty's earlier matrimonial alliances proved their worth when the county of Castille was inherited by Sancho on the death of the last count in 1028. The final stage of this rapid expansion occurred in 1030, when Sancho, disputing the succession, invaded the kingdom of León and overran most of it, leaving its last independent king, Vermudo III, with only Galicia. By the time of his death in 1035 he was, with some justification, entitling himself *rex Hispaniarum*, 'king of the Spains'.[3]

In itself this would warn us that in the eleventh century, no more than in the ninth and tenth, was this monarchy self-consciously Basque, despite the origins of the dynasty. The bulk of the population of Navarre, Vizcaya, Guipúzcoa, Alava and the territories across the Pyrenees, together with a significant percentage of that of Aragón and Castille, may safely be assumed to have been Basque speakers at this time, but, with the exception of one mid-eleventh-century charter, this could not be detected in the official records. All legal and administrative documents were drawn up in Latin. At the same time, the earliest evidence of the vernacular Romance speech that was to develop into Spanish dates from this period, and is testified to by some glosses in a manuscript written in the Riojan monastery of San Millán de la Cogolla.[4] These show some slight traces of Basque influence, but this region was probably already outside the area in which that language predominated.[5] Castillian, or Spanish Romance, had a remarkable future ahead of it in the Middle Ages, as a medium in which was to develop an extensive literature in both prose and verse. Basque, on the other hand, did not. It cannot even be called a literary language before the fifteenth century, at which point a small group of poems were written in Basque.[6] Even this proved to be something of a false start, as it was to have no representation in the 'Golden Age' of

[3] *Cartulario de San Millán de la Cogolla*, ed. A. Ubieto Arteta (Valencia, 1976), doc. 193 (1030).

[4] Full colour facsimile of the text in J. B. Olarte (ed.), *Las glosas emilianenses* (Madrid, 1977); see also R. Menéndez-Pidal, *Orígenes del Español*, 3rd edn (Madrid, 1950), pp. 1—9.

[5] R. Wright, *Late Latin and Early Romance* (Liverpool, 1982), p. 205.

[6] Texts in J. C. de Guerra, *Oñacinos y Gamboinos* (San Sebastián, 1930), quoted in J. A. García de Cortázar et al., *Introducción a la historia medieval de Alava, Guipúzcoa y Vizcaya en sus textos* (San Sebastián, 1979), text 45, pp. 146—8.

Spanish literature in the sixteenth and seventeenth centuries. At this time printed texts in Basque were confined to a small number of translations, mostly of catechisms and devotional works, and original composition in the language was not to be resumed until the nineteenth century.[7] This is not to deny the probable existence of an oral culture that expressed itself in songs, ballads and stories, but this never made its mark in print and has effectively failed to survive.

Obviously Basque presented particular problems as a potential literary language. It was incomprehensible beyond the circle of its own speakers, and the nature of earlier Basque society had been such that the language lacked a range of vocabulary in a number of key areas, particularly in relation to the conventions of courtly and urban life. This has always remained a problem, to which in the nineteenth century a response was made in the form of the invention of a large number of jarring and overly learned neologisms, many of which are now being replaced by more sympathetically constructed alternatives. Such problems are not unique to Basque, and some other relatively small and culturally distinctive medieval societies did produce a distinguished literature. The best example of this is probably Wales, where a tradition of vernacular poetry flourished under the patronage of both court and church.[8] This, however, is the main point of distinction. Neither Latin culture nor urban society was established in Wales, especially the north, in the course of the Roman period. On the other hand, as has been seen, the end of Roman rule over the Basque regions was followed by a phase of antagonism and mutual hostility between the Latinized town dwellers and the upland tribes, who surrounded them. The kingdom of Pamplona may have been essentially the creation of the descendants of the former group, and earlier attitudes continued to exist as far as language was concerned. The early charters of the Basque regions, both north and south of the Pyrenees, when required to record a toponym in its traditional or non-Latin form, either for reasons of greater clarity or because no alternative existed, always use such a

[7] J. Haritschelhar, 'La creation littéraire, orale et écrite', in his *Être Basque* (Toulouse, 1983), pp. 267—309.

[8] See the papers collected in I. Williams, *The Beginnings of Welsh Poetry*, 2nd edn, ed. R. Bromwich (Cardiff, 1980).

phrase as *rustico dictu* or 'in peasant speech'. Basque was the language of rural farmers and pastoralists, not of upper-class society in town and court. This is not necessarily to imply that the leaders of that society were unable to speak Basque. Evidence from later in the Middle Ages indicates that their equivalents in that period probably did.[9] But Basque was not regarded as appropriate for administrative or literary purposes, for which Latin and in due course a Latinate vernacular were available, the use of which stretched back 1000 years to the period of Roman rule.

This makes it difficult to speak of the Navarrese kingdom as being a Basque one, in that the language was consciously rejected as a vehicle for high culture. This was not helped by the Basques' lack of a dominating sense of their own racial identity. Judging by the present state of the numerous dialects, the language was probably uniformly comprehended, despite the varieties of local form, by all speakers. However, the dialectal range that can now be measured in a language spoken by such a relatively small population and in such a limited geographical area is evidence of the intense localization of Basque society in previous centuries, a phenomenon accentuated by geographical features breaking the region down into components sometimes no larger than an individual valley. Today dialects are recognized for each of the four Spanish and three French provinces containing Basque-speaking population, with the valley of Roncal having a separate one of its own; the subdivisions were probably once more extensive.[10] Linguistic divergences mirror a strong sense of distinction based upon local allegiance, which may be rooted in antiquity. The separation of Vizcaya and Guipúzcoa is clear from their very first emergence in the sources, and the Navarrese and (Basque-speaking) Gascons are always distinguished. The author of the early-twelfth-century guide for pilgrims travelling to the shrine of St James at Compostela comments on the identity of language but separateness of identity of these groups.[11] Even more localized patriotisms

---

[9] See below, p. 256.

[10] R. M. de Azkue, *Diccionario Vasco-Español-Francés* (2 vols, Bilbao, 1969), pp. xxviii—xxx, for the distribution of the various dialects at the beginning of this century, when the dictionary was first compiled (1902).

[11] J. Vielliard (ed.), *Le guide du pélerin de Saint-Jacques de Compostelle* (Macon, 1938), pp. 28—33.

doubtless existed, but these do not make a mark in the early evidence. In addition, the limitations of native institutions of government and the lack of indigenous traditions in high culture, notably art and literature, left court and town society in Navarre peculiarly open to penetration by cultural influences from outside, principally from France.[12] This in due course accentuated the sense of distinction between Navarre and the other regions in which Basque customs remained more firmly entrenched.

The lack of an overriding sense of common identity and of identification between the monarchy, looking to older traditions of Roman and Visigothic Hispania and influenced by newer procedural and cultural ones from beyond the Pyrenees, and the bulk of its subject population, proved a source of weakness to both. On the death of Sancho the Great his augmented realm was split up into its component parts and divided between his sons. One of them, Fernando, took Castille and within two years had overthrown the restored Vermudo III and taken his kingdom. A separate monarchy emerged in Aragón under his brother Ramiro, and a truncated Navarre, inherited by a third brother García III, was rapidly overshadowed by both the Leonese-Castillian and the Aragonese kingdoms.[13] With the Aragonese conquests of Huesca (1096) and Zaragoza (1118), the main potential route of expansion open to Navarre, in other words down the Ebro valley, was effectively cut. In the twelfth century the rising power of Castille brought Alava, Vizcaya and most of Guipúzcoa into the hands of its kings, detaching these western Basque regions from the control of Navarre. Likewise, from the mid eleventh century on the rise of the dukes of Aquitaine, and subsequently the Angevin kings of England, confined Navarrese interests north of the Pyrenees to a tiny area centred on St Jean Pied de Port, which came to be known as Basse-Navarre. Bayonne was once more briefly occupied, captured in 1122 by Alfonso I the Battler, who had reunited the Navarrese and Aragonese kingdoms, but his successors were unable to retain it. Thus, hemmed in on all sides by increasingly powerful neighbours, Navarre became the smallest of the

[12] See below, p. 256.
[13] But see J. M. Lacarra, 'El lento predominio de Castilla', *Revista Portuguesa de Historia*, 16 (1978), pp. 63—81.

Muslim cavalry sculpted on a twelfth-century capital in the former royal palace at Estella, Navarre

peninsula monarchies; and, as before the days of Sancho the Great, the Basques once more found themselves subjects of at least three separate monarchies.

Abbot and landowner in the eleventh century

The eleventh century provides the first clear evidence of the workings of Basque society and its economy since the days of Strabo. Indeed, this is the very first period in which the Basques can be said to speak for themselves. Information comes in the form of charters, which, beginning as a trickle in the late tenth century, steadily grow in range and volume as the next 100 years unfold. Such materials have their problems, both at a general level in terms of interpretation and technically in terms of authentication. The retarded development of the use of charters in the regions of Navarre and Aragón, let alone Guipúzcoa and Vizcaya, in which they are significantly out of step with the rest of the Christian north of the peninsula and with Catalonia, had important consequences. There are very few early charters, something that is not just due to the accidents of survival; moreover, when they do start to appear in reasonable numbers, an unusually high proportion of them can be shown to have been forged or interpolated at a date later than that claimed in their texts. Thus, of the two principal monastic houses established in these regions in the early period of the kingdom of Pamplona, no more than one of the charters of Leire dating to before the turn of the millennium is authentic, and, although this is not fully accepted, most of the documents of San Juan de la Peña from this time are equally flawed.[14] In the eleventh century the position is considerably improved, though unsound texts still abound. The relative profusion of forgeries amongst Navarrese and Aragonese texts is unique in the Spanish context. Although scribal errors are frequent, mendacious and interpolated charters are rarely to be encountered in Leonese, Castillian and Catalan collections. Galicia is notable for a small number of quite notorious forgeries, but its major collections are generally reliable.[15] The causes of this descrepancy are easily understood: the lack of early charters in the western Pyrenees meant that, subsequently, monasteries, cathedral churches and other clerical and lay landowners found it expedient to have charters fabricated. From the eleventh century on they were living in an age in which a documentary record was the best proof of title to property, and in which the procedures of the legal system operated on that basis.[16] Thus, if

---

[14] For these collections see A. J. Martín Duque (ed.), *Documentación medieval de Leire* (Pamplona, 1983), especially docs 1—14; and *Cartulario de San Juan de la Peña*, ed. A Ubieto Arteta (2 vols, Valencia, 1962), especially docs 1—32.

[15] The forgeries are those associated with the promotion of the cult of Santiago; see T. D. Kendrick, *St James in Spain* (London, 1960), chs I—III.

[16] R. Collins, '*Sicut lex Gothorum continet:* law and charters in ninth- and tenth-century León and Catalonia', *English Historical Review*, 100 (1985), pp. 489—512.

they lacked a charter proving their rights to some possession, it was advisable to obtain one, even if this meant having one drawn up that had to claim an antiquity or an authority that it actually lacked. In general the forgers sought to express what they believed to be the truth about property rights and possession in the pre-documentary age; anything too flagrant could usually be disproved by witnesses. Even some quite extraordinary claims, such as that of the monks of Leire to exemption from episcopal oversight on the grounds that their abbots had anciently always held the office of bishop of Pamplona in plurality, could develop out of misguided antiquarianism, as well as an eye to the main chance.[17]

Such problems aside, the growth in the numbers of charters relating to the Basque areas south of the Pyrenees, and in which, for example, Guipúzcoa makes its first appearance by name, provides much necessary evidence for such things as the formation of monastic estates, land use, prices and forms of exchange, as well as patterns of settlement. In quantity they are still considerably fewer than those available for such studies relating to the other parts of Christian Spain, and the evidence is also highly localized. The texts come almost exclusively from the fringes of the Basque regions, and principally from the Aragonese frontier with the Islamic powers in the Ebro valley, from the south of Navarre, where the kingdom had expanded to the Ebro, from the Rioja and Alava, and from those parts of Vizcaya that confronted Cantabria. Hardly any texts refer to northern Navarre, Guipúzcoa and the Pyrenean valleys. This is unlikely to be accidental. Those areas had long been occupied by the Basques, conceivably for millennia, and thus provided limited opportunities for new exploitation. Any movement of population had to be outwards towards the periphery, where new settlement was taking place in the tenth to twelfth centuries, just as it had in the seventh and eighth. Tenacity of family holdings, and perhaps the existence of traditional forms of sale and exchange to which the possession of documents were alien, have meant that no charters of any form now exist relating to these central areas from this period. It is also clear that monastic landholdings in such regions were surprisingly few.

[17] J. Goñi Gaztambide, *Historia de los obispos de Pamplona* (2 vols, Pamplona, 1979), vol. I, pp. 441—54.

(Opposite) The monastery of San Juan de la Peña, Aragón

The eleventh-century crypt under the abbey church of the monastery of Leire, Navarre

All of the major monasteries of the southern Basque regions developed in the frontier areas in the tenth and eleventh centuries. San Juan de la Peña, Leire, Irache, Iranzu, Santa María de Nájera and Valpuesta all conform to this pattern (see map 20).[18] In part this was a reflection of their founders' and benefactors' interests in such regions, where not only was land relatively plentiful, but also the monasteries could be expected to play an important role in the development and administration of newly conquered or repopulated territories. However, it is notable that such houses, once established, subsequently acquired hardly any property by sale or benefaction in the western Pyrenean heartlands; nor did any significant monastery come into existence in these regions. The only exceptions to this were urban monasteries, such as San Telmo in San Sebastián, that were created in the newly developed towns of the Biscay coast in the later medieval centuries, and the Augustinian house at Roncesvalles patronized by King Sancho the Strong of Navarre (d. 1234), which grew from the needs of pilgrims on the route to Santiago.[19] The existence of one or two small monasteries in the Pyrenees and inland Guipúzcoa can be detected from the documents, but they never developed, and in most cases cannot be traced subsequently. This contrasts markedly in volume and distribution with the proliferation of monasteries of varying size and significance that can be found all over western Alava in the same period of the tenth to twelfth centuries. Whilst important as a feature in its own right, and having a bearing on social conventions and landownership in the western Pyrenees, this has inevitably limited the amount of information available that concerns those regions, and makes necessary a somewhat disproportionate concentration of attention on the frontier and peripheral areas of the Basque regions.

One rather complicated story, drawn from a charter, does shed a little light upon what has been hitherto the darkest of the component parts of Vasconia, the future province of Guipúzcoa. At some point before 1035 a certain Sancho entered San Juan de la Peña as a monk, and he put under the control of the

[18] See the collections cited in note 14, and J. M. Lacarra (ed.), *Colección diplomática de Irache* (2 vols, Zaragoza, 1965); and for Nájera see the eighteenth-century transcript of its cartulary, Madrid, Archivo Historico Nacional, sección de códices, 105B.

[19] For the hospital at Roncesvalles see Goñi, *Historia de los obispos de Pamplona*, vol. I, pp. 358—62, with references.

*Roncesvalles: the church of the Augustinian monastery and pilgrim hospital,
burial place of King Sancho the Strong of Navarre, c.1230*

monastery a church, dedicated to St Euphemia, which he had built at Biniés in Aragón, in the modern provice of Jaca. At some time a little later, a lady called Galga *ex regione Ippuzka* asked Abbot Paternus of San Juan to send Sancho to her in Guipúzcoa, and once there he was put in charge of the monastery of San Salvador *de Ippuzka* by King Sancho the Great. On the strength of that, Sancho arrogated to himself the title of abbot, and tried to transfer authority over St Euphemia at Biniés, the monastery he had founded, away from San Juan and back to himself in his new capacity as head of San Salvador. Not surprisingly, San Juan de la Peña objected, but Sancho now had the backing of Galga's daughter Blasquita and her husband Sancho Fertungonio, and it was not until 1049 that a compromise was reached whereby it was agreed that they would retain control of St Euphemia for the rest of their joint lives, but on their deaths it would revert to San Juan.[20]

As well as providing the first documentary reference to the region of Guipúzcoa, this text is interesting in other respects. For one thing the property-owning rights of women are made quite clear by it: in both stages of these events the ladies Galga and Blasquita emerge as the dominant parties, and the compromise agreement on the usufruct of St Euphemia is drawn up in the name of the latter. The implication of the document is that San Salvador *de Ippuzka*, the first monastery recorded in Guipúzcoa, though its site is not now known, was founded by the lady Galga or her family. She certainly possessed another monastery, Santiago de Luquedeng 'in Pamplona', which she bequeathed to San Juan de la Peña in 1048, and which had been given to her by her parents and brothers.[21] Equally interesting is the apparent relationship, across the breadth of the Basque regions, between an area in Aragón and an unspecified part of Guipúzcoa. The document describing the ensuing dispute of 1049 makes it clear that Galga had asked specifically for the monk Sancho by name, and it is tempting to wonder if a family relationship did not exist between her and another Blasquita, whose nephew and heir had a legal quarrel with San Juan de la Peña over property in Biniés *c.* 1042.[22] It is also noteworthy

[20] Cartulario de San Juan de la Peña, Ubieto, doc. 98.
[21] Ibid., doc. 96.
[22] Ibid., doc. 79.

that, in this and other instances recorded in charters from the Basque regions, inheritance by nephews is a very common feature; this is a classic symptom of a society following matrilineal inheritance customs. Property is thus passed not from mother to son, and thereby out of the custody of the original lineage and into that of the father, but rather from a mother to the son of her eldest brother, retaining it within the family.[23]

The episode of Galga and the monk Sancho is also symptomatic of a wider, though short-lived, development in the same period. This was the attempt, under royal patronage, to promote monastic reform in the kingdom of Navarre. In 1025 King Sancho the Great had sent Abbot Paternus, Galga's correspondent, to the great Burgundian monastery of Cluny, to imbibe of the reformed monastic customs that were being promoted there, and, on his return, to introduce them into San Juan de la Peña.[24] From San Juan the Cluniac reforms were to be disseminated to other houses in the kingdom. Galga's appeal and King Sancho's appointment of the monk Sancho to San Salvador *de Ippuzka* may have been part of the same process. It is also likely to be found behind the small number of donations of Guipuzcoan monasteries and other property to San Juan de la Peña that feature in a number of documents of the 1040s and 1050s. Thus, *c.* 1053 a monk called Sancho gave his monastery 'that is called Arezeta, that is to say St Michael' in Bergara to San Juan, together with fields and orchards in two villages and all his herds.[25] Another such donation, made in 1055, of the monastery of Ollazabal, in the vicinity of Azpeitia in Guipúzcoa, by the *senior* García Azenáriz and his wife Gayla is particularly interesting for its linguistic content.[26] It contains the only piece of written Basque dating from before the fifteenth century. After a standard and formulaic opening in Latin, to the effect that García and Gayla were donating their monastery in Ollazabal and all of its possessions, and that they had determined the boundaries of its lands, it proceeds, as is normal with such charters, to describe them: 'Gaharraga Orer urte Alvizt urre,

---

[23] For example, C. Lévi-Strauss, 'Social structures of central and eastern Brazil', in his *Structural Anthropology* (English trans., London, 1963), pp. 120—31.

[24] A. Linage Conde, *Los orígenes del monacato benedictino en la península ibérica* (3 vols, León, 1973), vol. II, pp. 887—913.

[25] *Cartulario de San Juan de la Peña*, Ubieto, doc. 108.

[26] Ibid., doc. 117.

super Lascurende, alia parte inferiorem vel de Ainarte, de Areiz nabar sub Arzagicorin usque vera sibia in finem manzaneto de senior Garcia Azenariz, haralarre Heziza zaval, alia Hezi caray cum arrandari Sanzoiz, manzaneto de Ugarte Zuhaz nabar cum ossavio de medio manzaneto, ipsos tradimus.'

This is an extraordinary mixture of Basque and Latin that cannot easily be persuaded to make sense. Generically, the nearest equivalent to this unique text are those Anglo-Saxon charters which open and conclude with Latin formulae but put the intermediate passages, describing the bounds of lands being sold or donated, into the vernacular.[27] In such cases it is likely that the scribes either used a formulary, or understood that solemn Latin phraseology was necessary to make such documents look suitably formal, but left the crucial delineation of the property being disposed of in the native speech because this is what the owners of the land and/or the necessary witnesses to the transfer would have understood. There was thus less risk of ambiguity, when such texts had immediate practical importance in a society in which Latin was a learned language and its Romance forms not the normal speech. Something similar must have underlain this Guipuzcoan charter, but here it takes the form of a clumsy mixing of the two languages. Latin was used for the conjunctive phrases and to provide the overall structure, but Basque was employed to describe the vital boundary markers as well as for personal names. Not all of it can be translated, possibly as the result of scribal errors that arose in the making of the twelfth- and thirteenth-century copies of the original, the only form in which this text now survives, by non-Basque-speaking notaries. Some words seem clear enough, and fit the context of the description, as with *urre* (near), *nabar* (dark or grey) and *zabal* (large).[28] It is possible that more such bilingual charters once existed, but this is the last of the series of Guipuzcoan documents preserved in the San Juan de la Peña archives, and a substantial lacuna exists in the documentary record of the Biscay regions between the mid eleventh century and the later Middle Ages. In addition, the disproportionately heavy loss of archival materials from these areas in recent times,

---

[27] For example, *Charters of Rochester*, ed. A. Campbell (London, 1973), docs 26 (868) and 31 (995).

[28] de Azkue, *Diccionario*, vol. II, pp. 68, 375, 398—9.

Map 23   Vizcaya and the charter of 1053

as the results of both war and accident, has made the historian's task all the harder, and such lucky survivals as these texts preserved in Aragón all the more to be appreciated.

Another of these documents, dating to 1053, relates to Vizcaya, which, although attached to the kingdom of León in the tenth century, had become part of the much expanded Navarrese realm during the reign of Sancho the Great. It records the gift of estates made by one Enneco (Iñigo) López and his wife Tota Ortiz to the monastery of San Juan de la Peña and its abbot, Zianno.[29] The properties given are all in the region of Bermeo, on the Vizcayan coast north of Guernica. This deed of gift was combined with another donation, made at the same time by one Lope Garzéiz de Arratia. Both were made 'in the presence of all of the *seniores* of Vizcaya', who were its 'sureties, hearers and corroborators' — in other words, witnesses who could testify to it should the gift ever subsequently be challenged in court. The appended list of names — 'Sancio Ortiz de Auleztia, Sancio Garzeiz de Vellela, Sancio Nunasoz de

[29] *Cartulario de San Juan de la Peña*, Ubieto, doc. 107.

Garaunna, Didaco Munnicoiz, abba Monio de Mungia, Munnio Ezteriz, Munnio Gideriz, Mome Azenariz, Sancio Azanariz, Lope Sancoiz, Sancius Sansoiz, Lope Gidavoziz' — apart from testifying to the popularity of the name Sancho at this time, gives some evidence of the upper echelons of the social structure of mid-eleventh-century Vizcaya. It is also the only such evidence. Twelve men are named in this list of *seniores*, to which should doubtless also be added the two donors whose gifts were being witnessed. Of this 14, four are given an epithet by being described in terms of a place-name, and one being a donor the other three are placed first in the list of witnesses. Both of these features would seem to indicate special prominence on their part. One of the *seniores* is an abbot, probably of Munguía, situated inland from Bermeo and almost in the centre of the large promontory that divides the estuaries of the rivers Arratia and Mundaca (see map 23). He is almost certainly to be identified with the *Mome Munchiensis abba* who witnessed a charter of 1051 in favour of Bishop García of Alava, made by the same Iñigo López and his wife Tota, who are the donors in the San Juan document.[30] The 1051 text has additional relevance in that it reveals that Iñigo and Tota were of comital rank. In the charter the donor merely refers to himself as *senior*, but both King García III in confirming the gift and the Bishop of Nájera in witnessing it entitle him 'count'. This document was drawn up in Alava and relates exclusively to property in that region, so it is no surprise that the other Vizcayan *seniores* do not feature in it. The gathering of the latter in 1053 at a place called Tuga, and at which the king was not present, looks like some form of council, as it is otherwise hard to understand why so many men of local influence should have so conveniently forgathered to be able to witness the charter. Not all of the locations referred to can now be identified, but the centre of Sancho Ortiz's seigneurie at Auleztia is likely to be the modern Aulestia, ten kilometres east of Guernica.

The dearth of such charter material makes it impossible to say how much property any of these *seniores* might have

---

[30] Twelfth-century copy of lost original, in archive of Cathedral of Calahorra, given by I. Rodríguez de Lama, *Colección diplomática medieval de la Rioja* (3 vols, Logroño, 1976), vol. II, doc. 10; see, for a later reference, *Cartulario de Albelda*, ed. A. Ubieto Arteta (Zaragoza, 1981), doc. 43 (1061).

owned, let alone how it was distributed. Collectively, though, they can be regarded as the leading men of the region, holding some measure of governmental authority in it. It is possible that royal power had played a role in this region, as in the Ebro valley, in building up the seigneuries, but the Vizcayan *seniores* do not appear to have been frequenters of the court, unlike their Riojan and southern Navarrese equivalents, who featured regularly as signatories of royal charters. Nor may there have been any substantial royal landholding in Vizcaya, where the role of the principal official, the count, is distinctly underplayed. But for the Alavan charter of 1051, the existence of a count in Vizcaya at this time would have gone undetected.

Royal interest was closely involved in the building up of the position of dynasties of office-holders able to act as the local representatives of the monarchy in the provision of justice, maintenance of order, and oversight of the collection of various dues owing to the king. These dues were probably initially limited to revenues from royal estates, as there is no evidence for taxation either on land or on persons. When it does appear it comes principally in the form of duties on goods brought into royal towns. Therefore royal interest and the making of profit tended in the tenth and eleventh centuries to be concentrated on the newly acquired territories on the southern fringes of the Navarrese and Castillian kingdoms, where land and loot were to be obtained. The king's rights to these were tempered by the need to use such resources to pay for the military support that made such conquests possible. On the other hand the patronage and ties of mutual dependence thus created gave the monarchy such economic and military power as it possessed.[31]

As well as on the frontiers, the kings, and under them the counts and *seniores*, also had opportunities for extending their authority and their resources by the development of hitherto deserted or unappropriated areas of land. The sea coast of southern Biscay looks to be one region that attracted attention in this way in the eleventh century, as testified to by the Guipuzcoan documents from San Juan, and also the cartulary of Santa María del Puerto, which became a dependency of

[31] For the political history of this period see J. M. Lacarra, *Historia política del reino de Navarra desde sus orígenes hasta su incorporación en Castilla* (3 vols, Pamplona, 1972—3), vol. I.

Nájera in 1052. Much of the Pyrenees and the inland areas of the central Basque regions were long divided up into family holdings, or in some cases lands were owned communally, but the coastal zones seem to have been previously little used for agricultural and pastoral purposes, and they were therefore open to new exploitation. There would also generally have been areas of ambiguous ownership, where individuals and groups had traditionally pastured their flocks but without acquiring a legally recognizable title to the land. This would be a consequence of the late development of the charter in the Basque regions. Thus they were in no position to make an effective challenge if the king were to make a grant of the land to someone else. It is likely that the introduction of charters and written title to property created a period of considerable confusion and the opportunities for the unscrupulous annexation of land by the more powerful.[32] To this oral testimony as to long possession could be offered as a counter, but social pressure and a tendency to favour documentary title could outweigh older traditions when a dispute was brought to court. Such considerations may underlie the royal charter granted to Santa María del Puerto, which laid down drastic penalties against those who pastured their flocks on its lands without the abbot's consent.[33] This could well be a case in which an artificial and newly created piece of landholding cut across traditional rights. It is also notable that a number of monasteries found it necessary to include as much of the earlier history of an estate as they knew of when drawing up their first charter of ownership.

Whilst such new creation might cut across older rights and patterns of landholding, the new settlements, estates and monasteries, particularly in freshly conquered frontier territories, all required population to inhabit, work and defend them. Here those prepared to migrate to such areas or to move into settlements that lords wished to establish were in a strong bargaining position. The lack of a servile class in Basque society meant that all of the available manpower was of free status. At the same time the practice of passing the whole of a family

[32] For a case illustrating the advantage a ruler, here the count of Castille, could obtain from intervening in a legal dispute, and the need by the weaker party for his support, see J. del Alamo (ed.), *Colección diplomática de San Salvador de Oña* (2 vols, Madrid, 1950), vol. I, doc. 3 (944).

[33] See below, p. 204.

inheritance to one selected heir rather than dividing it up meant that there was a substantial reserve of manpower, not firmly attached to family property in the central Basque areas, which was able to take advantage of the expanding opportunities on the frontiers and newly developed areas. The Basques thus classically produced a surplus of 'younger sons', some of whom remained in a subordinate but free capacity in the family household, but others of whom were ready to export themselves to create their own fortunes elsewhere. This had been behind the creation of Gascony, and in the same way the Basques were to play a large and distinguished part in the expansion overseas to both North and South America from the sixteenth to the nineteenth century.

Royal charters and patterns of settlement

The agreements made between kings or lesser lords and their prospective settlers are the documents known as *fueros*. In form these began as simple charters in which the lord guaranteed certain rights and privileges to the inhabitants of a newly created settlement. In due course the size and complexity of such grants increased, as did the societies for which they were intended. Some of the later urban *fueros* could fill a book. However, in their earliest form, as charters of immunity, they are much simpler, and generally do little more than stipulate the inhabitants' freedom from outside judicial interference and lay down a tariff of monetary compensation to be paid for homicides and injuries. Of the latter some went to the victim or his family, but in many cases the lord also received a percentage by way of a fine. The earliest set of *fueros* now extant is that granted to the Castillian town of Castrojériz in 974.[34] In present form they consist of 16 original clauses, together with a preface, followed by another clause added subsequently by the original grantor, Count García Fernández of Castille; two more from his son and successor; then, jumping almost a century, two more on the part of King Alfonso VI of León-Castille; two more from Alfonso I the Battler of Aragón, briefly ruler of Castille; and

[34] G. Martínez Díez, *Fueros locales en el territorio de la Provincia de Burgos* (Burgos, 1982), pp. 119—22.

finally another four clauses added by Alfonso VII (d. 1157). Thus, as now preserved, the *fueros* date from the mid twelfth rather than the late tenth century. However, they have at least been organized in such a way as to make it possible to separate the different historical layers, and there are no grounds for doubting that the first 16 clauses do represent the original grant of 974. In other cases, though, where extant *fueros* claim to be no more than confirmation of earlier ones, it is not possible to be sure that the text has not been interpolated, and in some cases such 'confirmations' can be shown to be fictitious, and entirely untrustworthy as evidence for the earlier stages of a town's history.

The granting of *fueros* became a practice that was widespread throughout the whole of the Iberian peninsula in the Middle Ages, but it is tempting to speculate that the underlying principles may be traceable back to the conventions of Basque society. This may seem paradoxical in that the central Basque regions were amongst the last to receive *fueros* in written form. On the other hand, these are the only areas in which it is possible to show that customary law once existed. Elsewhere in Christian-ruled Spain and amongst the Christian communities of Al-Andalus the principles and procedures of the Visigothic law code, the Forum Iudicum, were consistently applied from the seventh to the eleventh centuries.[35] It is also significant that the *fueros* and the concessions which they embody first appear in Castille, at the time it was thoroughly penetrated by Basque settlers and under the influence of the kingdom of Navarre. Comparable conditions existed in other frontier zones between the Christian and Muslim powers, such as in Galicia and southern León, but these do not feature as areas producing the earliest grants of foral law.

Regrettably the earliest sets of *fueros*, with their particular concentration on immunities and judicial exemptions, give little evidence of the nature of the economy in the Basque-occupied regions; also, their distribution is somewhat erratic. Both Castille and Alava are well represented in the corpus of known early examples of such texts, whilst Guipúzcoa and Vizcaya only

---

[35] R. Collins, 'Visigothic law and regional custom in the settlement of disputes in early medieval Spain', in W. Davies and P. Fouracre (eds), *The Settlement of Disputes in Early Medieval Europe* (Cambridge, 1986), pp. 85—104.

start to appear later, when new towns begin proliferating in the two provinces.[36] Navarre displays peculiar features of its own, which will be examined later. Thus it is once again to charters that recourse must be made for evidence concerning the economic life of the central Basque areas south of the Pyrenees. In general, deeds of donation and sale tend to use formulae to indicate that all forms of land and its cultivation are being included within the act represented by the document. Thus such a text might read that the donor or vendor was disposing of the estate named X 'with all its fields, vineyards, woods, pastures and streams', intending thereby to indicate an all-embracing title. However, when additional specifications are added to such formulae, which are not otherwise found in the general corpus of Spanish and southern French charters, it looks as if local peculiarities are being carefully catered for, to ensure that there should be no legal loopholes left in the drafting of the documents. Thus, in charters from the coastal region of the Basque areas north of the Pyrenees, such all-embracing formulae generally include the term *landes*.[37] This is a late Latin word for moorland or, as in this case, areas of uncultivatable sand and couch grass, such as those giving the French province of Les Landes, just north of the Adour, its name. References to *landes* are not found in the charters of the Basque regions south of the Pyrenees, where such terrain does not exist. What is distinctive of documents from many of those areas are the large numbers of references to orchards: *mazanares* and *pomares*.[38] This generally accompanies a lack of mention of vineyards. The same features may be found in some of the charters from further west in Cantabria and the Asturias, but not other parts of Spain. The reasonable deduction, confirmed by modern practices, is that the Basques of Guipúzcoa and Vizcaya, like the Asturians, were cider rather than wine drinkers. Navarre, on the contrary, particularly in the Ebro valley, is, like Alava, a land of vineyards.

Another notable feature of the documents is the frequency of references to *ganatum* or livestock, specially distinguished in the body of the text, but rarely giving details of numbers or specific

---

[36] For the early fueros of Alava see G. Martínez Díez, *Alava Medieval* (2 vols, Vitoria, 1974), vol. I, pp. 217—88. Earliest text is 1140.

[37] For example, the foundation charter of Saint Sever: *Gallia Christiana*, vol. I, ed. D. Sammarthani (Paris, 1715); *Instrumenta Ecclesiae Adurensis*, 1 c. 182.

[38] For example, *Cartulario de San Juan de la Peña*, Ubieto, doc. 108 (*c.* 1053).

The survival of pastoralism: goats at Ruente

types of animal. The prominence of *ganatum* is also a feature of the Castillian texts of the twelfth century onwards, but Castille has long been recognized as the principal focus of pastoralism in the whole of the peninsula, and the region in which transhumance came to be practised on a large scale and whose social and political institutions were profoundly affected by it.[39] But it should not be forgotten that the Basque regions were noted for their pastoral economy, ever since the first references to it were made by the classical geographers. The terrain in the Pyrenees and the Biscayan provinces is very different to that of the expansive and open plains of Castille, so the scale on which

[39] C. Wickham, 'Pastoralism and underdevelopment in the early Middle Ages', *Settimane di Studi sull'Alto Medioevo*, 31 (Spoleto, 1985), pp. 445—6.

pastoralism was practised varied substantially between the two.[40] Long-distance movement of herds and flocks was much more difficult in the more mountainous and heavily wooded Basque regions, where the problems of acquiring additional grazing land on which to pasture herds were also great.

Such difficulties could lead to conflict. A charter from the monastery of Santa María del Puerto at Santoña, on the very easternmost fringe of Cantabria, provides an example.[41] The monastery, which had been flourishing in the ninth century, was abandoned for reasons that are unknown in the course of the next 100 years, but it was resettled by an Abbot Paternus in *c.* 1040. Initially welcomed by the local landowners, the *seniores terrae*, by whom he was elevated to the abbacy, he rapidly forfeited their support by his attempts to recover property that had belonged to the monastery in the ninth century by taking his neighbours to court. Hearing that they were planning to eject him and his monks, he went to King García III of Navarre and placed his monastery 'in the hands of the king', who in 1042 granted him and his successors a remarkable charter of immunity. Amongst other things, this contains a quite unprecedented decree that if anyone were to bring cows or pigs to pasture on the monastery's lands without the consent of the abbot they should be killed; no one should hold a judicial enquiry into their deaths, and it should be accounted no homicide. This is an extraordinary concession to make, and it is remarkable that the king felt himself to have the authority to allow one group of his subjects to kill others with legal impunity. At the very least it must indicate the seriousness of the problem to which so savage a measure was held to be the necessary remedy. The monastery for its part looks to have been anxious to preserve its pasturage for its own exclusive use, whilst pasturing by outsiders irrespective of property rights was sufficiently frequent for the monks to need to take steps to prevent it. This document is also indicative of the ways in which the kings, whose own position in these regions was severely circumscribed by local customs and a lack of a large stake in the

[40] D. A. Gómez-Ibañez, *The Western Pyrenees* (Oxford, 1975), pp. 1—39; R. Pastor de Togneri, 'La lana en Castilla y León antes de la organización de la Mesta', *Moneda y Crédito*, 112 (1970), pp. 47—55.

[41] Preserved in the eighteenth-century transcript of the cartulary of Santa María de Nájera, Madrid, Archivo Historico Nacional, sección de códices, 105B, ff. 38r—39r.

Abbot Asnar's charter, c.1046

land, could play an increasingly important role. By being able to provide remedies and defences, however drastic, the monarchy could offer an attraction to landowners, notably ecclesiastical ones, not otherwise able to defend themselves.

There are clear indications that the rearing of livestock — sheep in the Pyrenees and cows and pigs in the Biscayan regions — retained a central place in the Basque economy, and at the same time presented problems both of order and of land-hunger. The latter also provided opportunities for the expansion of royal authority over societies previously unused to monar-chical power. The physical extension of the Leonese and Navarrese kingdoms, either at the expense of their Muslim neighbours or in the recolonization of such depopulated regions as the Duero valley and much of northern Castille, gave their monarchs ways of increasing their influence on the more traditionalist communities of the central Basque regions. This can be illustrated by an example from Navarre, taken from a charter in the collection belonging to the monastery of Leire.[42]

[42] Madrid, Archivo Historico Nacional, sección de clero: carpeta 1404, doc. 5.

In an unusually full and circumstantial account of how he had acquired his property, a monk called Aznar, in making a donation of it to Leire in 1046, recorded how a great-uncle of his, the Abbot Galindo *clericus ac magister* to King Sancho Abarca (i.e. Sancho Garcés II), had asked the monarch for 'the mountain which in rustic speech is called Ataburu'. In return he had given the king 'two very beautiful sheep and a huge bull of the finest quality'. *Mons* or 'mountain' does not here imply a vast pile of rock, but is generally used in such charters to signify uncultivatable upland — in other words, land suitable for summer pasturage in the traditional Basque pastoral cycle.[43] As Abbot Galindo used his new estate to found and endow a monastery, it is likely that that is just what he wanted his 'mountain' for. Remote and rocky retreats may be very suitable for hermits, but functioning monastic communities require a sound economic footing. In the conditions of the Pyrenees this means herds as well as fields, and herds need summer pasture.

The monastery and its property was passed by Abbot Galindo to a nephew called Sancho Gentiles, selected by him from a range of possible heirs, and in due course Sancho did the same in bequeathing it to Aznar. Galindo as *clericus* and then abbot may well have had no heirs of the body, but Sancho is said to have selected Aznar out of a range of 'sons and daughters and other relatives'. Likewise at a later stage Aznar was chosen by a woman called Tota Fortuniones 'from amongst her heirs' to receive half of her property. Here again there look to be traces of matrilineal inheritance procedures, by this stage giving way to the more common inheritance through primogeniture. Aznar, having obtained the abbacy and the property that accompanied it, was able to develop and expand his holdings. As he himself put it, he was like the good and faithful servant to whom two talents had been given and who was able to return them to his Lord together with two more, thereby also meriting his admission to heaven! By the time of his drawing up this charter in 1046 his property consisted of buildings and land in a number of different localities (see map 24). The location of the *mons* of Ataburu and the site of the monastery there that Abbot Galindo had named Larresoin is not certain: it has been thought to be in the valley of Yerri, on the skirts of the mountains north of

[43] Wickham, 'Pastoralism and underdevelopment', pp. 439—40.

Map 24   Abbot Aznar and his property in 1046

Estella, but the lack of any other territorial acquisition in that area is perhaps reason for doubt. An alternative location might be in the vicinity of the village of Larrasoana in the Arga valley, around which Aznar was to build up his most substantial property holdings.[44] But otherwise, with the exception of one estate, the *monasteriolus* of Antulla, which an old cleric presented to Aznar and his monastery of St Augustine of Larresoin, all of the other properties can be located. In terms of distance the geographical distribution of the monatery's holdings was over an area no greater than 50 to 60 km wide, but this covered

[44] For Larresoin see C. E. Corona Baratech, *Toponomía navarra en la edad media* (Huesca, 1947), p. 77, and Goñi, *Historia de los obispos de Pamplona*, vol. I, pp. 183—4; the document has been misdated by reason of a scribal error, which would make it seem to have been written in 1006: J. Goñi Gaztambide, *Catálogo del Becerro antiguo y del Becerro menor de Leyre* (Pamplona, 1963), no. 27.

two distinct regions: the heartland of the kingdom around Pamplona and up the Arga valley, and the newly developed territories in the region of Estella, itself only a tiny settlement before 1090.

As well as this distinction, another should be made between the upland and the lowland estates. Of the latter Badostain, just south-east of Pamplona, is the most striking. Here Aznar had purchased a *domus* or manor house, together with a cellar, accompanied by fields and vineyards, as well as its farmyard *(curtis)* and granary *(horreo)*. He expanded his holdings here by further purchases of fields *(agros)* and vineyards. For one of the latter the price paid was a horse. The granary alone would suggest that this was envisaged as an agricultural enterprise, though a reference to *terras* could imply not only fields for cultivation but also lands suitable for winter pasture for herds. The upland properties that Aznar acquired by inheritance, purchase or, in one instance, by gift from the king give no indications of having been able to support arable farming, and may in some cases have served exclusively as granges for summer pasturing. In what figures in the charter almost as a kind of postscript, Aznar disposed of his livestock as well as his lands. He commanded that his 'fourfooted beasts . . . horses, cows, sheep and pigs' be divided equally, half going to Larresoin and half to the 6 sisters of Assitur'. This codicil, together with a later royal grant that links both Larresoin and Assitur, raises the possibility of the existence of a double monastery, but there is insufficient evidence relating to Assitur to be certain. The making of a distinct specification for the bequest of the livestock is notable; this is something also found in Guipuzcoan charters. In the circumstances of most other societies of western Europe herds might be expected to be disposed of together with the lands on which they were being reared, but in a transhumant pastoral economy they would move from holding to holding over a wide area, and might indeed be in movement at the time of their owner's demise and not on any of his lands.

Amongst other revealing details in this charter is the phrase used to describe how the 'old cleric' put himself and his monastery of Antulla in submission to Aznar and Larresoin: 'He commended himself between my hands.' This is the language and these are the procedures of vassalage, here making their

earliest appearances in sources for the Basque regions south of
the Pyrenees. By this time such practices were long established
in France, where the earliest recorded oath of vassalage is
reported in the *Royal Frankish Annals* under the year 757.[45] In
general the would-be vassal made himself his intended lord's
'man' by kneeling before him and placing his hands between the
lord's, whilst swearing an oath of fidelity to him. This created
ties of dependence, but also of mutual obligation. In its most
developed form such commendation became related to a grant
by the lord to his vassal of a fief (Latin *feudum* — hence
'feudalism') or estate in return for various services, generally of
a military nature. The classic French forms of vassalage and
feudalism, with their distinctive practices and terminology,
were slow in making an impact upon the Iberian peninsula
other than in Catalonia.[46] Their appearance in this document of
1046 is particularly striking in that such submissions of one
monastery to another or of a monk to an abbot were long
known in Spain, but were normally recorded in the form of a
legally enforceable charter of donation. This text of Aznar's
deed of gift to Leire thus combines within itself evidence both of
the anciently established economic and inheritance practices of
Basque society and of new ways of thinking and forms of social
organization that were starting to make themselves felt in
Navarre in the early eleventh century. Such practices, borrowed
from across the Pyrenees, were starting to make an increasing
impact on this society, so located geographically as to be
vulnerable to invasion and to the currents of cultural influences
from without and yet in many respects so impervious to change.
French ideas and French practices served the interests of the
kings of Navarre, still developing their role in a society to which
the institution they represented was alien. Frequent charter
references at this period to the king and *suos varones*, 'his men',
suggest how such ties of dependence through vassalage were
being promoted in the upper echelons of society, and this is
matched by the appearance of titles such as *pincernarius* (butler,

[45] *Annales Regni Francorum*, ed. F. Kurze, *MGH, Scriptores Rerum Germanicorum*
(Hanover, 1895), p. 14.

[46] See in general H. Grassotti, *Las Instituciones Feudo-Vasalláticas en León y Castilla*
(2 vols, Spoleto, 1969); L. G. de Valdeavellano, 'Las instituciones feudales en España',
in his *El Feudalismo hispánico y otrol estudios de historia medieval* (Barcelona, 1981),
pp. 63—162.

stabularius (groom) and *maiordomus* (major-domo) granted to members of the palatine nobility, all of which had Frankish antecedents.[47] So too at this time were the kings looking outwards for French help in reforming and 'modernizing' the Church in their domain. Cultural borrowings may have come first, but personnel followed soon after, and by the early twelfth century some of the Basque regions south of the Pyrenees were not only being opened up to new ideas and practices but also receiving a veritable migration of new population from the north.

[47] For example, A. J. Martín Duque (ed.), *Documentación medieval de Leire* (Pamplona, 1983), docs 31 and 32 (1042), and regularly thereafter; *Cartulario de San Millán de la Cogolla*, Ubieto, doc. 171 (1020).

7

Forces of Change

The French in Navarre

It was not only French ideas and institutions, and even French forms of writing, that were making themselves increasingly felt in eleventh-century Navarre, but also growing numbers of Frenchmen. They came in two ways and for two purposes. The first was as pilgrims, *en route* to the rapidly developing shrine of St James at Santiago de Compostela (see map 25). Although the greatest expansion of this cult may be associated with the period of Archbishop Diego Gelmírez in the first half of the twelfth century, it was certainly attracting its devotees, willing to make the long and arduous journey to Galicia, as early as the mid tenth century. This opened up a two-way channel of communications, as evidenced by the manuscript of St Ildefonsus of Toledo's *De Perpetua Virginitate*, written by the scribe Gomesanus and possibly in the Riojan monastery of Albelda in 951 for the Frankish bishop Godescalc of Le Puy, who visited the region on his way to Compostela and then collected the completed manuscript from its scribe on his route home.[1] Obviously, Navarre was no more than a point of passage for such pilgrims, and one not highly thought of by at least some of the travellers. The twelfth-century pilgrims' guide describes the Navarrese as being uncouth, barbarous in speech and much given to bestiality.[2] The standard route from western France

[1] M. C. Díaz y Díaz, *Libros y liberías en la Rioja Altomedieval* (Logroño, 1979), pp. 57—60.

[2] J. Vielliard (ed.), *Le guide du pèlerin de Saint-Jacques de Compostelle* (Macon, 1938), pp. 26—31.

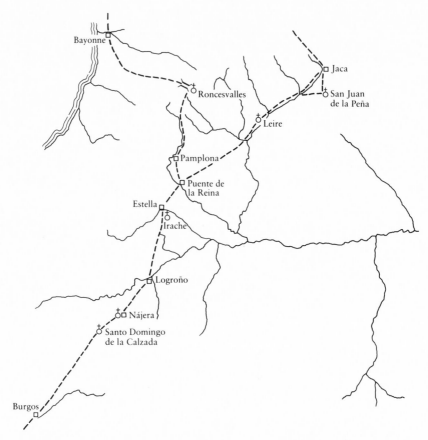

Map 25   The pilgrim route to Santiago de Compostela through Navarre

hardly brought the pilgrims into touch with Guipúzcoa or Vizcaya at all. Nevertheless, whatever their attitude towards the local inhabitants they encountered, their influence, and especially the interest that the great reforming monastery of Cluny in Burgundy took in the cult and the pilgrim route, exercised a considerable effect upon the areas through which they normally passed. This manifested itself particularly in architecture. More cosmopolitan styles, notably in church building, began to make themselves felt in Navarre: thus when the abbey church at Leire was rebuilt in 1098 the plan followed was that previously adopted for a number of similar buildings in the Limousin,

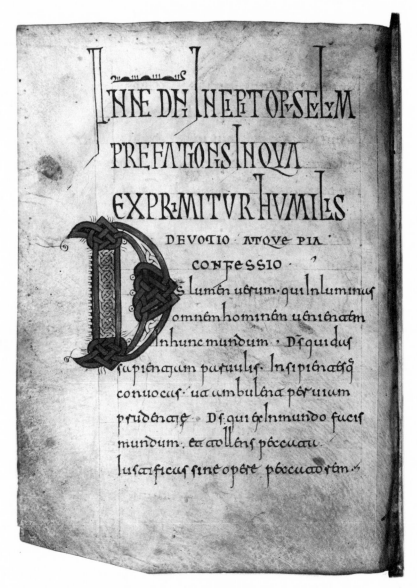

A folio from the MS of Ildefonsus, De Virginitate, *written for Bishop Godescale of Le Puy at Albeda in 951*

Estella, Navarre: the city gate and entry to the French quarter

towards the northern end of the pilgrim route from France.[3] Civil architecture could also be affected by the needs of the pilgrims, as evidenced in the fine medieval bridge over the Arga at Puente de la Reina, where two of the routes to Compostela converged.

The establishment of monasteries pertaining to the new religious orders that were becoming increasingly popular in

[3] For the architecture of the pilgrimage route see K. J. Conant, *Carolingian and Romanesque Architecture, 800—1200*, 2nd edn (Harmondsworth, 1966), pp. 157—90. There is no full study of Leire, but see W. M. Whitehill, *Spanish Romanesque Architecture of the Eleventh Century* (Oxford, 1941), pp. 205—8.

western Europe in the twelfth century, such as the Cistercian houses of Irache and Iranzu in southern Navarre, not only testified to the willingness of the kings to patronize the reformed monasticism and the currents of ideas and learning that went with it, but also created centres of such cultural irradiation within the kingdom. Abbots and monks to people such houses were drawn initially from across the Pyrenees, and the Navarrese monasteries continued to attract recruits from France. At the same time the clear intellectual predominance of Paris and the schools of northern France led many aspiring Navarrese clerics to seek their training there.[4] Both the ecclesiastical and the court culture of the kingdom of Navarre became predominantly French — a process intensified when in the thirteenth century, as the result of marriages and the failure of the direct male line, the monarchy passed into the hands of the counts of Champagne and then into those of the kings of France.

By this time there was also a substantial element in the population of southern Navarre that was of French origin. This was particularly true of Estella, south-west of Pamplona, which had so significant a proportion of French settlers that a special district of the town, known as Lizarra, was created for them, and their distinct identity was recognized in the *fueros* granted to Estella in 1090 by King Sancho Ramírez, now known only through the text of their confirmation in 1164 by Sancho the Wise.[5] Estella itself became a favourite royal residence in this period, and some of the former royal palace buildings can still be seen, displaying in their design and ornamentation further evidence of the strong French artistic and cultural influences then fashionable in the upper echelons of Navarrese society. Generally confined to the southern fringes of Navarre, such settlements had little effect on the Basque populations further to the north, but they did help to ensure that the Ebro valley and other reconquered areas even further south failed to receive any distinctive Basque imprint. The evidence of both personal

[4] For example, Bishops Pedro de Paris (a native of Artajona) and Remiro de Navarra of Pamplona: J. Goñi Gaztambide, *Historia de los obispos de Pamplona* (2 vols, Pamplona, 1979), vol. I, pp. 433ff. and 551ff.; Archbishop Rodrigo Jiménez de Rada of Toledo was also of Navarrese origin and trained in Paris.

[5] J. Yanguas y Miranda, *Diccionario de antigüedas del Reino de Navarra* (3 vols, Pamplona, 1840—3; reprinted with altered pagination, Pamplona, 1964), vol. I, pp. 316—51.

Estella: the remains of the twelfth-century royal palace of the kings of Navarre

names and place-names in the documents relating to these regions suggests that the Basque element was not able to make an impression in the expanding southern frontier of the Navarrese kingdom after about the middle of the eleventh century. The same is true of Castille, where the overtly Basque population, initially so strong in the texts of the tenth century, has effectively disappeared by the twelfth and thirteenth. In neither of these regions are there good grounds for believing that the Basque language was still in use by the end of the twelfth century. One possible exception might be Silos, the settlement that grew up

French sculptors at work in Navarre: a detail of the north portal of the twelfth-century church of San Miguel, Estella

around the important monastery of Santo Domingo de Silos, which received a contingent of immigrants from Gascony, after whom the district of Barbascones (Barrio of the Vascones) took its name.[6] There may have been other such groups from the Basque regions to the north of the Pyrenees amongst the 'Francos' who were established on the rapidly developing frontiers of the Spanish Christian kingdoms, but if so they were insufficiently numerous to have preserved a distinctive linguistic and cultural identity in our sources.

More significant for the future development of the Basque regions proper was a French presence on the Biscay coast, which resulted in the foundation of the first major town in Guipúzcoa at San Sebastián, which received its *fueros* in 1180.[7] With the exception of the Roman fort at Lapurdum, no major settlement existed on the coast of the Basque regions both north and south of the Pyrenees before the emergence of Bayonne in the eleventh century and of San Sebastián in the twelfth. The early records of both of these towns are few in number, and those of Bayonne in particular are bedevilled by problems of authenticity. However, their existence as distinctive social and economic units, different in size and character to all other settlements in their regions, is clear. This is particularly striking when contrasted with the generally undeveloped nature of the whole Biscayan area, from the mouth of the Garonne to Galicia, in previous centuries. It is possible that small fishing settlements had existed in the various natural harbours and river mouths of the region since antiquity. These grew in importance and certainly feature more prominently in the records in the later Middle Ages, but their existence does not explain the particular development of the two major cities of the coastal area, to which Bilbao was added as a third only in 1300. Town dwelling is an art, and requires the practice of certain skills and a legal and social framework quite different from those of a rural population. The new towns of the Biscay coast, in particular San Sebastián but also subsequently an increasing number of smaller settlements such as Bermeo and Fuenterrabía, depended upon the expertise of inhabitants already adjusted to this style

---

[6] M. Férotin (ed.), *Recueil des chartes de Silos* (Paris, 1897), pp. 388 (document of 1338) and 460 (1407).

[7] J. L. Banus Aguirre, *El Fuero de San Sebastián* (San Sebastián, 1963).

The harbour at San Sebastián

of existence. The population of the Basque regions, hitherto almost totally unurbanized except in the upper Ebro valley, thus hardly provided suitable material for attracting into the towns. This need probably explains why the kings of Navarre were so keen to import substantial numbers of French settlers, not just into their new foundations in the south such as Estella but also into the Biscay coast. In particular the area extending from San Sebastián to Fuenterrabía was given to them for settlement, and in the towns of that region a French dialect predominated until at least the sixteenth century.[8]

[8] S. de Múgica, 'Los Gascones en Guipúzcoa', in *Homenaje a D. Carmelo de Echegaray* (San Sebastián, 1928), pp. 1—29.

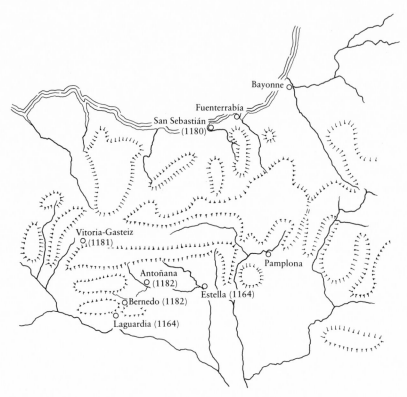

Map 26   Urban fueros in Navarre in the late twelfth century

Urban growth in the twelfth century

Thus once again this period of the eleventh to thirteenth
centuries, which saw the first significant urban development of
the Basque regions since the time of the Roman Empire and was
marked by the influx of new ideas, institutions and elements of
population, principally from northern France, accentuated the
divisions between the Basque rural society and that of the
towns, the Church and the court. However much the urban may
have depended upon the rural in economic terms, the cultural
divide was extended by the French predominance. On the other
hand the evidence of the numerous surviving sets of *fueros*
granted in this period shows that even in areas of almost

exclusively Basque occupation the size of settlements was increasing and social organization was becoming more complex and varied. In the continuing absence of substantial charter collections relating to such areas the texts of *fueros* can provide the best viewpoint for the study of Basque local society in this period.

Good examples may be found in the *fueros* granted to Bernedo and Antoñana, two small towns recently founded in Alava, which received their privileges from King Sancho the Wise in January 1182.[9] The two fortified settlements, little over 10 km apart, lie near the point of convergence of two major routes. One, coming eastwards from the upper Ebro and the plains of northern Castille, passes through Bernedo on its way to Estella and Pamplona; the other, coming south from the recently founded Vitoria-Gasteiz, passes through Antoñana before meeting the first road just to the east of Bernedo. Both as strategic locations controlling access from Castille into Navarre, and as toll levying points, the two towns, tiny as they are today, were of considerable importance in the 1180s, when they received *fueros* in the same decade as both Vitoria and San Sebastián (see map 26).

The two sets, preserved now only in later cartulary copies, are virtually identical and basically apply to the two foundations the rights and concessions in respect of law and mercantile activity that had previously been granted to the town of Laguardia, just across the southern slopes of their valley and in the Rioja, which had been conceded in 1164. The principal difference between the Antoñana-Bernedo *fueros* and those of Laguardia was that in the case of the former an additional annual payment to the king on the feast of St Michael of three solidi (a unit of value rather than a coin) per household was stipulated.[10] Such an extension of rights granted to one settlement and not to another was standard practice. There are only a limited number of original sets of *fueros*. Most grants consisted of such extensions of existing sets of concessions, amplified or modified to suit local circumstances. Those of Laguardia, like many of the others, having defined the boundaries of the town and its

---

[9] Texts in *800 aniversario de los fueros de población de Bernedo y Antoñana* (Vitoria-Gasteiz, 1983), pp. 11—26.

[10] G. Martínez Díez (ed.), *Alava Medieval* (2 vols, Vitoria, 1974), vol. I, pp. 219—22.

region, guaranteed the inhabitants freedom from forceful entry into their dwellings or seizure of their goods by royal and seigneural officials, notably the *saio*, an officer of the courts. Indeed it was stated that should one of these be killed attempting to make such a forbidden forcible entry no fine would be payable for his death. The amount of tax owed per caput was also stipulated and limited to one solidus per household, with no other service being owed to the king — unless offered voluntarily. Freedom of inheritance and the purchase and sale of property between themselves was also guaranteed. Much of the text was taken up with a tariff of compensations and fines for killings and injuries that the inhabitants might perpetrate. No murder fine was payable by the community if a man were to be found dead of unlawful causes within the boundaries of the town and its hinterland. Otherwise, for murder the killer had to pay 200 solidi, of which half was due *pro anima regis*, literally 'for the soul of the king', but indicating a fine payable to the fisc, whilst the rest went to the victim's heirs. At a less fatal if equally violent level of activity it was stipulated, for example, that if a woman hit another, seized her by the hair and tore her clothes, and if this were proved by the testimony of two other women witnesses, the offender had to pay 20 solidi, half going to the king. Equivalents of value are not easy to establish for this period, but it is worth noticing that a vineyard could change hands for less than a single solidus. These fines and compensations were by no means light. Various other penalties were also laid down, and thieves caught in the act were made liable to hanging, indicating that crimes of violence in hot blood within the community were regarded less seriously than offences against property.

The related *fueros* of Bernedo and Antoñana do in general follow those of Laguardia, but there exist a number of significant differences. Taking the Antoñana text as the example, the organized nature of settlement in the more densely populated Ebro valley, in which Laguardia was situated, is in marked contrast to the conditions to be encountered in the mountainous areas just to the north, in which Antoñana and Bernedo were placed. Thus the boundaries of Laguardia could be defined exclusively in terms of pre-existing properties, as for example 'from the coppice of Enego Galíndez within the settlement, with its boundaries, and from Uncina within the settlement as far as Lagoal, all of which is royal, as far as Buradon in the middle of the Ebro'.[11] On the other hand the *termini* of Antoñana generally consisted of natural objects, as in the case of 'from the bridge of Frameto to the tree *burandes*, thence to the dry tree'.[12] Man-made items used to define the boundaries consist exclusively of churches, free-standing crosses and a bridge; no reference is made to other settlements. It was particularly stated within the grant that the inhabitants had full and free access to the mountains (i.e. mountain pastures), grass and water contained within the specified boundaries, and, wherever grass were found, there they were permitted to pasture their animals. Moreover, within the area representing a day's travel beyond their own boundaries they would not be required to pay the tax called the *herbaticum*, paid for the privilege of pasturage rights. They were also allowed to take wood to build their houses from the royal *montes*. These do not look to have been reserved royal areas within the boundaries of Antoñana. Rather the kings seem to have succeeded in arrogating to themselves possession of all the uncultivated land within the kingdom not otherwise granted out, and thus these 'royal mountains' would be those upland pastures and woodlands not already conceded to the exclusive use of other settlers.

The tariff of compensations for injuries, although related to that given to Laguardia 18 years previously, was both heavier and more complex. Thus homicide in Antoñana would cost 250 solidi, and the king reserved the right to 'have justice' on the killer, in other words apply the death penalty. Likewise a woman throwing another woman out of her house or seizing her by the hair faced a fine of 30 solidi. New injunctions include one whereby a woman who seized a man by his beard, hair or genitalia had to 'redeem her hand' (by a payment?) or face a flogging. It was also stated that the inhabitants did not have the 'customs of fire, of water, or of battle'. These were forms of ordeal used in judicial processes, particularly in the kingdom of León, to determine innocence either as a supplement to or instead of the provision of proof by witness. These seem to have become increasingly unpopular, especially in Castille, from the

[11] Ibid., p. 219, clause 1.
[12] *800 aniversario*, p. 24.

eleventh century onwards, and thus not to have to resort to ordeal (i.e. not to have it as a local 'custom') was a valued privilege. Likewise, if involved in law cases with their lord or an outsider, which would require them to appear in the king's court, the inhabitants of Antoñana were not to be obliged to go unless it were being held in a small number of sites, such as Vitoria or Estella, relatively local to their town. Their own judicial tribunal was held in the town gate, and there was a jail in which, amongst others, outsiders who infringed local rights would be held until they bought their freedom with a fixed fine.

The organization of local government is not set out in detail in these and similar *fueros*, as the purpose of such texts was to put on record the ameliorations and exemptions from the general law, still that of the Visigothic *Forum Iudicum*, that the recipients were to enjoy. However, the Antoñana *fueros* do guarantee the inhabitants free right of election of their mayor, the *alcalde*, whose stipend was to be paid by the lord out of fines received for homicides and injuries. He also paid the *saio*, who had to be a local man, out of the same funds. The existence of some form of council may be assumed, and there was certainly a resident judge. Overall the town was under the patronage of the lord appointed by the king, whose principal roles were to defend it and to collect what was owing in taxes and fines to the ruler, but whose power over the individual citizens was restricted by the stipulations of the *fueros*.

Very similar in character were the *fueros* granted to the inhabitants of Vitoria in 1181, though it was stated that they were receiving the concessions given to Logroño rather than those of Laguardia.[13] The differences between the plains of central Alava around Vitoria, and the mountains to the south dividing them from the Rioja and in which Antoñana and Bernedo are situated, are made obvious by the lack of references to *montes*. The inhabitants of Vitoria were permitted to take wood for building and for fuel from wherever they found it, other than from 'known defences'. Otherwise, the tariffs for offences, the freedom from forcible entry, liberty of inheritance and so forth were identical concessions to those granted to Antoñana and Bernedo in the following year. Likewise the town

[13] Martínez Díez, *Alava Medieval*, vol. I, pp. 223—6; *Documento facsimil del fuero de población de Vitoria* (Vitoria-Gasteiz, 1980).

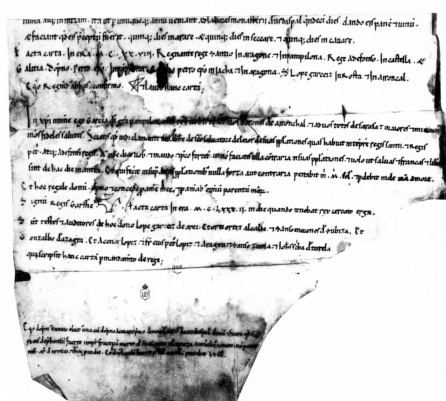

A copy of two royal charters, one of Sancho Ramírez of 1090 and the other of García IV of 1144, below which is an undated fuero *granted by the lords Iñigo and Aznar to the inhabitants of Urdaspal*

was to have an elected *alcalde*, paid by the lord out of fines, and the citizens were not subject to ordeals, which are here specified as being *iron*, hot water and battle.

Economy and charter in rural settlements

While in general this period of the second half of the twelfth century saw a small but significant number of such grants of *fueros* to new settlements on the expanding frontiers of the kingdom, and to such towns as the kings found it necessary to develop for military and mercantile purposes, it was also

Map 27   *Valley and town fueros of the reigns of Sancho the Wise and Sancho*
the Strong

marked by the concession of a substantial body of less complex
sets to small settlements in the heartlands of Navarre. Thus in
the *Archivo General del Reino de Navarra* in Pamplona, in
whose records there seems to exist a lacuna in respect of the
traditional Basque regions in the period *c.* 1085—1190, there is
preserved an unprecedented corpus of grants of *fueros* to
settlements and to rural areas in northern Navarre in the years
1192 and 1193. In this brief period *fueros* were conceded to the
inhabitants *(moradores)* of Esteribar, Agorreta, Aniz, the valley
of Gulina, the valley of Odieta, Larraun, Basaburúa, Erasún
and Labayen, Soracoiz, Imoz, Beunza, Berroeta, Berasain and

Arostegui, amongst others.[14] This was followed, at a more leisurely pace, by similar grants made by the succeeding king, Sancho the Strong, to the inhabitants of Ustés in 1195 and 1198, to those of Aspurz in 1199, to the *moradores* of Olaiz, Osacáin and Beráiz in 1201, to the hunters (*cazadores*) of Esteribar *c.* 1203, and to the *moradores* of Areizaga, Guiçairudiaga, Irurzun, Latorlegui, Yabar and elsewhere in 1210.[15] The series may be said to end in 1211 with a grant of *fueros* to the *moradores* of the valley of Ulzama (see map 27).[16]

All of these places are to be located to the north of a line drawn from Pamplona to Estella, and some of them are found in the remoter Pyrenean valleys such as the Baztan and the Salazar, which thereby make their first appearance in historical sources. The texts themselves are generally very brief and as a whole can appear somewhat repetitious. They relate principally to the taxes due per household or by each individual. Thus in 1192 in the *fuero* of Basaburúa the king stated that each royal villein (*villanus*) would have to pay him four solidi together with six measures (*arrobas*) of oats, that a seigneurial villein owed him three solidi and three measures of oats, and that for widows without such a taxpayer in their household, four of them would be regarded as the equivalent of one man.[17] Rates varied from place to place: in the same year in Erasun the *fueros* granted there required payment of only four solidi per head, and with no additional oats, whilst in the valley of Odieta royal villeins had to produce 15 solidi per annum plus six measures of oats. In addition those possessing a yoke of oxen had to pay a further two solidi.[18]

Such information from a relatively wide area but very close in time provides the basis for some interesting comparisons between the productive capacity of the different parts of the region, the prevalence or otherwise of cereal crops, and so forth. Important too is its bearing on social organization. Somehow, by the late twelfth century, the kings of Navarre had managed to impose

---

[14] J. R. Castro, *Archivo General de Navarra. Catalogo de la Sección de Comptos: Documentos*, vol. I (años 842—1331) (Pamplona, 1952), nos 98, 99, 101—5, 107—9; see also no. 110.

[15] Ibid., nos 115, 124, 126, 129, 131, 147, 148.

[16] Ibid., no. 151.

[17] Archivo General del Reino de Navarra (Pamplona), cajón 1, no. 57.

[18] Ibid., cajón 1, no. 59; cajón 1, no. 55.

themselves as landlords over areas in which it might be thought there had been continuous cultivation or occupation during several previous centuries and where there is no earlier evidence of their special interest or activity. Moreover in a number of these settlements or areas, some being villages and some whole valleys, an intermediate level in the social hierarchy had been introduced in the person of the *senior*, whose own villeins still owed dues to the king as well as to their immediate lord. How the system worked is thus relatively clear, but how it came into existence is not. The emergence of a class of villeins, effectively tied tenants owing services and/or rents in cash and kind to the lord from whom they held their land, is not easy to understand in the context of early Basque society. The lack of any evidence of a long-established native aristocracy makes it certain that the role of the monarchy must have been central to this process. But were there just a limited number of royal estates in which the monarchy was able to develop a rural equivalent to the urban settlements of the southern and western frontiers, granting lands on them to new settlers, with or without the introduction of a local lord, in return for specified payments and services? Or did a royal claim to ownership extend over all of the kingdom, encompassing all of those lands not already granted out under some form of tenure? Did the kings in effect seize all landed property to which an alternative (written?) title of ownership could not be produced?

The map of the areas encompassed within these sets of *fueros* is very revealing (see map 27). With the exception of two specified locations in the Salazar valley, all of the documents relate to a series of valleys north and north-west of Pamplona. Moreover, in the course of the period 1192—1210 all of these valleys became subject to *fueros*. The only exception is the Baztan valley, for which there exists just a document addressed to the inhabitants of Aniz alone, whilst the whole of the smaller tributary valley of Doneztebe may well have been encompassed within the *fueros* of Erasún. It is quite conceivable that more such texts existed once and have not survived. But overall it looks as if the royal intention was to establish fixed rates of taxes and dues owed to the crown by its villeins and those of the local *seniores* throughout the whole of this area of northern Navarre. This programme was not extended eastwards into the regions between Pamplona and Leire, and the valleys of the

Erro, the Aezkoa and of Roncesvalles have provided no such documents for this period. A similar process of the granting of *fueros* was, however, also being conducted for the more urbanized south of the kingdom, particularly in the reign of Sancho the Strong (1194—1234).[19]

It is clear that the productive capacity of the different parts of the northern region was understood to be variable. Thus the inhabitants of the Odieta valley were faced with the very high rate of 15 solidi per head, plus six measures of grain, whilst in the northern extremity of their own district, the confluent valley of the Ulzama, the tax rate was only one solidus per person and with no additional requirement in grain. This corresponds exactly to the geological variations in the composition of the soil and its possible uses between the two contiguous parts of the same region. The Odieta valley is capable of cereal production, whilst the Ulzama, rising on to mountain slopes, is stony and only able to support forest.[20] Further localized modifications could obviously sometimes be obtained as the result of special pleading. Thus in 1201 Osacáin and Beráiz, two of the settlements within the Odieta valley, were able to gain individual *fueros* of their own, in which the level of the personal contribution was lowered to six solidi, as opposed to the 15 set by the general *fueros* of the valley of 1192.[21]

The origins of medieval taxation still remain little studied, but it seems that there was only slight continuity between late Roman imperial taxes and those that later came to be levied by western European monarchies. Only in respect of various tolls and indirect taxes on the transportation of goods do the rights of the successor kings seem to correspond with those of their imperial predecessors. The development of direct forms of taxation looks to have been gradual, and in most parts of western Europe in the twelfth century royal revenue derived largely from exploitation of demesne, the taking of the profits of justice and a limited number of tolls and taxes on merchandise. As previously suggested, the Navarrese monarchy should if anything have been worse placed than most as the result of its relatively recent creation, the long pre-establishment of patterns

[19] See C. de Marichalar, *Colección diplomática del rey don Sancho VIII (el Fuerte) de Navarra* (Pamplona, 1934).

[20] A. F. Samanes and A. M. Duque (eds), *Atlas de Navarra*, 2nd edn (Barcelona, 1981), maps on pp. 20, 24, 25.

[21] Archivo General del Reino de Navarra, cajón 1, no. 72.

of settlement and ownership in much of its territories, and the absence of the kinds of royal rights created by antiquity of existence or by conquest. However, these late-twelfth-century *fueros* indicate that a substantial body of rights in respect of taxation did exist, and that these extended beyond the simple matter of the king exerting seigneurial powers over his villeins by way of payments and services in return for their tenancies. Several of the *fueros*, such as those given to the inhabitants of the valley of Gulina, make it clear that everyone living within the area encompassed by the grant was required to make the stipulated annual render, and that additional obligations were laid upon the royal and seigneurial villeins living in the valley.[22]

Such an impression is enhanced by the large number of different forms of taxation that can be found to be at the king's command. Some of these only feature in the relatively more abundant documentation of the later Middle Ages, but of these a number were then regarded as being onerous and archaic, and their appearance in the sources at that time is often in the context of a monarch freeing the population of a particular area from the obligation to pay these 'evil customs'. Interestingly, quite a number of these taxes, particularly some of the older and more obscure ones, many of whose character and purpose remain mysterious, had Basque names. Amongst others the taxes thus recorded include those entitled the *anubda*, referred to in 1208, the *opilarinzada* (1217), the *escanciania* (1168), the *ozerate* (1393), the *azaguerrico*, the *basto*, the *escuranina* or *crisuelu*, the *beraurdea*, the *irurdea*, the *gailurdirua*, the *ozteinto* and the *baturrata*. The last eight feature in very late documents, from the fourteenth-century *fuero general* onwards, but most of the names are clearly Basque, and when their purposes can be elucidated, which is not always possible, they constitute taxes of a fairly archaic kind.[23] Thus, for example, the *irurdea* was a charge on pigs being permitted to pasture on the king's *montes* — something regarded as a grantable privilege at the time of the Antoñana and Bernedo *fueros* of 1182.[24]

It is probable that some of these dues were of considerable antiquity, though the appearance of Basque names for them in

[22] Ibid., cajón 1, no. 54.
[23] Yanguas y Miranda, *Diccionario de Antigüdades*, see under 'Pechas', vol. II, pp. 325—94.
[24] Ibid., pp. 353—4.

the late medieval sources may be only another facet of the greater self-confidence of the vernacular at this time. But even if the *irurdea* be no more than the Basque translation of a Latinate form for a tax well known elsewhere in parts of western Europe, notably in the Anglo-Norman state where it went under the name of pannage, the number of such taxes that can be shown to have been available to the Navarrese kings by the end of the twelfth century was substantial. They included, in addition to the kind of hearth tax envisaged in some of the *fueros* of the 1190s, obligations to provide hospitality for the king. This was commuted into an annual levy known as the *cena*. Thus in 1192 the inhabitants of Aniz, as well as having to raise 600 solidi between them for the tax on households, were also required to produce 100 solidi in *cena*. In the Odieta valley *cena* was calculated at two solidi per head, but only payable on the part of those possessing a yoke of oxen.[25] In the same valley the inhabitants collectively had to find another 22 solidi for an animal tax known as the *adadura*.[26] Military service or a tax in lieu of it called the *fonsadera* also appears to have been a general obligation, but one from which many of the mountain communities were dispensed in their *fueros*.[27]

It is quite conceivable that the *fueros* of the 1190s and their numerous successors from other parts of Navarre represent rationalizations and compromises whereby the inhabitants of the different valleys compounded with the kings to provide fixed renders, basically by way of hearth and hospitality taxes, in order to be freed from a complex network of older taxes and services whose existence can be detected in some of the other sources. In general many of the agreements reached at the end of the twelfth century remained in force for the rest of the Middle Ages. In a number of cases these *fueros* were confirmed by later kings in the thirteenth and fourteenth centuries, when royal power was somewhat weaker than it had been at the time of the indigenous ruling house.[28] The survival of the documents

---

[25] Ibid., pp. 342—4.
[26] Ibid., pp. 338—9.
[27] Ibid., pp. 344—5.
[28] For the history of the kingdom of Navarre in the late Middle Ages, see J. M. Lacarra, *Historia política del Reino de Navarra desde sus origines hasta su incorporación a Castilla* (3 vols, Pamplona, 1972—3), especially vol. III; also J. Zabalo Zabalegui, *La administración del Reino de Navarra en el siglo XIV* (Pamplona, 1973).

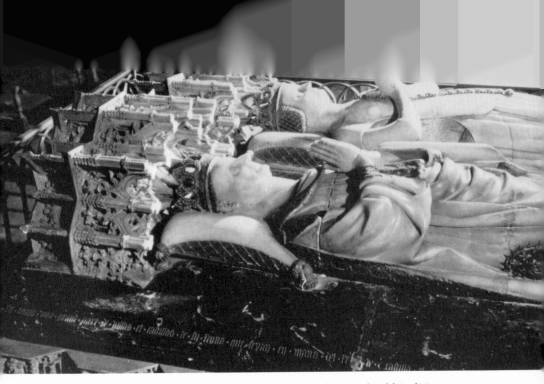

The tomb in Pamplona cathedral of Carlos III 'el noble' of Navarre, a descendant of Philippe IV of France and of the comital lines of Champagne and Evreux

themselves is testimony to the continuing value placed upon them for long after the time of their original concession; over a span of centuries what may have seemed harsh exactions could become valued liberties in altered economic circumstances. In general the Navarrese kings were relatively little interested in the mountainous northern heartlands of their kingdom. Their preferred residences and the areas of their greatest activity remained in the south, in the Ebro valley. After the merging of the Navarrese dynasty with the line of the counts of Champagne in 1234 and with the royal line of France in 1284 such tendencies were accentuated, and some of the monarchs became effectively non-resident (see the accompanying genealogy). One result of this is a lack of source material relating to the more Basque regions of the kingdom — something hardly compensated for in those parts of Basque territory outside Navarre and under the rule of the kings of Castille. In consequence the Navarrese *fueros* of the 1190s, with their surprising evidence of the operation of royal rights and authority in the mountainous

The later monarchs of Navarre

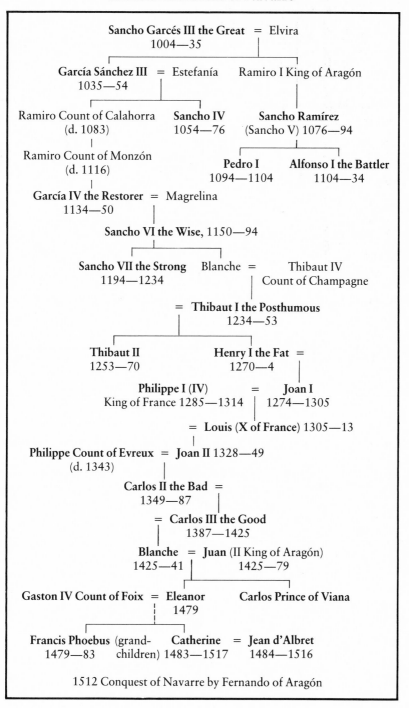

Sancho Garcés III the Great = Elvira
1004—35

García Sánchez III = Estefanía   Ramiro I King of Aragón
1035—54

Ramiro Count of Calahorra   Sancho IV   Sancho Ramírez
(d. 1083)   1054—76   (Sancho V) 1076—94

Ramiro Count of Monzón   Pedro I   Alfonso I the Battler
(d. 1116)   1094—1104   1104—34

García IV the Restorer = Magrelina
1134—50

Sancho VI the Wise, 1150—94

Sancho VII the Strong   Blanche =   Thibaut IV
1194—1234   Count of Champagne

= Thibaut I the Posthumous
1234—53

Thibaut II   Henry I the Fat =
1253—70   1270—4

Philippe I (IV)   =   Joan I
King of France 1285—1314   1274—1305

= Louis (X of France) 1305—13

Philippe Count of Evreux = Joan II 1328—49
(d. 1343)

Carlos II the Bad =
1349—87

= Carlos III the Good
1387—1425

Blanche = Juan (II King of Aragón)
1425—41   1425—79

Gaston IV Count of Foix = Eleanor   Carlos Prince of Viana
1479

Francis Phoebus (grand-   Catherine = Jean d'Albret
1479—83   children) 1483—1517   1484—1516

1512 Conquest of Navarre by Fernando of Aragón

zones, stand virtually alone as evidence for Basque rural society at this time. A little more can be known of urban life.

Gascony in the Angevin period

Pastoralism and cultivation in a mixed economy may have been the dominant features of the Basque lifestyle in most of the areas of their habitation, but the coastal regions of the Bay of Biscay produced alternatives. How long established were the fishing communities of the coast cannot be determined, but several of them received *fueros* in the thirteenth and fourteenth centuries. The existence of a number of natural harbours, notably on the river mouths, together with an abundance of fish in the coastal waters, may have made Bermeo, Motrico, Zarauz and their like obvious places of settlement from an early age. Certainly by the eleventh century charter evidence suggests that much of the Biscay region was being developed, and the earliest Vizcayan and Guipuzcoan texts relate to it. More adventurous forms of fishing in deeper waters may also have been practised, and whaling was certainly a regular feature of Basque maritime activity by the twelfth century if not earlier. In the foundation charter of Zarauz granted by Fernando III of Castille in 1237 the king reserved a royal right to a portion of every whale that the inhabitants might catch 'as is the custom'.[29] In the same way the Scottish kings had claimed rights over whales caught by their subjects, keeping for their portion the creatures' tongues.[30]

It has been argued that such activities as whaling and deep-sea fishing took the Basques of these coastal settlements far out into the Atlantic, and it thus comes as no surprise to find them joining the Welsh and the Vikings in claiming a prior discovery of America to that of Columbus.[31] However, the Bay of Biscay itself may have provided sufficient resources for their needs, and the annual migrations, particularly of some of the smaller forms

[29] Text given in J. A. García de Cortázar et al., *Introducción a la historia medieval de Alava, Guipúzcoa y Vizcaya en sus textos* (San Sebastián, 1979), no. 19, pp. 85—6 (1237).

[30] *Regesta Regum Scottorum I: the Acts of Malcolm IV*, ed. G. W. S. Barrow (Edinburgh, 1960), no. 118, pp. 182—5.

[31] For an account of Basque maritime activity in the Middle Ages, see J. Caro Baroja, *Los Vascos y el mar* (San Sebastián, 1981).

of whale, would have brought them within easier reach of the Basque fishermen than the Moby Dick imagery of whaling might suggest. Even making allowance for some modern exaggerations, the Basques of Vizcaya and Guipúzcoa were long regarded as being more than competent seamen, and in 1492 some of them played important roles in Columbus's first voyage, as well as in many of the subsequent expeditions to the Americas. It was not, though, exclusively or even primarily in fishing and whaling ventures that the Basques gained their reputation as seafarers or undertook their most demanding voyages. From at least the late twelfth century their ships were playing an important role in the maritime trade between both Spain and south-west France and northern Europe. In this the rise of the coastal cities of Bayonne, San Sebastián and then Bilbao was crucial, and the trade in turn fomented their growth.

Of these Bayonne was by far the oldest, even ignoring its likely identity with the Roman fort of Lapurdum. The previously peripatetic 'Bishopric of the Basques' (*c.* 980—1030) had finally settled itself there by 1030, arguing the prior existence of some form of settlement; an admittedly somewhat suspect charter suggests that the bishops exercised their authority over a number of the hinterland valleys, including some across the Pyrenees in Guipúzcoa, much of the eastern part of which remained within the diocese of Bayonne for the rest of the Middle Ages.[32] Other early documents are all too few, but that the dukes of Gascony played a central role in the earliest development of the town is indicated by a charter of Duke William VII of Aquitaine (1088—1127), whose ancestors had inherited the duchy of Gascony in 1058, by which he gave half of Bayonne to its bishop and the canons of the cathedral church of St Mary.[33] An earlier bishop, Raymond II, had already recovered episcopal control over various churches and properties previously held by the viscount of Bayonne (*c.* 1060).[34] This included the church that was to become the cathedral, four-tenths of all tithes, and a section of the town itself 'from the eastern gate to the gate of St Leo'. Thus prior secular aristocratic

---

[32] *Le Livre d'or de Bayonne*, ed. V. Dubarat (Pau, 1897), doc. 1, pp. 1—3.

[33] *Gallia Christiana*, vol. I, ed. D. Sammarthani (Paris, 1715), *Instrumenta Ecclesiae Baionenses*, doc. II, p. 201.

[34] Ibid., doc. I, pp. 200—1.

control over the settlement came increasingly to give way to that of the recently established bishops. This was matched by the rise of the cult of St Leo, a possibly entirely fictitious figure, said to have been a bishop of Rouen displaced from his see, who then established himself at Bayonne and began to evangelize the countryside before suffering a martyr's death at the hands of the Vikings (*c.* 900).[35] There seem to be no grounds for credence in any element in this tale, but the cult that it fostered was clearly gaining ground in Bayonne by the middle of the eleventh century.

By 1150—70 Bishop Fortunerius, with the support of the viscount of Bayonne, was able to lay down a tariff in livestock that the inhabitants of Labourd (the French Basque province in which Bayonne stands, and which derives its name from Lapurdum) were required to give to the church of Bayonne at the time of their death 'for the salvation of their souls':[36]

Whosoever has two horses should give one to the bishop. He who has only one horse and four ploughing oxen should give either the horse or the best ox; whoever has four oxen and no horse at all should similarly give the best ox; whoever has as many as two ploughing oxen and another ten head of oxen should either leave a pregnant cow or the ox of a pregnant cow to the bishop; whoever has two ploughing oxen but does not have another ten head of oxen but has pigs and sheep should give five solidi.'

It is interesting that the bishop should want horses and ploughing oxen but not animals such as pigs and sheep that required pasture. For his part the bishop pledged himself to say a mass for the soul of the departed donor in the cathedral. All of this it should be noted was to be in addition to the normal tithes which would still be expected to be paid in full. Although notionally voluntary, this looks as if the bishop of Bayonne had been able to impose death duties and thus exercise lordship not only over the city but also over much of its related region, though not the whole of his diocese.

[35] The *Vita* of St Leo of Bayonne/Rouen may be found in *Acta Sanctorum, Martii,* vol. I (1668), pp. 93—7; see also L'Abbé Menjoulet, *Saint Léon, Apôtre de Bayonne* (Bayonne, 1876).
[36] *Gallia Christiana,* vol. I, Sammarthani, *Instrumenta Ecclesiae Baionenses,* doc. III, p. 201.

(Opposite) The walls and cathedral of Bayonne

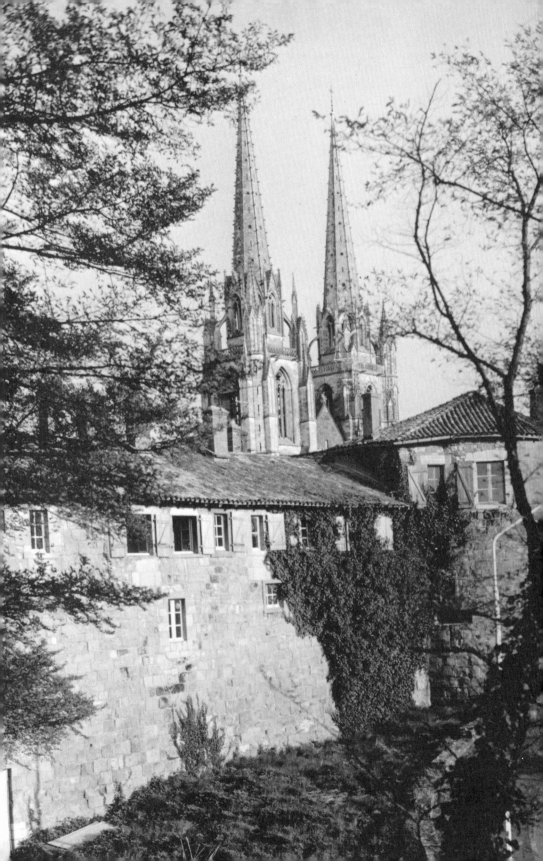

None of this indicates the existence of any alternative to a mixed pastoral and agrarian economy in these parts. Probably the most significant point in the development of Bayonne as a mercantile centre — for previously it looks to have been little more than the focus of the episcopal administration — was the acquisition of the duchy of Aquitaine, and with it therefore Gascony, by the Angevin dynasty of kings of England. In theory it became linked to the English crown by the accession of Richard I in 1189, as the heir to both Henry II and to Eleanor duchess of Aquitaine, but in practice the region was dominated by Henry since their marriage in 1152.[37] The growth of trade from Gascony to England, particularly in wine, provided great opportunities and incentives for the development of shipping in Bayonne, whose fleet, in rivalry with that of Bordeaux, came to dominate the trade route between the two parts of the Angevin empire. Only once such an alternative economy had developed could the growing and increasingly wealthy commercial class in the city successfully challenge the lordship of the bishop. The needs of warfare also stimulated the maritime potential of Bayonne. Thus the city provided a substantial contingent of ships to assist in the transportation of Richard I off to the Third Crusade in 1190, but this was provided under the authority of and led by Bishop Bernard II.[38] By the 1230s, though, the English government was negotiating with a mayor and council of citizens of Bayonne for such naval assistance. The emancipation from seigneurial authority, here represented by that of the bishop, was achieved and formally marked by the charter of the English king John of 19 April 1215, granting communal status to Bayonne.[39]

San Sebastián was initially more favourably placed than Bayonne, in that the latter was largely developed as an episcopal and vicecomital administrative centre, with resident lords whose

---

[37] For Aquitaine in the mid twelfth century see J. Gillingham, *Richard the Lionheart* (London, 1978), pp. 25—98.

[38] *Chronica Rogeri de Hoveden*, ed. W. Stubbs (Rolls Series, 4 vols, Oxford, Cambridge, London, 1870), vol. III, pp. 36 and 42.

[39] *Livre des Établissements* (Bayonne, 1892), doc. 4, pp. 61—2; this text has survived in a later Gascon French translation. It details the powers to be exercised by the mayor, jurisdictions, the procedures for the settlement of disputes, claims etc. For naval agreements see *Calendar of the Close Rolls Preserved in the Public Record Office*, vol. II, p. 104 (a reference to letters sent to the mayor and *Homines Probi* of Bayonne), and vol. IV, p. 501 (a summons of the galleys of Bayonne, 1242).

interests were not necessarily coterminous with those of the inhabitants. San Sebastián, on the other hand, within the diocese of Bayonne could not become the centre of a bishopric, and it was in the interests of its non-resident lords, the kings of Navarre, to develop its economic potential as rapidly as possible, as this became their principal source of profits from it. Some impression of this can be gleaned from the *fueros* granted to the town by Sancho the Wise in 1180. In these are recorded the duties that would be payable to the king on merchandise brought in through the port. The goods thus detailed include copper, tin, lead, fish, pepper, skins of various kinds including those of both wild and domestic cats, wax, cotton, and wool.[40] This complexity of detail suggests that the settlement was already functioning, indeed thriving, by the time the *fueros* were granted, and certainly indicates something of the mercantile activity taking place in San Sebastián in the late twelfth century, but the lack of surviving archival records makes it hard to reinforce such an impression with concrete examples. Bayonne is more fortunate, largely thanks to the preservation of substantial numbers of English royal records of the period from the twelfth century onwards. Documents preserved in Bayonne itself are few in number, but there are numerous references to the ships of Bayonne, as well as to those of Bordeaux and to a lesser extent those of Dax, to be found in the rolls of royal letters close and patent kept in the Public Record Office in London. These relate not so much to the specifics of trade as to matters of justice, war and tax. Thus safe conducts were issued to specified merchants and shipmasters of Bayonne allowing them to bring goods to England; orders could be issued to sheriffs and port officials commanding the seizure of ships if such documents had not been obtained, or in other words paid for, or if the king needed the vessels for war or to transport himself and his followers to Gascony. For example there is a letter close of Henry III of 1230 to the Sheriff Geoffrey de Lacy ordering him not to let the ship *Seint Salvadur* of Bayonne leave Portsmouth until its master Petrus Johannis had given pledges to have his ship ready for royal service the following Easter.[41] Occasionally the Bayonne

---

[40] García de Cortázar et al., *Introducción*, doc. 16, pp. 78—9 for that section of the fuero relating to tolls.

[41] *Calendar of Close Rolls*, vol. I, s.a. 1230, p. 291.

sea captains could suffer from the depredations of the king's own English subjects on privateering ventures. Thus in 1265 another Petrus Johannis of Bayonne had his ship, arms and goods returned to him by the barons of Winchelsea on the orders of Henry III.[42] The number of such references is in itself an indicator of the large scale of the commercial activity between England and Gascony, largely conducted by the ships of Bayonne and Bordeaux, from the thirteenth century onwards. The survival of licences to import granted to various shipmasters of these cities provides more specific evidence, and wine is the commodity most usually to be transported.[43]

Although such documents generally relate to the Gascon subjects of the English monarchy, outsiders from other Basque areas occasionally feature in such sources. One such is the merchant Bonamy of Pamplona, who appears in documents of 1225 and 1229. In 1230 the cog *Boni Amici* of Pamplona was licensed to bring wine to England.[44] In the same decade the king is found standing as surety for the debts owed by one of his subjects to two merchants of Pamplona, Simon Murde and Sancho of Pamplona, and in 1254 a number of merchants of Pamplona were licensed to trade in Gascony and were given safe conducts for four years 'unless open war breaks out between the king and the king of Navarre'.[45] Such periodic glimpses in the English records give the impression of a wider network of trade between the Spanish Basque regions and Gascony, and also between the former and England. Unfortunately, the very poor rate of survival of documents *in situ* throughout all of the Basque areas makes it impossible to provide the kind of detailed studies of commerce in respect of Navarre, Vizcaya and Guipúzcoa that have often been undertaken in the case of English trade with Gascony.[46]

In the case of the two Spanish Basque maritime provinces, which were annexed to Castille in the late twelfth century, the

[42] Ibid., vol. VIII, s.a. 1265, p. 34.

[43] For example, *Calendar of Patent Rolls Preserved in the Public Record Office*, vol. I, s.a. 1225, p. 515.

[44] Ibid., vol. II, s.a. 1230, p. 386.

[45] Ibid., vol. II, s.a. 1225 and 1229, pp. 4 and 242; vol. III, s.a. 1230, pp. 327 and 289; vol. IV, s.a. 1254, p. 322.

[46] There is much that is relevant to the Basque regions, and particularly the development of Bilbao, in W. R. Childs, *Anglo-Castilian Trade in the Later Middle Ages* (Manchester, 1978), especially ch. 5.

principal role of the shipmasters of their great ports was initially restricted to the carrying of goods. They provided the transport necessary to convey merchandise, generally wool, from northern Spain to markets in the Low Countries, France and England. The production and selling of the wool was controlled by the merchants of the Castillian corporation, the Mesta, that was centred in Burgos. In due course the decline in the monopolistic powers of this body later on in the Middle Ages did open the way for merchants of Bilbao and other Basque ports to take a more active role in overseas trading ventures on their own account. Once again it is only the fortunate survival of relevant documents outside the Basque regions, whose own archives have suffered so badly, that enables some details to be given concerning these Basque merchants and their activities. This is principally due to the survival in the archives of the Flemish city of Bruges of many of the records of the commercial consulate established there in the fifteenth century for the merchants of Guipúzcoa and Vizcaya. Although far from comprehensive, these documents provide pictures in close-up of the mercantile and social life of the Basques who traded to and from Bruges. Thus it is recorded in the year 1454 that a shipmaster, one Jehan Martines de Otasca from Bilbao, bringing a cargo of iron from Spain to Flanders, was forced to jettison some of it at sea because of the storms that his ship encountered. A dispute followed between the merchants who had entrusted the cargo to him as to the division of the remainder. This was between those merchants who had obtained written charters of freighting and those who, because of shortage of time, had not — with the former group laying claim to all of the surviving cargo. Arbitrators appointed in Bruges took depositions, looked at all of the relevant documents and took statements from witnesses in Spain. Their ensuing award divided the remaining iron between all of the investors in strict proportion to the ownership of the original cargo. A number of the merchants concerned were Catillian, as names such as Juan de Covarrubias would indicate, but by far the greater number had Basque names.[47]

Also recorded in the Bruges documents are a series of related episodes that are revealing of some Basque attitudes towards

---

[47] L. Gilliodts-van Severen, *Cartulaire de l'ancien Consulat d'Espagne à Bruges*, vol. I (1280—1550) (Bruges, 1901), pp. 58—60 (6 May 1454).

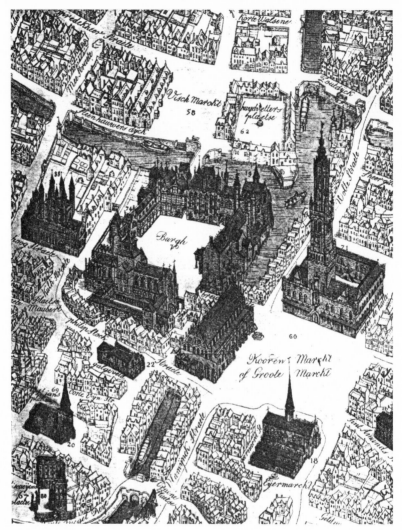

The Basque consulate in Bruges, as marked on a sixteenth-century map. The house is in the extreme bottom left corner, numbered 80

their ruler, the king of Castille, and their fellow subjects from other parts of his realm. In the early fifteenth century another consulate was established in the city in order to provide facilities for and look after the interests of other Spaniards in Bruges, notably the Castillians. By 1452 relations between this newer element and the consuls and merchants of the Basque community in the city had deteriorated to the point of open violence and much contentious litigation. In an attempt to remedy this five Castillians and seven Basques were appointed by their respective 'nations' to produce an agreement to unite the two consulates. This was finally signed on 2 August 1452 in the presence of seven merchants of Burgos and Castille and of 26 'from the coast of Spain', which may give some indication of the preponderance of the Basques in the city and in the trade. New consuls were appointed and a single chapel was henceforth to be used by both sides, who promised to act thereafter in unanimity (*como hermanos yuntamente*).[48]

However, on 9 February 1453 Fernando Dias de Toledo, *oydor* to King Enrique IV of Castille, issued a decree in the king's name expressing the royal anger that had been occasioned by learning that in the (newly united) chapel in Bruges the arms of the province of Vizcaya had been painted above the royal arms of León and Castille. The king ordered this to be remedied immediately and those responsible to be punished.[49] Obviously some form of reply was then sent from Bruges to the royal court at Burgos, for a royal letter of 29 August 1455 takes up the question of the arms in the Bruges chapel once more. The dispute there it seems from this text was between the merchants of Vizcaya on the one hand and all the rest on the other. The latter are said to include men from Burgos, Seville, Toledo, Segovia, Soria, Valladolid and Medina. The Vizcayans convinced the king that they had not insulted the royal arms, but what they had done was to prevent any of the other Spanish merchants from erecting their own city or provincial arms in the chapel. Some of the latter had probably then filed the charge against the Vizcayans that so incensed the king in 1453. The Vizcayans claimed this monopoly in the chapel because they had originally built it, and their arms had been displayed there *de tiempo syn memoria*. King Enrique, while stressing that the chapel was to be held communally by all of his subjects in Bruges and indicating his approval of the document of concord drawn up in 1452, agreed that only the royal arms and those of Vizcaya should be permitted to be displayed there. But he

[48] Ibid., pp. 50—2 (2 August 1452).
[49] Ibid., pp. 53—4 (9 February 1453).

further allowed that if members of other towns or provinces were in the future to work on, repair or ornament the chapel then they could erect their own arms in it, as long as this was not done in any way that was prejudicial to those of the king or of Vizcaya.[50] In the same letter the king agreed to the Vizcayans and Guipuzcoans electing two of their number apiece to bear the title of consul and to have jurisdiction in all legal cases and pleas relating to their communities, but without any authority over the other subjects of the crown. The administrative uniformity agreed to in 1452 thus proved short-lived.

Disputes between the Vizcayans and Guipuzcoans on the one hand and the 'Spaniards' on the other continued unabated. On 6 September 1465 another agreement worked out by arbitrators was signed by the consuls of Spain and those of the two Basque provinces. This arranged for meetings between the consuls, and also fixed the respective proportions of the dues owed to the duke of Burgundy, the ruler of Flanders, and of the damages due on the transportation of goods owned by foreigners. In both cases the Castillians took the lion's share, paying 31 of the 45 pounds of gold required for the new ducal ten-year safe conduct, and also taking responsibility for 38 crowns in every 60 of all damages that might have to be paid for the merchandise of 'strangers' carried in Spanish ships.[51] This may indicate a numerical and economic preponderance in Bruges on the part of the non-Basque merchants, or a strong bargaining position on the part of the Basques. In either case the size of the Basque interest is striking when it is considered how small a portion of the kingdom they represented in all other respects. None of these agreements appears to have been final or even long lasting. Even as late as 1500 there were still disputes over respective rights in the chapel, and consultations took place over the privileges and obligations of the Spanish 'nation' and the Vizcayan one in their communal chapel. In 1485 a further royal clarification had had to be issued at the request of the merchants of Burgos to define the power and responsibilities of the Vizcayan consuls in Bruges, who were clearly exceeding those that had been envisaged in 1455 and 1465. These new rules had

[50] Ibid., pp. 68—73 (29 August 1455).
[51] Ibid., pp. 84—6 (6 September 1465).

to be reissued with revisions in 1495, 1501, 1504 and 1505.[52] In Bruges, at least, the Vizcayans were difficult and contentious neighbours.

The perversity of the accidents of the survival of evidence that has so restricted and channelled information concerning the towns of the Biscay coast south of the Pyrenees has also denied us much desirable knowledge of Bayonne. Relatively few of the municipal documents of Bayonne or of the other towns of Gascony under English rule have survived. Of those that have, many are in London and are essentially royal instruments. There are some charters granted to individuals, such as that of Henry III of 14 February 1229, permitting one Oger de Murleus to set up two ovens in the suburb of St Andrew in Bayonne.[53] By the early thirteenth century the mayor and council, largely freed from the hold of the bishop though in a struggle of which we have little record, were seeking greater liberties from their distant overlord in Westminster. According to a letter they sent in 1219 to Hubert de Burgh, then the dominant figure in the minority council of Henry III, they had petitioned the late King John on the Easter before he died (1216) to be freed from having to pay any tolls and customs in his territories. Apparently he had promised then to make such a grant when he came to Bayonne on a proposed expedition to the Holy Land, but much to the regret of the mayor and council he had since died, and so they now requested a concession of this (extraordinary) privilege from the mentors of his successor.[54] John's political and military position in 1216 was so weak that he might have had to contemplate such a concession, though he clearly temporized, but conditions in 1219 were not as to make such a major loss of revenue necessary.

Although many of the names of bishops, shipmasters, king's serjeants and others associated with Bayonne in the English administrative records are not Basque or are not certainly so, and although the case of San Sebastián with its predominantly

[52] Ibid., pp. 194—7, 124—30.

[53] *Calendar of Charter Rolls Preserved in the Public Record Office*, vol. I, p. 91, 14 February 1229.

[54] *Inventaire-Sommaire des Archives Communales antérieurs à 1790 de la Ville de Bayonne*, ed. E. Dulaurens (Bayonne, 1894).

(Above and opposite) Examples of the typical fortified manor house of the lesser nobility of the Basque regions in the later middle ages: the fourteenth- or fifteenth-century castle of the Mendoza family (above), and the castle of the Salazar family at Nogroro (opposite), both in Alava

French-speaking population might suggest that a non-Basque-speaking element would predominate in a flourishing commercial city such as Bayonne, there are indications that a majority of the citizens probably did speak the language, at least in the thirteenth century. Thus, for example, in June 1254 Bertramn de Podenzac was appointed mayor of the city, and it was specifically recorded that he was 'of their tongue'.[55] This would hardly have been noteworthy if the Romance speech of the wider area of Aquitaine-Guienne was being referred to, and the appointment

[55] *Calendar of Patent Rolls*, vol. IV, June 1254, p. 302.

of a native speaker looks to have been made in response to
specific requests by the citizens.

In general the history of Gascony under English rule has been
subjected to substantial historical analysis, though this has
encompassed the whole of the area between the Garonne and the
Pyrenees, apart from the small Navarrese enclave north of the
mountains, whilst the limitations of records have meant that
little of such scholarship has been able to be directed at the
Basque-speaking areas south of the Adour.[56] The overall impressions of fidelity to the English crown in the fourteenth and
the first half of the fifteenth centuries may have been conditioned
more by hostility to the notion of rule from Paris than to
sentiments of loyalty to the alien and distant overlords in

[56] See in particular M. G. A. Vale, *English Gascony, 1399—1453* (Oxford, 1970).

England. Certainly, though, there were in the case of Bayonne solid commercial advantages to be gained from this allegiance. Moreover, as in the case of the appointment of Bertrand de Podenzac, the distant government in London could on occasion take notice of local conditions, or at least allow the local authorities and the nobility to go their own ways with only limited and periodic interference. That Bayonne remained the last stronghold of English rule in Gascony, holding out until 1453, was probably not accidental.[57]

Feud and faction in Navarre and Aragón

Turbulent as conditions may have seemed in southern Gascony in the final phases of the Hundred Years War, they were matched in the same period by those to be encountered in many of the Basque areas to the south of the Pyrenees. There spiralling faction fighting and local rivalries which central authority proved powerless to suppress resulted in widespread violence in both town and countryside which lasted for roughly half a century and which could at times amount to little less than localized civil war. In Navarre a weakened monarchy, whose titular holders were frequently absent from their realm, was unable to curb the struggles for power between the two noble confederacies of the Agramunts and the Beaumonts, the latter being descendants of a minor branch of the royal house.[58] Even more fissile were the factional struggles in Vizcaya and Guipúzcoa, where the cycle of inter-family violence was augmented by the logic of feud. Alava was only a little less disturbed, as its numerous surviving small late medieval noble fortresses demonstrate, but its history in this period is less well documented than that of the two maritime provinces. In the case of Vizcaya in particular the unusual wealth of detailed information that is available comes from a remarkable genealogical and local historical compilation entitled *Las Bienandanças e Fortunas*, written *c.* 1471 by Lope García de Salazar, himself a

[57] Compare the conclusions of M. G. A. Vale, 'The Gascon nobility and the Anglo-French War 1294—98', in J. Gillingham and J. C. Holt (eds), *War and Government in the Middle Ages* (Cambridge, 1984), pp. 134—46.

[58] Yanguas y Miranda, *Diccionario de Antigüedades*, vol. I, pp. 28, 95—101.

major protagonist in his own family's feuds and struggles for local power. This work is the principal source for what came to be known as the War of the Bands.[59]

Lope García began his book with an account of the *seniores* of Vizcaya, commencing with an origin legend similar to the much older one of the dukes of Gascony found in the Black Cartulary of Auch. According to his story the Vizcayans and the Leonese fought a great and bloody battle at Artiaga, in which the former were victorious. In consequence they were able to elect a *senior* of their own in the person of one Don Zuria, grandson of the king of Scotland, who swore at Guernica, the customary meeting place of the Vizcayans, that he would protect their freedoms and liberties. As the great-grandson of this Zuria is here said to have been the ally of the tenth-century count of Castille Fernán González (d. 971) in a totally unhistorical battle against Al-Mansūr of Córdoba (d. 1002), this foundation story looks to have been put into a late-ninth-century context.[60] The claimed origin of the line in the person of a foreign prince, together with hostility to a threatening local overlord, are features common to this and other origin legends, such as that of the dukes of Gascony. In both cases the myths incorporate the element of friendly relations with Castille, the descendants of whose counts were the royal overlords of Vizcaya in the time of Lope García, though it is probable that the story considerably antedates his time.

Not before the thirteenth-century section of the account of the *seniores* can any degree of reliance be placed upon this work, and even in that portion there are legendary elements, such as the banding together at Guernica of twelve men and their families who then overthrew the twelfth *senior*, nephew of Fernando III of Castille (d. 1252), who had sought to challenge the traditional liberties of the Vizcayans. More historical was the late-thirteenth-century crisis when the direct male line of the *seniores* died out and three years of fighting ensued between two rival claimants. Further succession crises ensued in the fourteenth century before the seniory was finally merged into

---

[59] *Las Bienandanças e fortunas que escribió Lope García de Salazar estando preso en la su torre de San Martín de Muñatones*, facsimile of the MS, with transcription by M. Camaraon (Madrid, 1884); unfortunately this entirely lacks pagination.

[60] The account of the line of the *seniores* is to be found on ff. 1—3v of the MS.

the crown of Castille in 1379. Even in the midst of this fairly
troubled period some of the *seniores*, notably a Lady María,
proved themselves to be effective rulers of the province. María
was responsible for a number of new urban foundations and for
the granting of various sets of *fueros*.[61] However, the royal
absorption of the seniory meant that the dominant landholder
in Vizcaya was thereafter not personally present in the province,
and the weakness of the Castillian monarchy for much of the
first three-quarters of the fifteenth century became also the
weakness of the *seniores* of Vizcaya. The controlling power that
might have been exercised by the principal noble family of the
province was thus removed. Similarly, other great noble families
of Basque origin, such as the Mendozas, were seeking power on
a much wider stage in the kingdom of Castille as a whole, and
played no part in the events in the coastal provinces, where
smaller lineages struggled for local control in the vaccuum left
by the absence of the greater.[62]

In the earlier fourteenth century, family feuds and factional
violence were not unknown, but from Lope García's accounts
these were generally quickly suppressed by the *senior* or by the
king and were prevented from spreading. Thus in 1300 when
the sons of Diego Pérez de Ligizamon took revenge for their
father's murder, they were publicly flogged on the orders of
the *senior*.[63] However, the civil wars between the sons of
Alfonso XI and the relative weakness of the ensuing Trastámara
dynasty, together with the effective elimination of the seniory in
1370, opened the way for a series of local power struggles and
acts of revenge between the rival lineages of the lesser aristocracy
and junior branches of some of the greater families. The
growing wealth of the new towns, particularly Bilbao and
Bermeo, also provided incentives and opportunities for factional
rivalry and bids for local ascendancy. Several of the feuds had
their origins in the more distant past. Thus the houses of
Ligizamon and Zamudiano, the former of which claimed an
ancestry going back to the Cid, were in a state of enmity by

---

[61] For a detailed history of the period see the materials in E. J. de Labayru y
Goicoecha, *Historia general del Señorió de Bizcaya* (3 vols, Bilbao-Madrid, 1895).

[62] For the Mendozas, see G. Bleiberg (ed.), *Diccionario de historia de España*, 2nd
edn (Madrid, 1968), vol. II, pp. 1001—2.

[63] *Las Bienandanças.*

1270, which still existed when Lope García wrote two centuries later. As is the wont with blood feuds, such inter-family vendettas escalated as other lineages became associated with one or other of the rival parties by marriage. Thus Lope García records an ancient enmity between the minor noble houses of Sant Pedro from Labourd in English Gascony and the Espeleta from Navarre. One facet of this was a private war in 1413 between Mosen Juan de Sant Pedro and the Navarrese house of Alzate, in the course of which the household head of the Alzate and one of his sons were killed. Soon after the head of a Guipuzcoan noble family, the Gamboinos, married his son to the daughter and heiress of the late señor of the Alzate. This made the Gamboinos the automatic enemies of the Sant Pedros, and this Fernando de Gamboino led a force of his followers to attack Mosen Juan de Sant Pedro and thus avenge his son's late father-in-law. In the event, however, the Gamboinos were defeated and Fernando killed. Lope García reports that 150 men died in this battle.[64] Thus a direct feud between the Gamboinos and the Sant Pedros came into being. At the same time the Gamboinos created a feud of their own by a night attack (*c.* 1420) on a rival Guipuzcoan family, the Onis, in the course of which the head of the Onis and nine others were killed when their house was burnt over their heads. This was on Christmas night. The Gamboinos and allied families then went on to ravage the lands of the Onis, but were themselves attacked by other families linked to the latter; in the ensuing affray one of the leaders of the Valda family, supporters of the Gamboinos, was killed by members of the Lescano. This in turn created a network of new feuds to supplement the existing one between the principals. Thus in 1446 a battle was fought in Zumarraga between the Valda and the Gamboinos on the one hand and the Lescano and the Onis on the other. The former group were defeated, their manor house at Escoitia was burnt and 70 men were killed, including 12 of the leaders of both of the parties.[65] Further battles took place in 1447 and 1448 in which the number of families involved increased. This particular spiral of violence only came to an end in 1457, when the *hermandades* of Guipúzcoa rose against both the Onis and the Gamboinos,

[64] Ibid.
[65] Ibid.

captured their fortresses and expelled their leaders from the province.

From just this one example, which could be multiplied many times over from the accounts given by Lope García, whose own family became involved in this group of conflicts through its marriage ties to the Sant Pedros, it can be seen how far the requirements of honour and revenge could, if unchecked, lead to a rapid escalation of violence and create an almost irremediable network of feuds. Moreover, although some of the conflicts, such as that between the Onis and the Gamboinos, might be restricted to a single province, they could easily extend themselves over the frontiers of the three kingdoms that coexisted in the vicinity of the western Pyrenees, between which there was anyway much interchange at the level of the aristocracy. Thus Mosen Juan de Sant Pedro was brought up at the court of Castille, was in the service of the king of England, and married the daughter of the constable of the kingdom of Navarre. The diversification of such families and the emergence of junior branches of them, carrying on the feuds of the senior line but also having the potential to create new ones of their own, further exacerbated the possibilities for conflict. To some extent such family networks and the pressures of a society that seems only able to have obtained justice through feud when central authority was weak, make this period of endemic violence comprehensible and logical in its own way. But other factors limiting the effect of alternative pressures towards concord and accommodation should not be overlooked. Some of the initial acts of violence that sparked off long and deadly feuds were the products of apparently trivial causes. Thus a bloody conflict between the Ligizamon and the Vasurta, that rapidly grafted itself on to other pre-existing feuds, was started by a disagreement over a salmon. On the other hand some of the antagonisms look to have been related to struggles for local authority, notably in the newly established towns of the coast; this is something that has its parallels in many other parts of the peninsula at this period. Thus in 1362 Lope García records fighting in Bilbao between the Ligizamon and the Zurbarán, and there was a battle between the same two rival clans in the market quarter of Bermeo in 1413. From this there ensued 20 years of fighting between them and their allies without any

A sixteenth-century engraving of an old lady in the costume of Vizcaya

truce. Not surprisingly the Vasurta appeared on the side of the Zurbarán. The fighting, much of which took place in the streets of Bilbao, clearly got worse in the 1440s, though the numbers of casualties remained low in comparison with those of the rural pitched battles. Thus in an affray in Bilbao in 1440 five men are reported as being killed, and in another in Bermeo in 1443 there were ten casualties.[66]

[66] Ibid.

The only force that seems capable at this time of interrupting or limiting the spread of factional violence was that provided by the *hermandades* (brotherhoods). These were confederacies of citizens, or in the countryside of members of the rural population at a level just below that of the lesser nobility, which were formed with royal consent to provide defence and local order. Such bodies, co-ordinated by a royal *corregidor*, took effective action against the noble families and their *bandos* in Vizcaya in 1390 and 1393.[67] Their Guipuzcoan equivalents were able to end the Onis—Gamboino feuding in 1457, and similar though less conclusive action was taken against the *bandos* in Bilbao and Mondragón in 1442. On occasion, however, use of the *hermandades* could prove a double-edged weapon: those of Vizcaya rebelled against the *corregidor* in 1415 when, on royal orders, he tried to divert Vizcayan wheat to the Asturias. As the king's representative the *corregidor* was able to draw upon the resources of the royal estates, and in this case he was able to defeat the *hermandades* in a pitched battle at Erandio, in which 60 men were killed.[68] In general, though, the *hermandades* could provide occasional and temporary relief from the violence and depredations of the noble *bandos*, but, as in the case of the rest of Castille, the problem was only solved by the reimposition of effective royal rule under Ferdinand and Isabella.[69]

Conclusion

Thus by the closing of the Middle Ages both the social and the economic structures of Basque society had undergone considerable transformation and an increase in complexity in comparison with their early medieval equivalents. Some features of rural life remained but little changed, as indeed they do to the present. These include the predominance of pastoralism in the mountainous zones, the association of families with a particular house, the special pre-eminence of the head of that household, and possibly distinctive funerary customs. In village life rural

[67] On the role of the *hermandades* and their organization in the late fourteenth century, see A. de los Santos Lazurtegui, *La Hermandad de Guipúzcoa y el Corregidor Dr Gonzalo Moro* (San Sebastián, 1935).

[68] *Las Bienandanças.*

[69] M. Sarasola, *Vizcaya y los Reyes Catolicos* (Madrid, 1950), especially pp. 111—30.

democracy took the form of regular meetings be̞tween the heads of households in front of the local church, from which feature such gatherings took the name of *anteiglesias*. These were institutionalized as part of the structure of local government in the Basque provinces other than Navarre in the fourteenth century by the *ordenanza* of 1394, but it is likely that the practice was considerably older.[70] At a special general meeting of the community, known as a *cruz parada* or 'paraded cross', local officers were elected; thus in Vizcaya were chosen the representatives to be sent to attend the *juntas generales*, which generally met at Guernica. In fact both urban and rural societies were drawn into a single framework of government at the apex of which, under the crown, stood the provincial or regional junta. In Vizcaya, as well as the juntas that met at Guernica, two regional subdivisions of the province, the Encartaciones and the Duranguesando, had juntas of their own which met at Avellaneda and at Astola or Guerediaga respectively. The juntas are first recorded in 1307, when an assembly met at Arechabalagana to discuss the succession dispute over the seniory. That such general assemblies were an older feature of Basque society cannot be proved, though by the time Lope García de Salazar was writing legend had made of them the ancient touchstone and defence of traditional Basque liberties.

Rural representatives dominated the juntas. Even as late as 1630 they had 72 out of 91 votes as opposed to the representatives of the towns who had only 21, although it has been calculated that the respective percentages of the population were in the region of 46 per cent compared with 31 per cent. The additional eight votes and 23 per cent of the population were those of the provincial subdivisions of the Encartaciones, Durango and the 'republicas unidas'.[71] In 1514 the towns made a fruitless bid to set up an independent representative assembly of their own. However, it would be unwise to stress town—countryside conflict or to suggest a lack of mutual interaction

---

[70] On the administrative structures of the seniory see G. Monreal, *Las instituciones públicas del Señorió de Vizcaya (hasta el siglo XVIII)* (Bilbao, 1974). For interesting comparisons that can be made with similarly constituted societies in the Alps, see P. Bozon, *Le Pays de Villards en Maurienne* (La Tronche-Montfleury, 1970), pp. 53—70, 93—100, 115—26.

[71] F. García de Cortázar and M. Montero, *Historia de Vizcaya* (2 vols, San Sebastián, 1980), vol. I, p. 85.

between the two. Obviously the rapid proliferation of urban settlements in the later Middle Ages created new markets for the products of the rural economy. Despite the near-monopoly of the Castillian Mesta it is hard to believe that Pyrenean wool did not enter the trade. Moreover the growth in trading in iron, so well represented in the Bruges records, represents the rise of a major Basque industry that was located in the countryside, particularly in Guipúzcoa.[72]

Overall the Basques remained, in the late Middle Ages as in the early, politically divided, subjects of different kingdoms and with no sense of nationhood of their own. Indeed such a concept is anachronistic if applied to them. Their language, the key to any such sense of an identity greater than those of the separate provinces and smaller divisions into which they were broken up, remained largely unregarded as the vehicle for any form of higher culture. The appearance of a small amount of vernacular literature in the fifteenth century proved to be a false start. However, this does not imply that the language itself was yet in decline. Letters written in Basque by a Navarrese royal secretary in the fifteenth century suggest its continuing or even expanding use in the upper echelons of society for purposes other than literary.[73] Equally notable is the fact that the Basque noble and Franciscan missionary St Francis Xavier (d. 1545) relapsed into his native speech on his death-bed.[74] Even the gradual northwards retreat of the language, which has now removed its use almost entirely from Alava and has restricted its survival in Navarre to the mountainous areas north of Pamplona, looks to be a more recent process than is often allowed. Nineteenth-century observers record its continuing use as far south as Olite in the period of the Napoleonic wars.[75]

This lack of an overriding sense of a Basque identity and a low level of regard for the language in sophisticated circles were first seriously challenged in the later sixteenth century, probably as an indirect consequence of the period of discoveries in the

[72] The late medieval Basque iron industry is treated exhaustively in L. M. Díez de Salazar, *Ferrerías en Guipúzcoa (siglos XIV—XVI)* (2 vols, San Sebastián, 1983).

[73] F. Idoate, 'Una carta del siglo XV en Vascuense', *Fontes Linguae Vasconum*, I (1969), pp. 287—90.

[74] G. Schurhammer, *Frances Xavier. Vol. IV: Japan, 1549—52*, tr. M. J. Costelloe (Rome, 1982), p. 642 and n. 11.

[75] F. Michel, *Le Pays Basque* (Paris, 1857), p. 5.

The portrait of the Basque historian Esteban de Garibay that appears in his
XL Libros del Compendio historial

Indies and the Americas. The interest thus aroused in the Indian
peoples whom the Spanish explorers and settlers encountered
created something of an ethnological revolution. This climate of
opinion helped to produce the first Basque historian, who was
also to be the first scholar to try to trace the history of the
Basque people and to explain the origins and special nature of
their language. This was Esteban de Garibay from Mondragón
in Guipúzcoa, who published the four volumes of his *Compendio*

Historial in 1571.[76] Garibay was *par excellence* a genealogist, as his other books and unpublished manuscripts attest, and much of his work was devoted to listing the pedigrees of the kings, not excluding the Ottoman sultans, who were held to have some connection with Spain.[77] He also discoursed parenthetically on heraldry, church councils, Spanish martyrs, the learned men of Spain 'y otras cosas muy notables'. He took up the notion, already popular with other Spanish antiquarians, that the Iberian peninsula had been populated by the descendants of Tubal, one of the sons of Japhet the son of Noah. However, he gave this legend a distinctive twist in making the Basque regions (which Garibay called Cantabria) the principal focus of Tubal's activity, and he 'proved' this thesis by claiming affinity between various Basque place-names and those in the Bible that were associated with Armenia, where the Ark had come to rest. This, he argued, was due to Tubal's own great affection for his earlier homeland, which led him to use its place-names for the toponyms of his new settlement in Spain. Amongst other examples Garibay cited Mount Gordeya in Armenia with its parallel in Gorbeya on the borders of Vizcaya and Alava, and the River Araxes with its equivalent in the Navarrese river Araica. Perhaps most preposterous of his arguments was his mention of a mill site close to his native Mondragón that was called Babylonia. All of this enabled Garibay to provide an origin for the Basque language in the speech of Tubal. This made of it one of the original languages of mankind, created after the fall of the Tower of Babel. He also made of it the first tongue to be spoken in Spain, and he showed that Cantabria and Navarre were the first regions of the peninsula to be inhabited after the Flood. Another argument to which he had recourse, and which shows some of the roots of his thinking in the outburst of ethnographic speculation that followed the discoveries in America, was that Vizcayan and Guipuzcoan sailors had been able to converse with the Indians with the

[76] Esteban de Garibay, *XL Libros del Compendio Historial de las Chronicas y Universal Historia de Todos los Reynos de España* (Antwerp, 1571). It was printed by Christopher Plantin 'a costa del autor'.

[77] See, amongst other unpublished works by Garibay, Madrid, Biblioteca Nacional, MS 3136, *Arboles de los Reyes de Oviedo, León, Castilla, Aragón, Navarra y Portugal hasta Felipe II*, and, applying his genealogical skills to political ends, Biblioteca Nacional, MS 9984, *Discursos sobre la Sucesión de Inglaterra*.

greatest of ease, and the latter, despite a lack of education, proved able to learn Basque with extraordinary facility.[78]

In other respects the sixteenth century promised to provide the opportunities for the Basques to assert themselves and to gain recognition of their distinctive identity. Their regional customs and liberties were recognized and systematized to a degree unknown to the medieval state. The production of such major and all-embracing compilations as the *fueros* of Vizcaya and those of Guipúzcoa, together with a revised version of the *Fuero General* of Navarre, gave the inhabitants of these regions distinct legal status and exemptions that singled them out from amongst the rest of the subjects of the Spanish monarchy. It is also thought that the entrenched privileges thus recognized in the foral laws made even the Inquisition chary of operating extensively in the Basque regions. The inquisitors were reluctant to intervene, even when specifically requested to do so by the local authorities, as in the case of some of the witch trials for which the regions became famous in the late sixteenth and early seventeenth centuries.[79]

On the other hand fear of heresy and suspicions of a language few could understand seem quickly to have stifled greater use of the language, and the economics of production limited printing in Basque to no more than a handful of the most popular and innocuous of devotional and catechetical works. The growing centralization of government, and the disappearance of such anomalies as the much shrunken kingdom of Navarre, which was absorbed by Castille in 1514, presented in the long term greater threats to Basque traditions than opportunities for their flourishing. In particular the division of the western Pyrenees between the mutually antagonistic powers of Spain and France, formalized by the Treaty of the Pyrenees in 1659, replaced the more numerous and looser political divisions of the Middle Ages by a single and more tightly controlled frontier. The Basques, who inconveniently straddled it, became objects of increasing suspicion to their masters in distant Madrid and

---

[78] Garibay, *Compendio Historial*, book IV, chs ii—iv, pp. 86—92.

[79] For an example of the difficulties of bringing charges against someone protected by these foral laws, see the case involving Garibay described in N. Alonso Cortés, 'Esteban de Garibay y el *Compendio Historial*', in *Homenaje a D. Carmelo de Echegaray* (San Sebastián, 1928), pp. 61—8. For the Inquisition and the witches see J. Caro Baroja, *The World of the Witches*, tr. O. N. V. Glendinning (Chicago—London, 1965), p. 152.

Paris. On the French side this was accentuated by memories of Gascon separateness and the involvement of a small but significant group of Basques in the cause of the Protestant Huguenots. On both sides of the frontier pressure was exerted to make the Basques either more fully French or more fully Spanish. Government-inspired attempts to undermine the continued use of the Basque language in the Spanish Basque regions was reported even in the nineteenth century: this was not just a phenomenon of Spain after the Civil War.[80] At the same time the late-nineteenth-century and twentieth-century industrialization of the Spanish Basque regions of the Biscay coast made them a magnet for job-hungry migrants from the south, to such an extent that the Basques, as identifiable by name and language, are now numerically a racial minority in their own provinces.[81] Immigration into the Basque regions was also paralleled by a widespread emigration that took large numbers of Basques not only to the Spanish speaking regions of Central and Southern America but also to the northern continent as well. In the latter, substantial concentrations of Basques established themselves on the west coast and above all in the State of Nevada. Although their use of the language has inevitably declined, awareness of Basque origins has remained strong amongst the descendants of the late-nineteenth and twentieth-century settlers, and numerically they now outnumber the residual European Basque population.

The separate identity of Navarre, accentuated by the long survival of its independent kingdom, has also been affected by the recent rapid decline in the number of its Basque speakers, and by differences of loyalty in comparison with the Basque provinces of Alava, Vizcaya and Guipúzcoa during such episodes as the Carlist Wars in the nineteenth century and the Civil War in the present one. Even the French Basque nationalists, who have been making increasingly common cause with their more violent counterparts across the frontier, have very different perspectives to those of their Spanish equivalents. For them their three provinces of Labourd, Soule and Basse Navarre (the rump of Navarre not swallowed by Castille in 1514) are

[80] Michel, *Le Pays Basque*, p. 5.
[81] For the industrialization of the Basque provinces (but not Navarre), see J. Harrison, 'Heavy industry, the state and economic development in the Basque region', *Economic History Review*, 36 (1983), pp. 535—51.

underdeveloped 'third world' regions only exploited for their tourist potential and denied the necessary government funding and investment to develop their economy and provide jobs. On the other hand, Basque nationalism on the Spanish side of the frontier is largely conditioned by the problems of an industrialized society in rapid decline, and with its Basque population in danger of losing its cultural distinctiveness in the face of a growing immigrant element, until recently abetted by a central government that regarded the unique Basque racial and linguistic heritage as a threat to the greater national unity of Spain. The problems remain. All sides in these arguments have tended to turn to history for proofs of their claims, and have often distorted it in the process. Bad history may make good politics, but it should be resisted. One comfort the lessons of the past can certainly give: however unconscious of it they may have been, the Basques have preserved a distinct identity, and in their small corner of the world and in many places beyond it they have made a unique contribution to the complex web of human history. May they long continue to do so.

Index